How
Intranets
Work

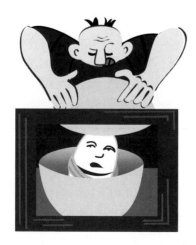

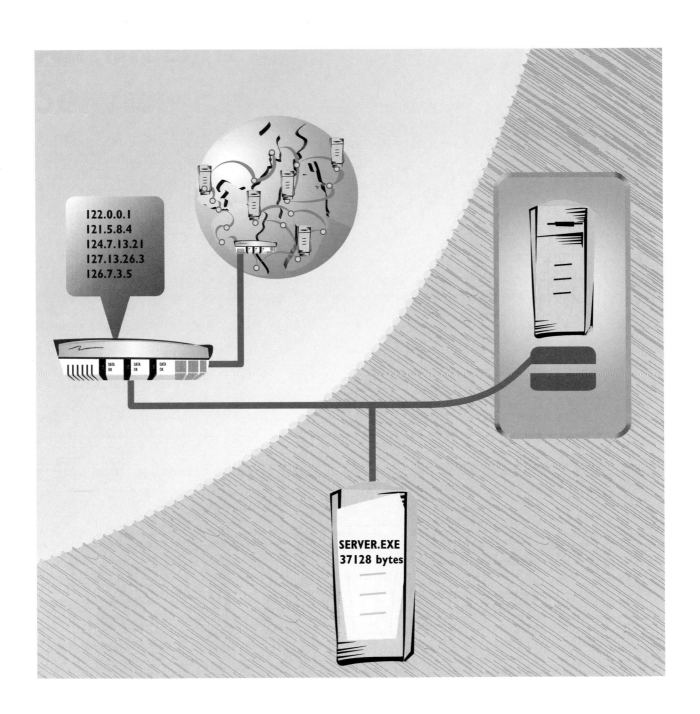

How Intranets Work

Preston Gralla

Illustrated by Mina Reimer

Ziff-Davis Press
An imprint of Macmillan Computer Publishing USA
Emeryville, California

Publisher	Stacy Hiquet
Associate Publisher	Juliet Langley
Acquisitions Editor	Lysa Lewallen
Development Editor	Paula Hardin
Copy Editor	Margo Hill
Technical Reviewer	Mark Butler
Production Editor	Barbara Dahl
Proofreader	Jeff Barash
Cover Illustration	Mina Reimer
Cover Design	Regan Honda and Megan Gandt
Book Design	Carrie English and Bruce Lundquist
Lead Illustrator	Mina Reimer
Contributing Illustrators	Sarah Ishida, Karl Miyajima, Joan Carol, and Chad Kubo
Page Layout	M.D. Barrera
Indexer	Valerie Robbins

Ziff-Davis Press, ZD Press, the Ziff-Davis Press logo are trademarks or registered trademarks of, and are licensed to Macmillan Computer Publishing USA by Ziff-Davis Publishing Company, New York, New York.

Ziff-Davis Press imprint books are produced on a Macintosh computer system with the following applications: FrameMaker®, Microsoft® Word, QuarkXPress®, Adobe Illustrator®, Adobe Photoshop®, Adobe Streamline™, MacLink®*Plus*, Aldus® FreeHand™, Collage Plus™.

Ziff-Davis Press, an imprint of

Macmillan Computer Publishing USA

5903 Christie Avenue

Emeryville, CA 94608

ISBN 1-56276-441-1

Manufactured in the United States of America

10 9 8 7 6 5 4 3 2 1

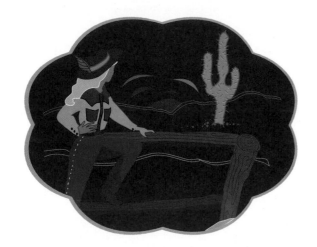

THIS book wouldn't have been possible without a host of people working on it. I'd like to thank acquisitions editor Lysa Lewallen for getting the ball rolling, and editor Valerie Haynes Perry for her initial work on the book. Editor Paula Hardin wields a sharp pen and tightened the writing and thinking tremendously. Technical editor Mark Butler, as always, vetted the work for accuracy. And thanks also to Mina Reimer, illustrator; Barbara Dahl, production editor; Margo Hill, copy editor; and M.D. Barrera, page layout artist. Also thanks to Carol Burbo for keeping track of everything.

And, as always, I'd like to thank my family, Lydia, Mia, and Gabriel, for putting up with my occasional absences into the dark recesses of my office, as well as ignoring my odd behavior as I mumbled too much about the domain name system or Virtual Secure Private Networks.

THE Internet has been hailed by many as the most revolutionary technology that computing has seen. It's a technology that affects not just the computing world, but the noncomputing world as well: You can't turn on your television without seeing Web locations flash across your screen, or read a newspaper without seeing a story about the latest Internet startup that made its young entrepreneurs instant millionaires.

The truth is, though, that Internet technology may have its greatest impact in the next several years not on general culture, but rather on corporations. It has already begun to revolutionize the way that companies operate and do business—and most people agree that we've only seen the very beginnings of the its effects on corporate culture and on the way corporations function.

When Internet technology is applied and used inside a corporation, and open only to its employees, it is referred to as an *intranet*. The same technologies that underlie corporate intranets form the basis of the larger Internet. The only difference is that the company has put up a wall around its intranet to keep intruders out. This wall that a company builds around its intranet is known as a *firewall*.

An intranet uses the same basic underlying architecture and network protocols as does the Internet. Protocols such as the Transmission Control Protocol (TCP), the Internet Protocol (IP), the Simple Mail Transfer Protocol (SMTP), and many others are what make it all possible. Most intranet technologies, like those on the Internet, are client/server based. In many instances, however, the way the technology is applied on the intranet differs from the way it is applied on the Internet.

Intranets are generally more complicated than the Internet itself, for many reasons. One reason is that these Internet-specific protocols have to coexist and cooperate with other network protocols such as IPX. Another is that intranets are often composed of a variety of different local area networks, and they all must be hooked together seamlessly. And in order to serve businesses, intranet applications—such as workgroup applications—are often required to be far more complex than those generally found on the Internet.

Because the Internet itself changes so fast and can be confusing, and because intranet technology is that much more complex, it often seems impossible to ever truly understand how an intranet actually works. Proxy servers, filtering routers, Virtual Secure Private Networks, firewalls, password protection schemes—it can all seem a jumble.

This book will help make it all much clearer. It will show you, in carefully detailed illustrations, how the Internet actually works. Whether you're an intranet administrator, or just someone who wants to know more about how a modern corporate network works, you'll find it a great help.

The book is divided into four major sections. In Part 1, "An Intranet's Building Blocks," we'll take a look at the underlying technologies that make an intranet possible. We'll begin by taking a global look at an intranet, and see how all the pieces fit together and interact with the

Internet. We'll take a close look at how the Internet's two most important protocols—TCP and IP—work. And we'll also see how those protocols fit in and interact with other network protocols. In Part 1 we'll also see how some of an intranet's most important hardware works. We'll examine how routers and bridges transfer data packets inside an intranet, between an intranet and the Internet, and how they make sure that the packets don't get lost. We'll also take a look at intranet Web servers, and gain an understanding of how they deliver Web pages to intranet Web browsers, and how they also interact with Internet Web servers.

Part 1 also takes a look at the underlying technology that makes sending and receiving data on an intranet possible, the Domain Name System. And we'll see how e-mail works on an intranet, and see not just how the mail is delivered to other intranet users, but also to people out on the Internet and on other intranets.

And in Part 1, we'll also look at two extremely important technologies that allow intranet administrators and programmers to write customized programs that can form the basis of an intranet. We'll see how the Common Gateway Interface works, a technology that allows the Web to interact with other resources, such as corporate database. And we'll look at Java, a programming language that allows people on an intranet to build truly interactive applications.

In Part 2, "Security and Intranets," we'll turn our attention to what for many is the most complex part of any intranet—the hardware and software that protects intranets against outside intruders. Hackers and crackers on the intranet often feel it a badge of honor to break into corporate computers, and security systems are what keeps them out, while still allowing people inside the intranet to get access to the Internet.

In this part, we'll look at how firewalls use a variety of techniques to keep out intruders. We'll see how filtering routers examine all packets coming into the intranet, and based on what they find, allow some packets—and people—in, while keeping others out. We'll take a close look at bastion servers—heavily fortified intranet servers designed to be a primary line of defense against hackers. Proxy servers, which allow people from inside the intranet to get at Internet resources, are examined as well. The book details how authentication systems work. These systems allow qualified users to log in by using passwords, while keeping others out.

Other security issues we'll look at include the touchy issue of how to block intranet users from visiting objectionable Internet sites, such as those containing pornography. The book will also examine in detail Virtual Secure Private Networks, an important emerging security technology that allows intranets to communicate with each other securely. Finally, we'll see how server-based virus scanning tools can keep in intranet as virus-free as possible.

Part 3, "Intranets and Groupware," shows how some of the newest intranet technology works—a kind of software that has been lumped together under the general term of groupware. Groupware is admittedly somewhat of a fuzzy term, and is thrown around with great abandon—

and with great imprecision—these days. Generally, however, intranet groupware refers to intranet technology that allows people in a corporation to collaborate with each other electronically. It covers everything from simple messaging to complex applications that lets people see what is on each other's computer screens.

We'll get an overview in this section of all the important intranet groupware technologies, and see how they work together to make people communicate more efficiently.

Intranet discussion software also gets a close examination in this section. Discussion software allows people to communicate with each other on what are, in essence, sophisticated computer bulletin boards. But these discussion areas, as well see, allow people to do more than merely talk. They also can contain links to other corporate resources, such as Web pages and corporate databases.

Videoconferencing systems are covered here as well. With videoconferencing, people across the country from each other can see each other and talk to each other on their computers. It allows for one-on-one conferencing, as well as large group conferencing as well.

A related technology, whiteboards, lets people see what others have on their computer screens, and allows them to mark up those documents, and talk to them about what they're marking up. In this way, people separated geographically can work together on the same document—a proposed budget for example.

The final section of the book, Part 4, "Applying the Intranet," looks at how corporations can apply the technology to their businesses. We'll see, for example, how an intranet allows people to get access to corporate databases by using simple forms on intranet Web browsers.

Usually an intranet is built well after a corporation has databases and networks in place, and so in this section we'll also see how these so-called legacy systems can be accessed from, or even integrated into, a corporate intranet.

This section of the book also looks at intranet search tools—systems that allow people to sift through the vast amounts of information on an intranet and find the precise information they need. And we'll see how intranets can be accessed not just from corporate offices, but from people's homes and while they are traveling as well.

We'll invent a mythical corporation in this section of the book, the CyberMusic record company, and look at how an intranet helps CyberMusic work better. We'll see how CyberMusic uses an intranet to market itself, do business with its customers, and do business with other businesses. And we'll also see how CyberMusic uses an intranet to deliver corporate news and information to its employees, and how it uses the intranet for training as well.

P A R T

AN INTRANET'S BUILDING BLOCKS

THE architecture underneath your computer, the wires, the technology, the hardware and the software—what you might think of as the "plumbing"—
is what makes an intranet possible. In the first part of this book we will look at these basic building blocks of an intranet. We'll examine the underlying technnologies, such as TCP/IP, that makes intranets possible. We'll also look at a variety of underlying networking hardware and software that allows intranets to function. Without technology such as routers and bridges—hardware/software combinations that send an intranet's packets and data to the proper places on an intranet—intranets couldn't function.

There are also a variety of specialized software technologies that form the basic building blocks of an intranet. Programming and scripting languages, such as Java and CGI, allow for custom applications to be built, and hook intranets into existing corporate resources, such as databases.

In Chapter 1 we'll look at every aspect of the networks—from how data is routed to how people work cooperatively on intranets, to how intranets are protected by a variety of hardware and software, including firewalls. We'll also look at how all the parts of an intranet fit together. In a single illustration, we'll get a global view of all the important technology and how it fits together into a single, functioning unit.

Chapter 2 examines the most basic underpinnings of an intranet, the protocols for communications among computers, including the foundation for these protocols, the seven-layer Open System Interconnect (OSI) model. The Transmission Control Protocol (TCP) and the Internet Protocol (IP) are based on the OSI model and are commonly lumped together into a single combined acronym, TCP/IP. We'll look at how TCP breaks every piece of information that travels across an intranet or the Internet into packets, at how IP takes those packets, encapsulates them, and then delivers the packets to the intended recipient. On the receiving end, we'll see how IP strips the "envelope" away and how TCP recombines the packets into their original, unified form. We'll also see how TCP makes sure that the data wasn't damaged en route—and if it was, asks that the damaged data be re-sent. The underlying TCP/IP protocols are what defines an intranet and differentiates it from any other kind of network.

In Chapter 3 and 4, we'll take an in-depth look at important intranet hardware, bridges and routers. Both route packets, but bridges can only route traffic between the same physical types of networks, such as Ethernet to Ethernet. Routers are considered more "intelligent" because they can identify and translate Ethernet to Token Ring. Both examine the IP header for the packet's destination address.

In Chapter 5, we'll turn to electronic mail, or e-mail. We'll look at how e-mail is delivered between intranets and to the Internet. The Simple Mail Transfer Protocol, or SMTP, underlies e-mail, and we'll look in detail at how SMTP works, as well as how it works in concert with a special mail delivery system called the Post Office Protocol (POP).

Chapter 6 turns to the part of an intranet that probably gets more publicity than any other—the Web. The World Wide Web has been one of the driving forces behind the establishment of intranets at many corporations, since it can so easily allow departments to publish information for employees as well as for customers.

In Chapter 7 we'll take a closer look at one of the more mysterious parts of an Intranet—the Domain Name System, commonly called DNS. It's a system that logically divides up all the addresses on the Internet and intranets. We'll see how *nameservers* are used to make sure that every time anyone addresses an e-mail message to someone or attempts to contact an intranet location, the request goes to the proper destination. And we'll look at how intranet nameservers cooperate with Internet nameservers.

Chapter 8 looks at the Java programming language. This compiled language, developed by Sun Microsystems, is expected to be used by intranet programmers to create a variety of specialized, customized intranet applications. It will be used as a way to allow people to access corporate databases, to help people navigate what can be large and confusing intranets, and also to create special search tools and multimedia, interactive content such as animations.

In Chapter 9, we'll turn to another kind of programming tool that is often used on intranets—the Common Gateway Interface, or CGI. CGI is a standard way to allow outside resources to interact with the Web. Most commonly, CGI is used to allow someone to use a browser to search a database, and then have the resulting information returned in Hypertext Markup Language (HTML) so that it can be viewed and used. A variety of tools and programming languages can be used to do this, such as the popular Perl scripting language. Programming languages such as C++ can be used as well.

Chapter 10 takes an inside look at subnetting. Subnetting is used to make an intranet easier to manage and maintain by dividing a single intranet into several smaller networks. Subnetting is sometimes required because of the physical limitations of network technology, and often required because it would be impossible for a central group to manage every aspect of a corporate network that spans many departments, and in some cases many countries. We'll look at how a special 32-bit number called a *subnet mask* makes subnetting possible.

Finally, Chapter 11 looks at a very real-world intranet problem: How do you convert an existing network into an intranet? We'll see that in many cases, NetWare technology and TCP/IP co-exist on the same network. The chapter will take a close look at how the Ethernet and TCP/IP technologies work together to create a single, unified network.

CHAPTER

1

A Global View of Intranets

WHAT exactly is an intranet? It's one of those terms that's more thrown around than understood, and has become more of a buzzword than a commonly understood idea. Simply put, an intranet is a private network with Internet technology used as the underlying architecture. An intranet is built using the Internet's TCP/IP protocols for communications. TCP/IP protocols can be run on many hardware platforms and cabling schemes. The underlying hardware is not what makes an intranet—it's the software protocols that matter.

Intranets can co-exist with other local area networking technology. In many companies, existing "legacy systems" including mainframes, Novell networks, minicomputers, and various databases, are being integrated into an intranet. A wide variety of tools allow this to happen. Common Gateway Interface (CGI) scripting is often used to access legacy databases from an intranet. The Java programming language can be used to access legacy databases as well.

With the enormous growth of the Internet, an increasing number of people in corporations use the Internet for communicating with the outside world, for gathering information, and for doing business. It didn't take long for people to recognize that the components that worked so well on the Internet could be equally valuable internally and that is why intranets are becoming so popular. Some corporations do not have TCP/IP networks, the protocol required to access the resources of the Internet. Creating an intranet in which all the information and resources can be used seamlessly has many benefits. TCP/IP-based networks make it easy for people to access the network remotely, such as from home or while traveling. Dialing into an intranet in this way is much like connecting to the Internet, except that you're connecting to a private network instead of to a public Internet provider. Interoperability between networks is another substantial bonus.

Security systems separate an intranet from the Internet. A company's intranet is protected by firewalls—hardware and software combinations that allow only certain people to access the intranet for specific purposes.

Intranets can be used for anything that existing networks are used for—and more. The ease of publishing information on the World Wide Web has made them popular places for posting corporate information such as company news or company procedures. Corporate databases with easy-to-build front-ends use the Web and programming languages such as Java.

Intranets allow people to work together more easily and more effectively. Software known as groupware is another important part of intranets. It allows people to collaborate on projects; to share information; to do videoconferencing; and to establish secure procedures for production work. Free server and client software and the multitude of services, like newsgroups, stimulated the Internet's growth. The consequence of that growth stimulated and fueled the growth of intranets. The ease with which information can be shared, and with which people can communicate with one another will continue to drive the building of intranets.

A Global View of an Intranet

An intranet is a private corporate or educational network that uses the Internet's TCP/IP protocols for its underlying transport. The protocols can run on a variety of network hardware, and can also co-exist with other network protocols, such as IPX. People from inside an intranet can get at the larger Internet resources, but those on the Internet cannot get into the intranet, which allows only restricted access from the Internet.

Videoconferencing is an important application that requires sending massive quantities of data. Intranets can be built using components that allow the extremely high bandwidths required for transferring such information.

Software that allows people to communicate with each other via e-mail and public message boards and to collaborate on work using work-group software is among the most powerful intranet programs. Applications that allow different corporate departments to post information, and for people to fill out corporate forms, such as time sheets, and for tapping into corporate financial information are very popular.

Often an intranet is composed of a number of different networks inside a corporation that all communicate with one another via TCP/IP. These separate networks are often referred to as *subnets*.

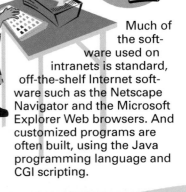

Much of the software used on intranets is standard, off-the-shelf Internet software such as the Netscape Navigator and the Microsoft Explorer Web browsers. And customized programs are often built, using the Java programming language and CGI scripting.

Intranets can also be used to allow companies to do business-to-business transactions, such as ordering parts, sending invoices, and making payments. For extra security, these intranet-to-intranet transactions need never go out over the public Internet, but can travel over private leased lines instead.

Intranets are a powerful system for allowing a company to do business online, for example, to allow anyone on the Internet to order products. When someone orders a product on the Internet, information is sent in a secure manner from the public Internet to the company's intranet, where the order is processed and completed.

Information sent across an intranet is sent to the proper destination by routers, which examine each TCP/IP packet for the IP address and determine the packet's destination. It then sends the packet to the next router closest to the destination. If the packet is to be delivered to an address on the same subnetwork of the intranet it was sent from, the packet may be able to be delivered directly without having to go through any other routers. If it is to be sent to another subnetwork on the intranet, it will be sent to another internal router address. If the packet is to be sent to a destination outside the intranet—in other words, to an Internet destination—the packet is sent to a router that connects to the Internet.

In order to protect sensitive corporate information, and to ensure that hackers don't damage computer systems and data, security barriers called firewalls protect an intranet from the Internet. Firewall technology uses a combination of routers, servers and other hardware and software to allow people on an intranet to use Internet resources, but blocks outsiders from getting into the intranet.

Many intranets have to connect to "legacy systems"—hardware and databases that were built before an intranet was constructed. Legacy systems often use older technology not based on the intranet's TPC/IP protocols. There are a variety of ways in which intranets can tie to legacy systems. A common way is to use CGI scripts to access the database information and pour that data into HTML formatted text, making it available to a Web browser.

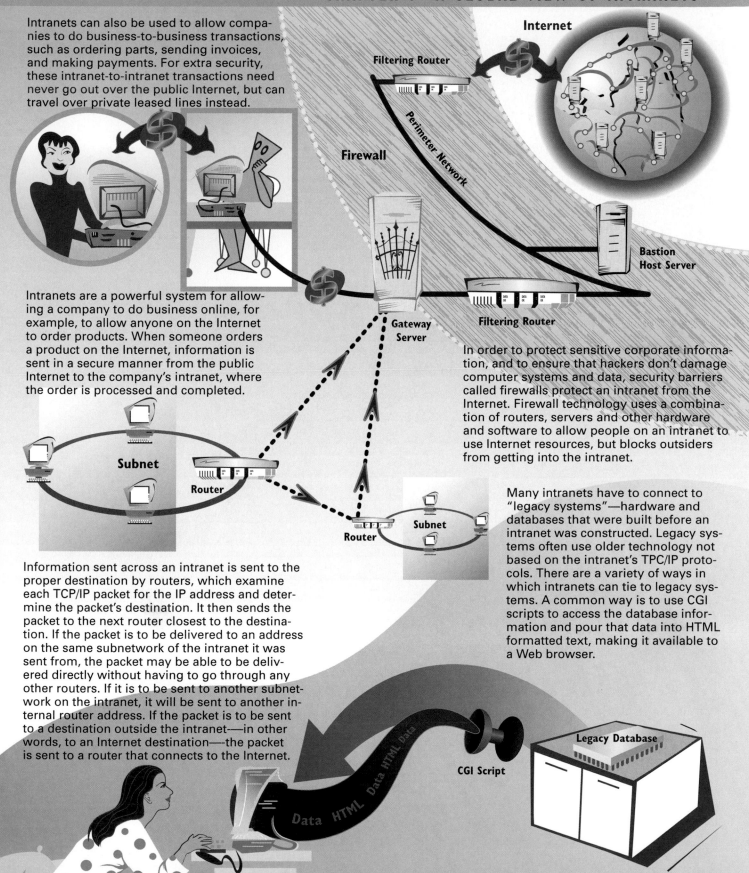

Internet

Filtering Router

Firewall

Perimeter Network

Bastion Host Server

Gateway Server

Filtering Router

Subnet

Router

Router

Subnet

Legacy Database

CGI Script

Data HTML Data HTML Data

CHAPTER

2

How TCP/IP Works

As we saw in Chapter 1, an intranet is a private network built using the Internet's technology and communication protocols. At the heart of this technology—and what makes all intranet communications possible—are two protocols for exchanging information: The Transmission Control Protocol (TCP) and the Internet Protocol (IP). Together, these protocols are known as TCP/IP. They are separate protocols, not a single one, although they are tightly woven together to allow for the most efficient communications.

These two protocols perform their magic by doing something that seems deceptively simple. They break data into sections called packets, deliver those packets to the proper destinations on an intranet (or onto the Internet), and after they've been delivered, they reassemble the packets into their original form so that they can be viewed and used by the recipient. TCP performs the work of separating the data into packets and reassembling it, while IP is responsible for making sure that the packets are sent to the right destination.

TCP/IP is used because intranets (and the Internet) are what is known as *packet-switched* networks. In a packet-switched network, information is sent in many small packets over many different routes at the same time and reassembled at the receiving end. Because packet-switched networks can always use the most efficient means of delivery by tapping into unused network resources, they make the best use of the network's resources.

By contrast, the telephone system is a *circuit-switched* network. In a circuit-switched network, there is a single, unbroken connection between the sender and the receiver. Once a connection is made to a resource on the network (as with a telephone call), even if no data is being sent (such as when a call is on hold), that physical connection remains exclusively dedicated to that single connection.

In order for personal computers to take full advantage of intranets, they need to use TCP/IP protocols. Winsock functions as an intermediary between the personal computers and intranet (and Internet) hosts. For Macintoshes, the software is called Mac/TCP. Winsock is an application program interface (API) that handles the sending and receiving data to the TCP/IP systems.

An intranet may not be the only network used within a corporation. An intranet may be connected to other corporate networks, in particular to NetWare-based networks. When this happens, the intranet can be used as a way to route data between the NetWare networks. To do this a NetWare network sends packets of data, and essentially disguises its own network protocols inside IP packets, and then uses IP protocols to send the data from one network to another. When an intranet is used like this, it is referred to as *IP tunneling*.

How TCP/IP and IPX Work on Intranets

What distinguishes an intranet from any other kind of private network is that it is based on TCP/IP—the same protocols that apply to the Internet. TCP/IP refers to two protocols that work together to deliver data: the Transmission Control Protocol (TCP) and the Internet Protocol (IP). When you send information across an intranet, the data is broken into small packets. The packets are sent independently through a series of switches called routers. Once all the packets arrive at their destination, they are recombined into their original form. The Transmission Control Protocol breaks the data into packets and recombines them on the receiving end. The Internet Protocol handles the routing of the data and makes sure it gets sent to the proper destination.

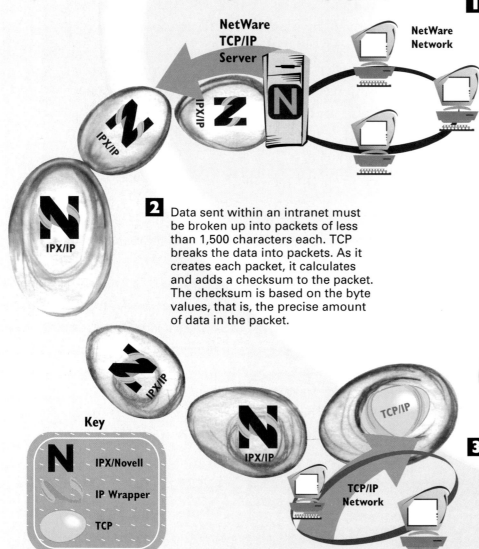

1 In some companies, there may be a mix of TCP/IP-based intranets and networks based on other networking technology, such as NetWare. In that instance, the TCP/IP technology of an intranet can be used to send data between NetWare or other networks, using a technique called IP tunneling. In this instance, we'll look at data being sent from one NetWare network to another, via an intranet. NetWare networks use the IPX (Internet Packet Exchange) protocol as a way to deliver data—and TCP/IP networks can't recognize that protocol. To get around this, when an IPX packet is to be sent across an intranet, it is first encapsulated inside an IP packet by a NetWare server specifically for and dedicated to providing the IP transport mechanism for IPX packets.

2 Data sent within an intranet must be broken up into packets of less than 1,500 characters each. TCP breaks the data into packets. As it creates each packet, it calculates and adds a checksum to the packet. The checksum is based on the byte values, that is, the precise amount of data in the packet.

Key

N IPX/Novell

IP Wrapper

TCP

3 Each packet, along with the checksum, is put into separate IP wrappers or "envelopes." These wrappers contain information that details exactly where on the intranet—or the Internet—the data is to be sent. All of the wrappers for a given piece of data have the same addressing information so that they can all be sent to the same location for reassembly.

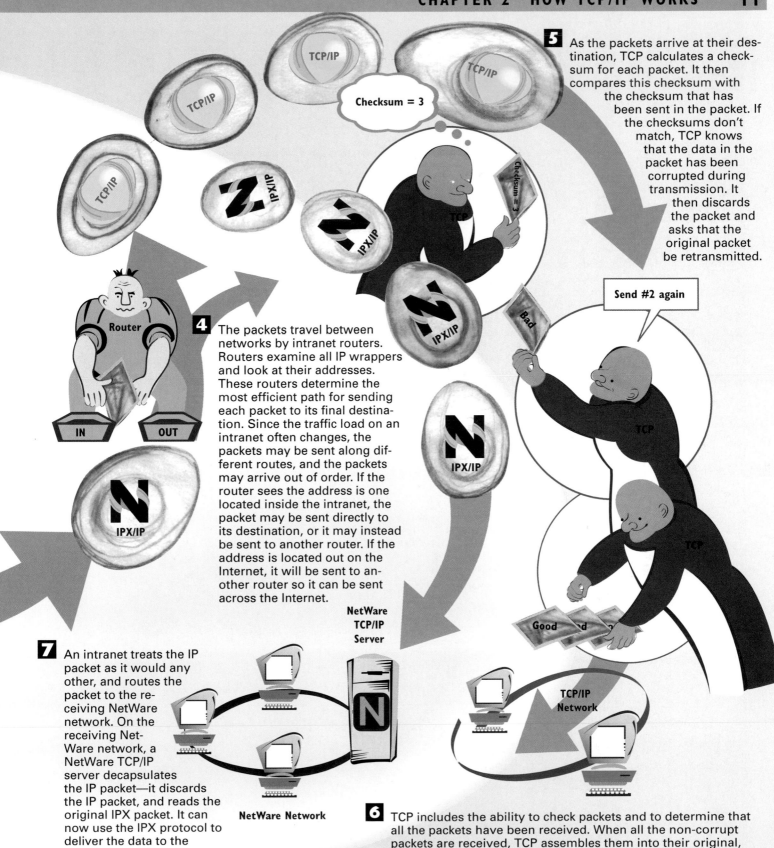

5 As the packets arrive at their destination, TCP calculates a checksum for each packet. It then compares this checksum with the checksum that has been sent in the packet. If the checksums don't match, TCP knows that the data in the packet has been corrupted during transmission. It then discards the packet and asks that the original packet be retransmitted.

Send #2 again

4 The packets travel between networks by intranet routers. Routers examine all IP wrappers and look at their addresses. These routers determine the most efficient path for sending each packet to its final destination. Since the traffic load on an intranet often changes, the packets may be sent along different routes, and the packets may arrive out of order. If the router sees the address is one located inside the intranet, the packet may be sent directly to its destination, or it may instead be sent to another router. If the address is located out on the Internet, it will be sent to another router so it can be sent across the Internet.

7 An intranet treats the IP packet as it would any other, and routes the packet to the receiving NetWare network. On the receiving NetWare network, a NetWare TCP/IP server decapsulates the IP packet—it discards the IP packet, and reads the original IPX packet. It can now use the IPX protocol to deliver the data to the proper destination.

6 TCP includes the ability to check packets and to determine that all the packets have been received. When all the non-corrupt packets are received, TCP assembles them into their original, unified form. The header information of the packets relays the sequence of how to reassemble the packets.

How the OSI Model Works

A group called the International Standards Organization (ISO) has put together the Open Systems Interconnect (OSI) Reference Model, which is a model that describes seven layers of protocols for computer communications. These layers don't know or care what is on adjacent layers. Each layer, essentially, only sees the reciprocal layer on the other side. The sending application layer sees and talks to the application layer on the destination side. That conversation takes place irrespective of, for example, what structure exists at the physical layer, such as Ethernet or Token Ring. TCP combines the OSI model's application, presentation, and session layers into one which is also called the application layer.

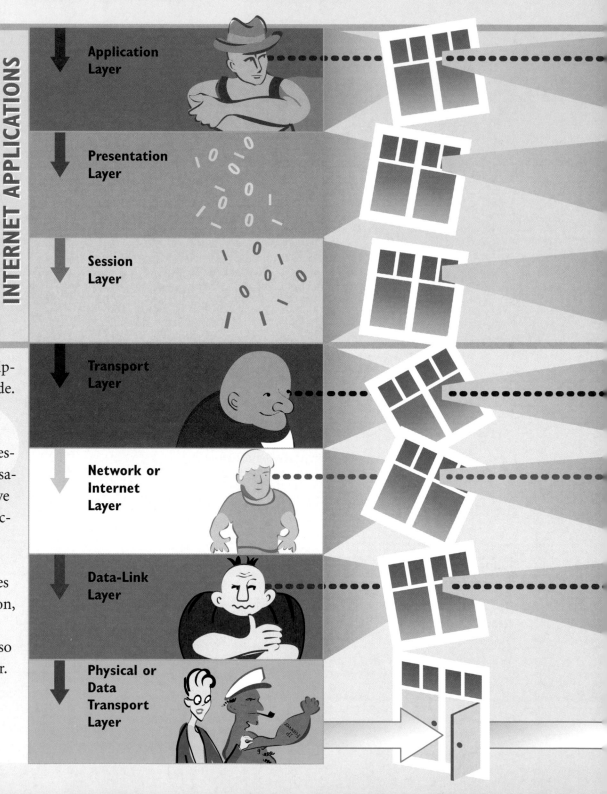

INTERNET APPLICATIONS

Application Layer

Presentation Layer

Session Layer

Transport Layer

Network or Internet Layer

Data-Link Layer

Physical or Data Transport Layer

7

The application layer refers to application *interfaces*, not programs like word processing. MHS (Message Handling Service) is such an interface and it operates at this level of the OSI model. Again, this segmentation and interface approach means that a variety of email programs can be used on an intranet so long as they conform to the MHS standard at this application interface level.

6

The presentation layer typically simply provides a standard interface between the application layer and the network layers. This type of segmentation allows for the great flexibility of the OSI model since applications can vary endlessly, but, as long as the results conform to this standard interface, the applications need not be concerned with any of the other layers.

5

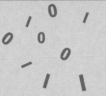

The session layer allows for the communication between sender and destination. These conversations avoid confusion by speaking in turn. A token is passed to control and to indicate which side is allowed to speak. This layer executes transactions, like saving a file. If something prevents it from completing the save, the session layer, which has a record of the original state, returns to the original state rather than allowing a corrupt or incomplete transaction to occur.

4

The transport layer segments the data into acceptable packet sizes and is responsible for data integrity of packet segments. There are several levels of service that can be implemented at this layer, including segmenting and reassembly, error recovery, flow control, and others.

3

The IP wrapper is put around the packet at the network or Internet layer. The header includes the source and destination addresses, the sequence order, and other data necessary for correct routing and rebuilding at the destination.

2

The data-link layer frames the packets—for example, for use with the PPP (Point to Point). It also includes the logical link portion of the MAC sublayer of the IEEE 802.2, 802.3 and other standards.

1

Ethernet and Token Ring are the two most common physical layer protocols. They function at the MAC (Media Access Control) level and move the data over the cables based on the physical address on each NIC (Network Interface Card). The physical layer includes the physical components of the IEEE 802.3 and other specifications.

How TCP/IP Packets Are Processed

Sending Computer

HTTP

Protocols such as TCP/IP determine how computers communicate with each other over networks such as the Internet. These protocols work in concert with each other, and are layered on top of one another in what is commonly referred to as a protocol stack. Each layer of the protocol is designed to accomplish a specific purpose on both the sending and receiving computers. The TCP stack combines the application, presentation, and the session layers into a single layer also called the application layer. Other than that change, it follows the OSI model. The illustration below shows the wrapping process that occurs to transmit data.

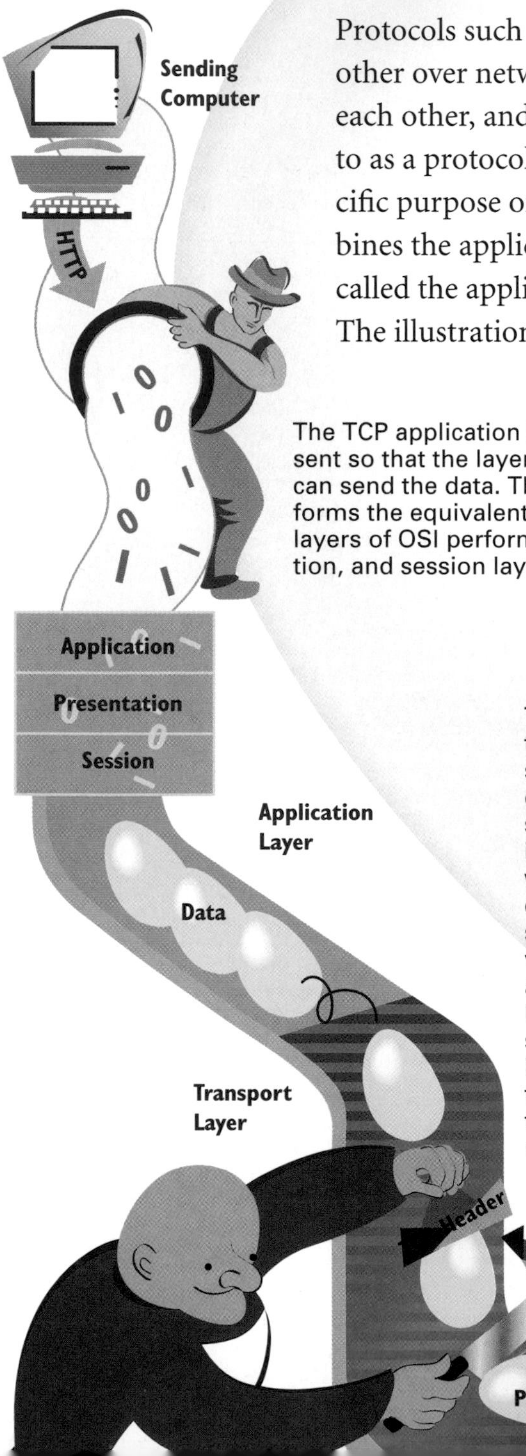

The TCP application layer formats the data being sent so that the layer below it, the transport layer, can send the data. The TCP application layer performs the equivalent actions that the top three layers of OSI perform: the application, presentation, and session layers.

Application

Presentation

Session

Application Layer

Data

Transport Layer

Header

TCP Packets

The next layer down is the transport layer, which is responsible for transferring the data, and ensures that the data sent and the data received are in fact the same data—in other words, that there have been no errors introduced during the sending of the data. TCP divides the data it gets from the application layer into segments. It attaches a header to each segment. The header contains information that will be used on the receiving end to ensure that the data hasn't been altered en route, and that the segments can be properly recombined into their original form.

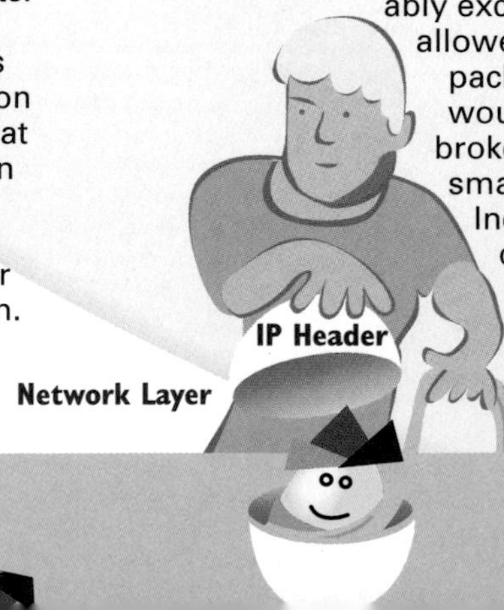

The third layer prepares the data for delivery by putting them into IP datagrams, and determining the proper Internet address for those datagrams. The IP protocol works in the Internet layer, also called the network layer. It puts an IP wrapper with a header onto each segment. The IP header includes information such as the IP address of the sending and receiving computers, and the length of the datagram, and the sequence order of the datagram. The sequence order is added because the datagram could conceivably exceed the size allowed for network packets, and so would need to be broken into smaller packets. Including the sequence order will allow them to be recombined properly.

IP Header

Network Layer

The Internet layer checks the IP header and checks to see whether the packet is a fragment. If it is, it puts together fragments back into the original datagram. It strips off the IP header, and then sends the datagram to the transport layer.

Network

Data

Physical

The physical network layer receives the packet. It translates the hardware address of the sender and receiver into IP addresses. Then it sends the frame up to the data link layer.

Physical Network Layer

The data-link layer ensures that the CRC for the frame is right, and that the data hasn't been altered while it was sent. It strips off the frame header and the CRC, and sends the frame to the Internet layer.

Transport

The transport layer looks at the remaining header to decide which application layer protocol—TCP or UDP—should get the data. Then the proper protocol strips off the header and sends the data to the receiving application.

http

On the receiving computer, the packet travels through the stack, but in the opposite order from which the packet was created. In other words, it starts at the bottom layer, and moves its way up through the protocol stack. As it moves up, each layer strips off the header information that was added by the TCP/IP stack of the sending computer.

The application layer gets the data and performs, in this case, an HTTP request.

Receiving Computer

The final layer is the physical network layer, which specifies the physical characteristics of the network being used to send data. It describes the actual hardware standards, such as the Ethernet specification. The layer receives the frames from the data link layer, and translates the IP addresses there into the hardware addresses required for the specific network being used. Finally, the layer sends the frame over the network.

The next layer down, the data link layer, uses protocols such as the Point-to-Point Protocol (PPP) to put the IP datagram into a frame. This is done by putting a header—the third header, after the TCP header and the IP header—and a footer around the IP datagram to frame it. Included in the frame header is a CRC check that checks for errors in the data as the data travels over the network.

Data-Link Layer

IP Datagram

Frame

C H A P T E R

3

How Bridges Work

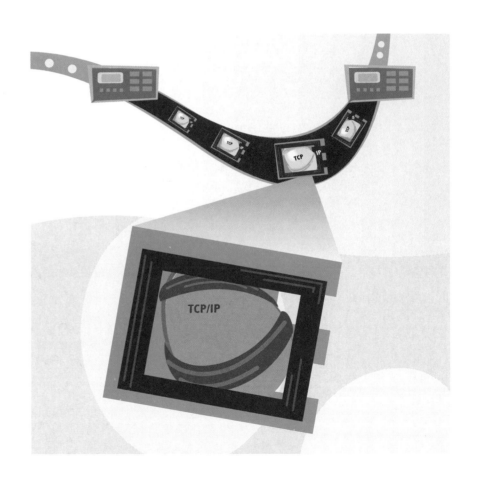

AN intranet—especially one in a large corporation—can be a remarkably complex endeavor, consisting of many networks, including departmental local area networks, as well as larger *subnetworks*, which each are in essence collections of networks.

Bridges connect networks. When bridges were first developed they could not connect incompatible networking architectures. Early bridges functioned at the media-access control (MAC) section of the data-link layer of the OSI model (discussed in Chapter 2). Ethernet and Token Ring architecture differ at the MAC section of the data-link layer, hence their incompatibility. Newer bridges function at the logical-link control (LLC) portion of the data-link layer. As long as the communication protocol on both networks is the same (IPX to IPX, for example), Ethernet and Token Ring networks can be linked by bridges. Connecting divergent networks is an essential requirement for intranets.

Bridges are also used to connect networks indirectly by long-distance, usually leased, lines. Remote bridges on Ethernet networks use a *transparent* routing technique to handle traffic. It is the destination address of each packet that is read to determine the action to be taken. If the destination is on the same network, bridges ignore the packet; bridges pass only packets that need to go to other networks. Token Ring operates somewhat differently in that it uses *source* routing. In this case, the bridge uses a test message to calculate the best path between the source and the destination.

In order to determine whether to pass or drop a packet, bridges refer to a table, which is basically a list of addresses. These tables originally had to be built manually, causing considerable maintenance every time a replacement or additional NIC address was put on the network. This led to the development of *learning* bridges, that is, bridges with software algorithms that could build these tables automatically. Today's bridges build and maintain their tables by listening to cable traffic and checking packets for source addresses.

Bridges are relatively simple to set up and maintain, and they can operate fairly fast since they simply decide whether to pass or drop the packet. In the next chapter a similar but more complex piece of equipment, the router, is discussed. Bridges are often used to segment and reduce local network traffic. Routers are usually used for connecting entire networks and subnetworks together.

Bridges and routers are sometimes combined into a single product called a *brouter*. A brouter combines the functions of both bridge and router. It examines the outermost address to see if the data needs to be sent to another LAN over a bridge, and delivers information that way if possible. If, instead, it needs to be sent using IP technology, it will act as a router does.

How Bridges Work

Bridges are hardware and software combinations that connect different parts of a single network, such as different sections of an intranet. They connect local area networks (LANs) to each other. They are generally not used, however, for connecting entire networks to each other, for example, for connecting an intranet to the Internet, or an intranet to an intranet, or to connect an entire subnetwork to an entire subnetwork. To do that, more sophisticated pieces of technology called routers are used. (See Chapter 4 for more information on how routers work.)

1 When there is a great amount of traffic on an Ethernet local area network, packets can *collide* with one another, reducing the efficiency of the network, and slowing down network traffic. Packets can collide because so much of the traffic is routed among all the workstations on the network.

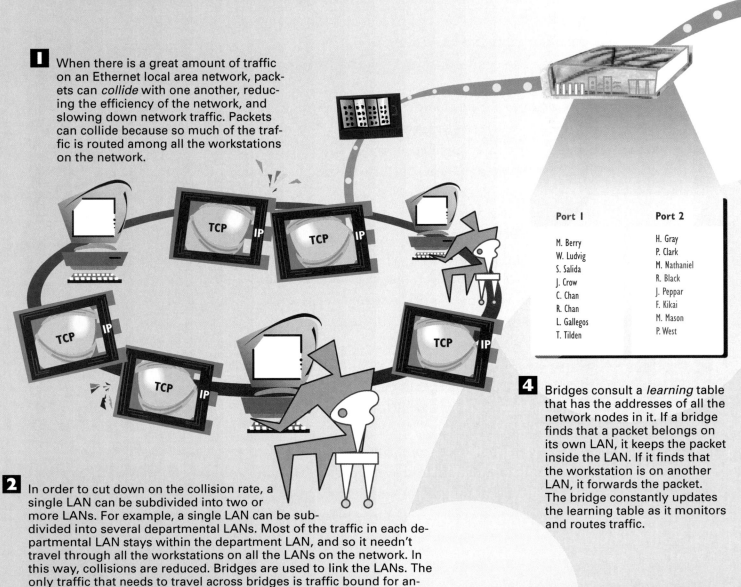

Port 1	Port 2
M. Berry	H. Gray
W. Ludvig	P. Clark
S. Salida	M. Nathaniel
J. Crow	R. Black
C. Chan	J. Peppar
R. Chan	F. Kikai
L. Gallegos	M. Mason
T. Tilden	P. West

2 In order to cut down on the collision rate, a single LAN can be subdivided into two or more LANs. For example, a single LAN can be subdivided into several departmental LANs. Most of the traffic in each departmental LAN stays within the department LAN, and so it needn't travel through all the workstations on all the LANs on the network. In this way, collisions are reduced. Bridges are used to link the LANs. The only traffic that needs to travel across bridges is traffic bound for another LAN. Any traffic within the LAN need not travel across a bridge.

4 Bridges consult a *learning* table that has the addresses of all the network nodes in it. If a bridge finds that a packet belongs on its own LAN, it keeps the packet inside the LAN. If it finds that the workstation is on another LAN, it forwards the packet. The bridge constantly updates the learning table as it monitors and routes traffic.

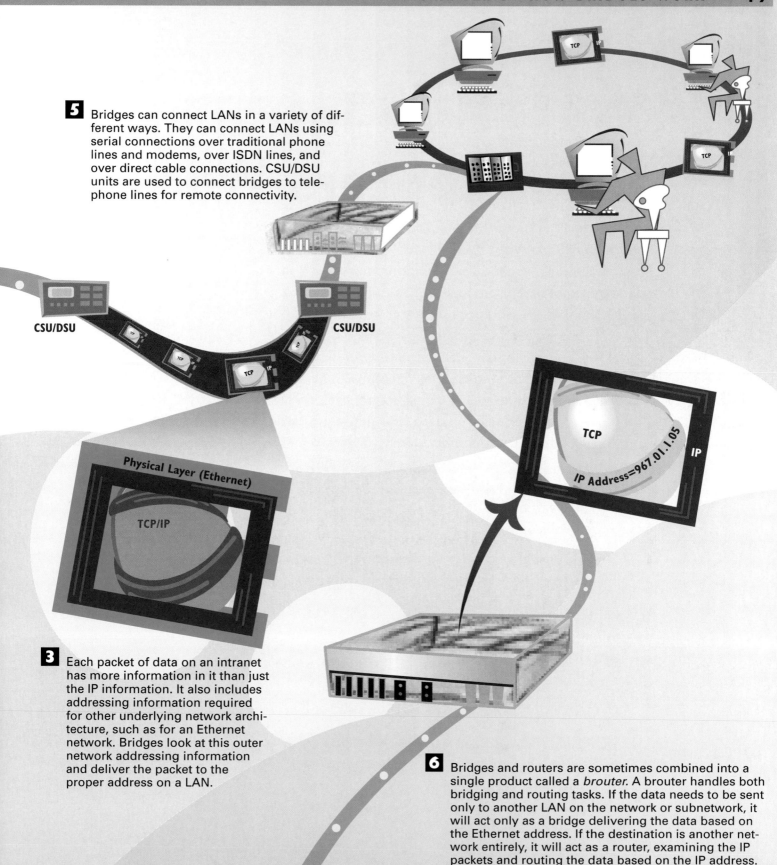

5 Bridges can connect LANs in a variety of different ways. They can connect LANs using serial connections over traditional phone lines and modems, over ISDN lines, and over direct cable connections. CSU/DSU units are used to connect bridges to telephone lines for remote connectivity.

CSU/DSU

CSU/DSU

TCP

IP Address=967.01.1.05

IP

Physical Layer (Ethernet)

TCP/IP

3 Each packet of data on an intranet has more information in it than just the IP information. It also includes addressing information required for other underlying network architecture, such as for an Ethernet network. Bridges look at this outer network addressing information and deliver the packet to the proper address on a LAN.

6 Bridges and routers are sometimes combined into a single product called a *brouter*. A brouter handles both bridging and routing tasks. If the data needs to be sent only to another LAN on the network or subnetwork, it will act only as a bridge delivering the data based on the Ethernet address. If the destination is another network entirely, it will act as a router, examining the IP packets and routing the data based on the IP address.

CHAPTER
4

How Intranet Routers Work

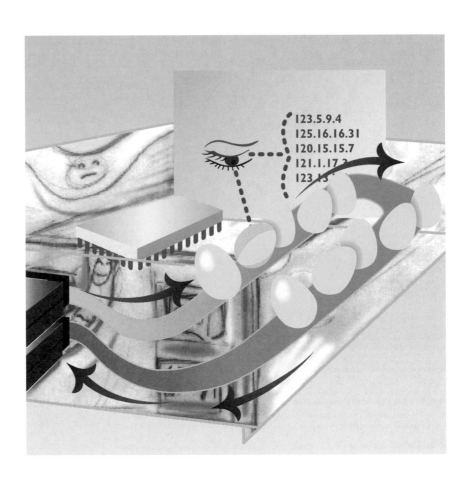

ROUTERS

are the traffic cops of intranets. They make sure that all data gets sent to where it's supposed to go and that it gets sent via the most efficient route. Routers are also useful tools to make the most efficient use of the intranet. Routers are used to segment traffic and provide redundancy of routes. Routers use encapsulation to permit different protocols to be sent across otherwise incompatible networks.

When you sit down at your computer on an intranet and send or receive data, that information generally must first go through at least one router, and often more than one router before it reaches its final destination. Routers can be simple or quite sophisticated. Factors that determine the required complexity of a router include the size of the intranet, the type and quantity of traffic on segments, and security concerns of the intranet. The more complex the intranet, and, in particular, the greater number of possible destinations for data, the greater the need for sophisticated router hardware and software.

Routers open the IP packet to read the destination address, calculate the best route, and then send the packet toward the final destination. If the destination is on the same part of an intranet, the packet would be sent directly to the destination computer by the router. If the packet is destined for another intranet or subnetwork (or if the destination is on the Internet), the router considers factors like traffic congestion and the number of *hops*—a term that refers to the number of routers or gateways on any given path. The IP packet carries with it a segment that holds the hop count and a router will not use a path that would exceed a predefined number of hops. Multiple routes within an acceptable hop count range are desirable in intranets to provide redundancy and assure that data can get through. For example, if a direct route between San Francisco and New York were unavailable, sophisticated routers would send data to New York via another router probably in another city on the intranet—and this would all be transparent to the users.

Routers have two or more physical ports: receiving (input) ports and sending (output) ports. In actuality, every port is bi-directional and can receive or send data. When a packet is received at an input port, a software routine called a routing process is run. This process looks inside the header information in the IP packet and finds the address where the data is being sent. It then compares this address against an internal database called a *routing table* that has information detailing to which port packets with various IP addresses should be sent. Based on what it finds in the routing table, it sends the packet to a specific output port. This output port then sends the data to the next router or to the destination itself.

At times, packets are sent to a router's input port faster than it can process them. When this happens, the packets are sent to a special holding area called an *input queue*, an area of RAM on the router. That specific input queue is associated with a specific input port. A router can have more than one input queue, if several input ports are being sent packets faster than the router can process them. Each input port will process packets from the queue in the order in which they were received.

If the traffic through the router is very heavy, the number of packets in the queue can be greater than the capacity of the queue. (The capacity of the queue is called the queue's *length*.) When this happens, there is a possibility that packets may be dropped and so will not be processed by the router, and won't be sent to their destination. This doesn't mean, though, that the information has be to lost. The TCP protocol was designed to take into account that packets can be lost en route to their final destination. If not all the packets are sent to the receiving end, TCP at the receiving computer recognizes that and asks that the missing packets be re-sent. It will keep requesting that the packets be re-sent until they are all received. Sophisticated routers can be managed and problems diagnosed and resolved using special software, such as SNMP (Simple Network Management Protocol). TCP can tell what actions to take because there are various flags in the packet, like the hop count in IP, that tell TCP what it needs to know to act. For example, the *ack* flag, set to "on," indicates that it is responding to (acknowledging) a previous communication.

A wide variety of routing hardware and software is available. In some cases, a variety of different kinds of routing software can be run on a given piece of hardware. For example, Novell's Multi Protocol Router is routing software that runs on router hardware. In other instances—and particularly when routers are high-performance routers—the routing software is built directly into a router's hardware or firmware.

There are several kinds of tables used in routing. In the simplest kind of intranet, an exceedingly simple routing table can be used, called a *minimal routing table*. When an intranet is composed of a single TCP/IP network, and when that network is not connected to any other TCP/IP network or to the Internet, minimal routing can be used. In minimal routing, a program called *ifconfig* automatically creates the table, which contains only a few basic entries. Since there are very few places that data can be sent, only a minimal number of routes need to be configured.

If an intranet has only a limited number of other TCP/IP networks, then a *static routing table* can be used. In this case, packets with specific addresses are sent to specific routers—the routers do not redirect packets to adjust to changing network traffic. Static routing should be used when there is only one route to each given destination. A static routing table allows an intranet administrator to add or take away entries in the routing table.

Dynamic routing tables are the most sophisticated routing tables. They should be used when there is more than one way in which data can be sent from a router to the final destination, and in more complex intranets. These tables constantly change as network traffic and conditions change, so that they always route data the most efficient way possible, taking into account the current state of traffic on the intranet.

Dynamic routing tables are built using routing protocols. These protocols are ways in which routers communicate with one another, giving each other information about the most efficient way of routing data given the current state of the intranet. A router with a dynamic routing table can automatically switch data to a backup route if the primary route is down. It can also always determine the most efficient way of routing data toward its final destination. Routers advertise their IP addresses and know the IP addresses of their neighbors. Routers can use this information in an algorithm to calculate the best route to send packets.

The most common routing protocol that performs these best-case calculations is known as RIP (Routing Information Protocol). When RIP determines the most efficient route for data, it calculates the hop count for the route. RIP always chooses the path with the lowest hop count as the route to send data over. It assumes that the fewer the hops, the more efficient the path. RIP will not allow any path with a hop count of over 16. If there is a hop count of over 16, it will discard the route. On most intranets this shouldn't be a problem.

The Exterior Gateway Protocol (EGP) is used for the Internet where many more routers might have to be traversed before a packet reaches its final destination. It will not be needed on an intranet since it's rare that an intranet would be so large that data would have to pass through more than 16 routers or gateways in order to be sent to the final destination.

The thing to keep in mind about intranets and routing technology is that it is not an either/or situation. Many different kinds of routing technologies can be used on a single intranet, depending on the needs of that particular part of the network. Some parts may be able to use routers with static routing tables, while other parts may require dynamic routing tables. As in anything having to do with intranets, the whole point is flexibility and using the right tool for the job.

How Intranet Routers Work

Just as routers direct traffic on the Internet, sending information to its proper destination, routers on an intranet perform the same function. Routers—equipment that is a combination of hardware and software—can send the data to a computer on the same subnetwork inside the intranet, to another network on the intranet, or outside to the Internet. They do this by examining header information in IP packets, and then sending the data on its way. Typically, a router will send the packet to the next router closest to the final destination, which in turn sends it to an even closer router, and so on, until the data reaches its intended recipient.

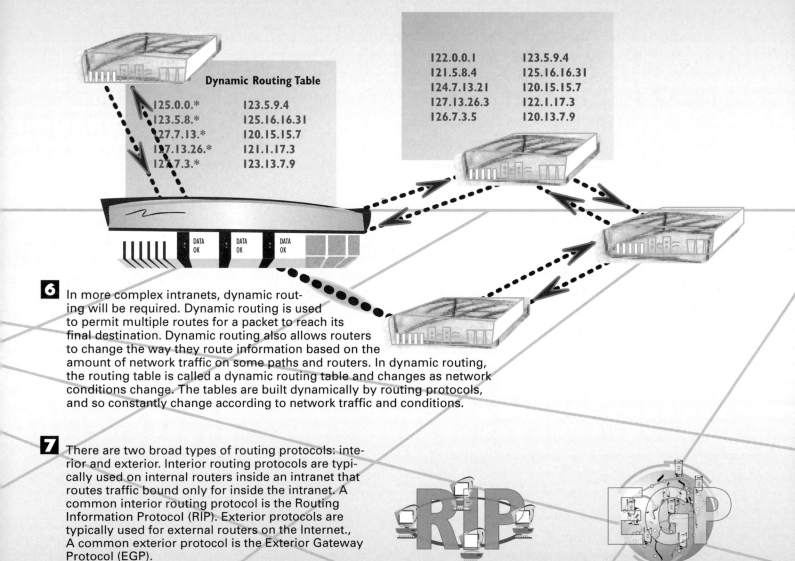

Dynamic Routing Table

125.0.0.*	123.5.9.4
123.5.8.*	125.16.16.31
127.7.13.*	120.15.15.7
127.13.26.*	121.1.17.3
127.7.3.*	123.13.7.9

122.0.0.1	123.5.9.4
121.5.8.4	125.16.16.31
124.7.13.21	120.15.15.7
127.13.26.3	122.1.17.3
126.7.3.5	120.13.7.9

6 In more complex intranets, dynamic routing will be required. Dynamic routing is used to permit multiple routes for a packet to reach its final destination. Dynamic routing also allows routers to change the way they route information based on the amount of network traffic on some paths and routers. In dynamic routing, the routing table is called a dynamic routing table and changes as network conditions change. The tables are built dynamically by routing protocols, and so constantly change according to network traffic and conditions.

7 There are two broad types of routing protocols: interior and exterior. Interior routing protocols are typically used on internal routers inside an intranet that routes traffic bound only for inside the intranet. A common interior routing protocol is the Routing Information Protocol (RIP). Exterior protocols are typically used for external routers on the Internet., A common exterior protocol is the Exterior Gateway Protocol (EGP).

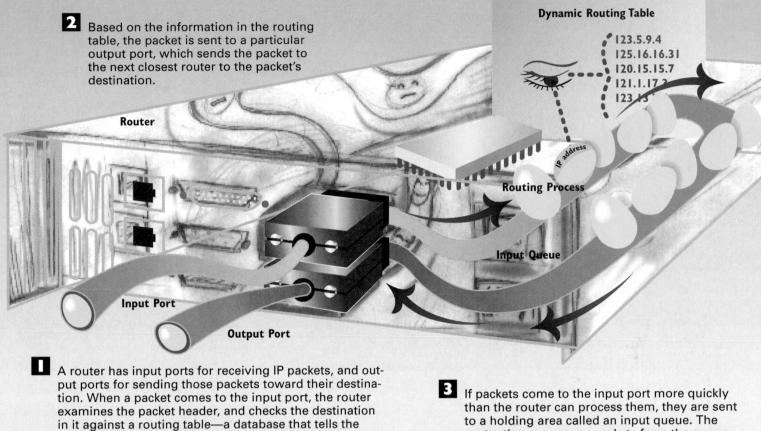

2 Based on the information in the routing table, the packet is sent to a particular output port, which sends the packet to the next closest router to the packet's destination.

Router

Dynamic Routing Table

123.5.9.4
125.16.16.31
120.15.15.7
121.1.17.3
123.13

IP address

Routing Process

Input Queue

Input Port

Output Port

1 A router has input ports for receiving IP packets, and output ports for sending those packets toward their destination. When a packet comes to the input port, the router examines the packet header, and checks the destination in it against a routing table—a database that tells the router how to send packets to various destinations.

3 If packets come to the input port more quickly than the router can process them, they are sent to a holding area called an input queue. The router then processes packets from the queue in the order they were received. If the number of packets received exceeds the capacity of the queue (called the length of the queue), packets may be lost. When this happens, the TCP protocol on the sending and receiving computers will have the packets re-sent.

Minimal Routing Table

125.0.0.1
125.0.0.1
127.7.13.21
127.13.26.3

4 In a simple intranet that is a single, completely self-contained network, and in which there are no connections to any other network or the intranet, only minimal routing need be done, and so the routing table in the router is exceedingly simple with very few entries, and is constructed automatically by a program called *ifconfig*.

Static Routing Table

125.0.0.1	123.5.9.4
125.0.0.1	125.16.16.31
127.7.13.21	120.15.15.7
127.13.26.3	121.1.17.3
127.7.3.5	123.13.7.9

5 In a slightly more complicated intranet which is composed of a number of TCP/IP-based networks, and connects to a limited number of TCP/IP-based networks, static routing will be required. In static routing, the routing table has specific ways of routing data to other networks. Only those pathways can be used. Intranet administrators can add routes to the routing table. Static routing is more flexible than minimal routing, but it can't change routes as network traffic changes, and so isn't suitable for many intranets.

CHAPTER

5

How Intranet E-Mail Works

INTRANETS

allow people to work together better by allowing them to communicate better. The most time-honored—and still the most popular—means of communication using computers is e-mail. Using e-mail, people can send messages to anyone else on the intranet—and, in fact, to anyone connected to the Internet as well, or connected to a computer network that has a connection to the Internet, such as an online service.

Intranet e-mail uses the TCP/IP protocol. The TCP protocol breaks your messages into packets, the IP protocol delivers the packets to the proper location, and then TCP reassembles the message on the receiving end so that it can be read.

You can also attach binary files, such as pictures, videos, sound, and executable files, to your e-mail messages. Since the Internet can't directly handle binary files in e-mail, the file must first be *encoded* in one of a variety of encoding schemes. Popular schemes are Base64 and uuencode. The person who receives the attached binary file must *decode* the file with the same scheme that was used to encode the file. Many e-mail software packages do this automatically.

When e-mail formats differ (and they often do, having developed from proprietary and incompatible products), *gateways* are used to translate the data into the appropriate format for the recipient. However, several standards have been developed that have been adopted by most e-mail companies today that allow the various products to communicate with each other. The Simple Mail Transfer Protocol (SMTP) and the X.400 MHS (message handling service) are the two most common protocols.

SMTP is based on a client/server model in which someone uses a mail client to create mail and read mail, while servers do the actual processing and delivery of the mail.

To create e-mail, you use a mail client, which is called a *mail user agent* or *user agent* (MUA or UA). There are multiple kinds and different agents for different types of computers. When mail is sent, the Message Transfer System (MTS) on a server uses a *mail transfer agent* (MTA) to examine the address of the person to which the mail is being sent. If the person can be found on the intranet, the mail is delivered to a *mail delivery agent* (MDA). The MDA then delivers the mail to the intended recipient. When you send e-mail to someone on another intranet or on the Internet, the message is instead sent by the MTA through the Internet. The message often has to travel through a series of networks before it reaches the recipient—networks that might use different e-mail formats.

Gateways are not attached to one particular machine or one combination of hardware and software, nor are they restricted to e-mail processing functionality. They can fulfill a variety of roles in addition to protocol conversion. One example of this is actually translating data from one format to another, as they do for PC to mainframe connectivity. Gateways differ from linking hardware such as bridges and routers by operating at higher OSI levels, although routers, because of their protocol conversion functionality, are also commonly called gateways.

How E-Mail Is Delivered within an Intranet

Probably the most heavily used part of an intranet has nothing to do with corporate databases, flashy Web pages, or multimedia content—it's the use of electronic mail. Corporate intranets can use a number of different e-mail programs, such as cc:Mail, Microsoft Mail, or Lotus Notes, among others. But the most common architecture underlying the use of intranet e-mail is the protocol called the Simple Mail Transfer Protocol, or SMTP. Illustrated here is how SMTP is used to deliver mail within an intranet.

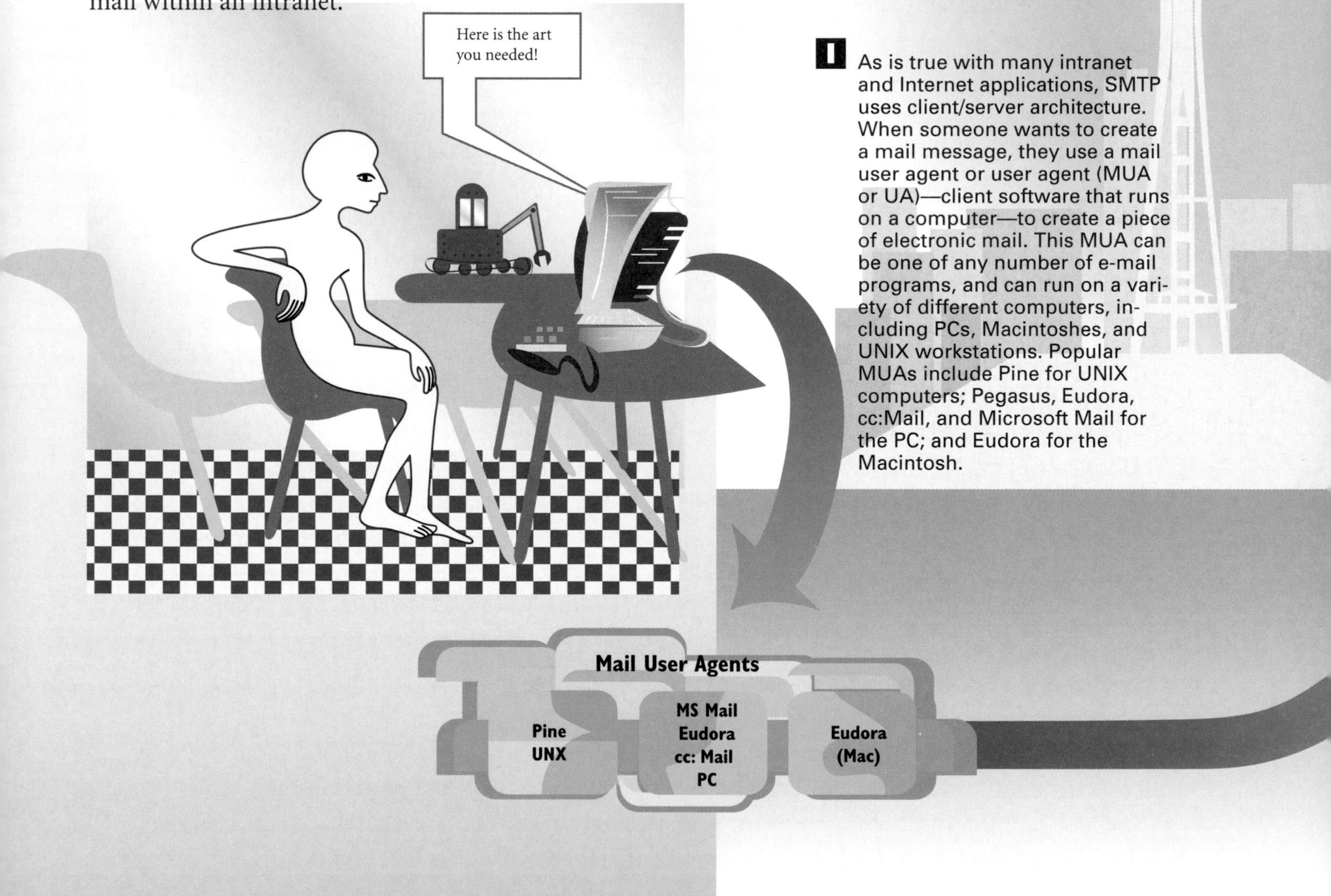

Here is the art you needed!

1 As is true with many intranet and Internet applications, SMTP uses client/server architecture. When someone wants to create a mail message, they use a mail user agent or user agent (MUA or UA)—client software that runs on a computer—to create a piece of electronic mail. This MUA can be one of any number of e-mail programs, and can run on a variety of different computers, including PCs, Macintoshes, and UNIX workstations. Popular MUAs include Pine for UNIX computers; Pegasus, Eudora, cc:Mail, and Microsoft Mail for the PC; and Eudora for the Macintosh.

Mail User Agents

| Pine UNX | MS Mail Eudora cc: Mail PC | Eudora (Mac) |

Uuencoded text

```
MITE&.#EAO`'(`/<```(`@@4`#0(&"080#@@0$&`0!(@`(@`((000(`@(*(*0(",P0( M-044+@@0(.04&I004/0022Q(!"!$$
-#A,")!`4("``+"AT.("T/%4,3%Q`Q`(-|`0 M.l`&2`P4|A`8.l`O3A<*/B,2/!4F+"4|*BTN(RPR-A$J0BDS0C$M/3$Y.0(?
M3@H@3Q`A3B`=3@XO3AXX32XO3"E$3D0C%48R'44N,D-&-3DNI$@UOC%!2Dl+
M0CDN3#$$Y4D(M2CPY3#9"3S%.4D9"2D-22@@57A869`@B8A0A:`8N7A4N6@LJ
M:Q@@I;PHY9A4Y8A@@]7A@Y:PHZ<Q@Y<!`]=Q$Z?2,>820K920U824Q="%`8R%"
M<QT^?B8\>$@@@$5S5&5TT[4Dl*4B\Y9BX\>#]6D(\9Q5.;")5:Cl37#%<4:T)*
M6D)*9T)24C]:8Dl.5D9:5DQ.7DY,:4l:6D):8T=::$=G$A0%*?B5*?QI/@!M> MA"Y/=3%%*@RM2@@RE8A#@14=T-
4=S%6C#Y3BC5J?49K>SlDCS]TE6$?$F,W$V0J
M(6(Q-%]*+5M72%M14UQQG4EU,75l:7E)C6EU=8%)H8%|C8UYG7F-K7E)::UY. M:UY::U)C:U)K:UlC:UlK:V-
G:UE6=U9C<UlG<UAC?U9K=V-K<UlK>UlKAWTl M'((]'W%&(XE&'W=/)'9=*(l3(HAD)W]#-
```

5 SMTP can only handle the e–mail transfer of plain ASCII text files. In order to send binary files such as spreadsheets, pictures, and word processing documents, they must first be converted into an ASCII format by encoding them. The files can be encoded using a variety of methods, including uuencoding and Base64. Some e-mail software will automatically encode binary files. When an encoded file is received by someone, they decode it and then can use or view the binary file. Again, many e-mail packages automatically decode encoded files.

4 The recipient of the mail can now use a mail user agent to read the mail, file it, and respond to it.

Mail Transfer Agent

Mail Delivery Agent

POP server

Mailboxes

Post Office Protocol (POP)

3 Some mail systems use another e-mail protocol called the Post Office Protocol (POP) in concert with SMTP. With POP, e-mail is not delivered directly to your computer. Instead, the mail is delivered to a mailbox on a server. To get the mail, someone logs onto the server using a password and user name, and retrieves mail with their mail agent.

2 After the message is completed, it is sent by the MUA to a program running on a server called a *mail transfer agent* (MTA). The MTA looks at the address of the intended recipient of the message. If the recipient of the message is on the intranet, the MTA sends the message to another server program on the intranet called a *mail delivery agent* (MDA). If, instead, the recipient is located on the Internet or another intranet, the file is sent over the Internet to the recipient. (See the next illustration on how mail is transferred among intranets.) The MDA looks at the address of the recipient, and sends the mail to the in box of the proper person.

How E-Mail is Delivered among Intranets

Often, e-mail created on an intranet will not be delivered to a computer on the intranet, but instead to someone on the Internet, to another intranet, or to an online service such as America Online, the Microsoft Network, or CompuServe. Here are the steps a typical message might take when being delivered from an intranet to another network or intranet.

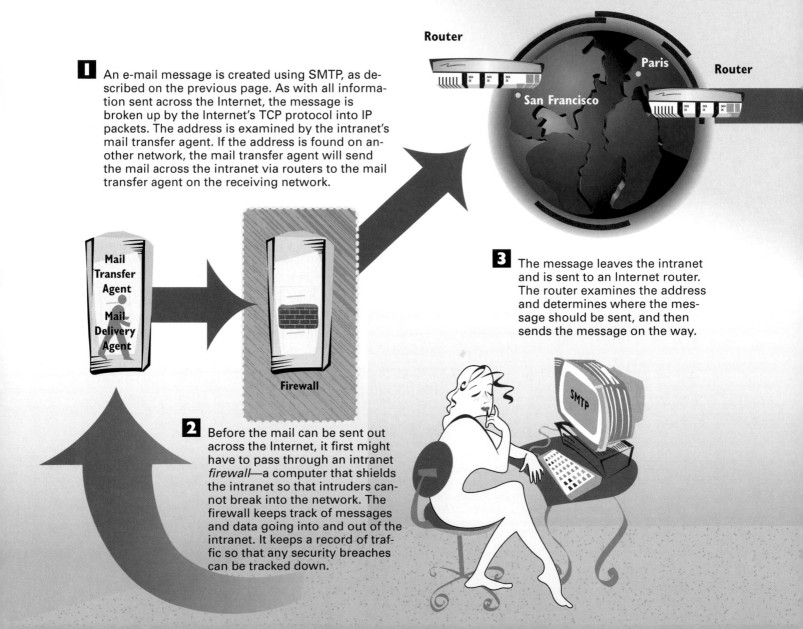

1 An e-mail message is created using SMTP, as described on the previous page. As with all informa-tion sent across the Internet, the message is broken up by the Internet's TCP protocol into IP packets. The address is examined by the intranet's mail transfer agent. If the address is found on an-other network, the mail transfer agent will send the mail across the intranet via routers to the mail transfer agent on the receiving network.

3 The message leaves the intranet and is sent to an Internet router. The router examines the address and determines where the mes-sage should be sent, and then sends the message on the way.

2 Before the mail can be sent out across the Internet, it first might have to pass through an intranet *firewall*—a computer that shields the intranet so that intruders can-not break into the network. The firewall keeps track of messages and data going into and out of the intranet. It keeps a record of traf-fic so that any security breaches can be tracked down.

4 The receiving network gets the e-mail message. A *gateway* there uses TCP to reconstruct the IP packets into a full message. The gateway then translates the message into the particular protocol the target network uses (such as CompuServe's mail format), and sends it on its way. The message may be required to also pass through a firewall on the receiving network.

5 The receiving network examines the e-mail address and sends the message to the specific mailbox where the message was intended to go, or uses the Post Office Protocol (POP) to deliver it to a mail server.

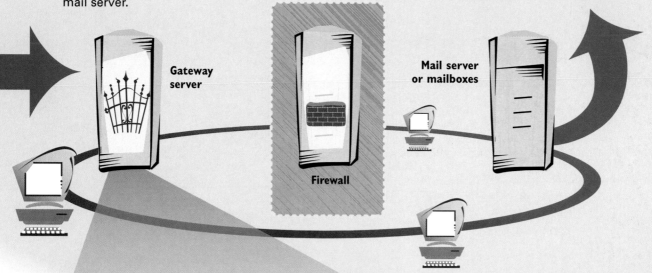

Gateway server

Firewall

Mail server or mailboxes

OSI	Layer	Hardware	Action
1	Application	Gateways	May convert data (CompuServe protocol to SMTP)
2	Presentation		
3	Session		
4	Transport		
5	Network/Internet	Routers	Do not change data
6	Data-Link	Bridges	
7	Physical	Repeaters	

6 Gateways can actually change data (if needed) for connectivity. For e-mail it may convert CompuServe protocol to SMTP. Gateways are also used to connect PC's to IBM mainframes for example, ASCII to EBCDIC.

C H A P T E R
6

How Intranet Web Servers and Browsers Work

WITHOUT the World Wide Web, there would probably be very few intranets. There are many forces driving corporations to set up an intranet, but the main one is the dominating presence of the World Wide Web. The Web has made it possible for companies to better communicate vital information among employees, departments, and divisions; to better communicate with customers; and to make it easy for those within a company to get at the vast resources often locked up in corporate databases and information centers.

The Web makes it easy to publish information because each Web page allows people to incorporate text, graphics, sound, animation, and other multimedia elements. In essence, each page is an interactive multimedia publication. This means that a company can easily publish simple documents such as personnel handbooks or expense reports. They can also create sophisticated pages that let people do more than just read a corporate annual report, and also let them see videos of the company in action or listen to speeches by corporate officers. The page at the top (or entrance to a site) is called a home page.

The Web is also a powerful intranet tool because of the way it can link corporate home pages to one another. *Hypertext* links any home page to any other home page, and to graphics, binary files, multimedia files, and any Internet or intranet resource. To jump to one home page from another, you merely click on a link on a home page, and you'll automatically be sent there. It is easy to create documents that allow employees to find specific company information and related material quickly.

The Web uses client/server architecture to work. To access the Web, a client uses a Web browser program. Clients are available for all common types of computers, including PCs, Macintoshes, and UNIX workstations. Popular browsers include Netscape and Microsoft's Internet Explorer. The client/server model works well for an intranet, since it allows many different kinds of clients on different computers to be run, and yet the same corporate resources can be made available to all clients from the same servers. The operating system of a server need not be the same as the operating system of a browser. Popular operating systems for servers include UNIX and Windows NT.

Corporations often standardize on a particular browser such as Netscape or Internet Explorer, so that everyone on an intranet will use the same kind of browser. This is done because the language of the Web—the Hypertext Markup Language—has not been truly standardized. Additionally, each browser has slightly different capabilities, so pages designed for one browser may not display very well in another browser.

Home pages on an intranet (and the Internet) are built using a page markup language called HTML (Hypertext Markup Language). This specialized language contains commands that tell browsers how to display text, graphics, and multimedia files. It also contains commands for linking the home page to other home pages, and to other Internet resources. HTML is a constantly evolving language, and with each new generation it gets additional capabilities. While there are HTML standards, there are also variations on the language, so those who build intranets have to be careful to use HTML commands that their company's standard intranet browser will easily understand.

It's the browser's job to contact Web servers, receive HTML pages, and then interpret and display those pages. Web locations on an intranet are specified by URLs—uniform resource locators. You type in the URL in your browser, or click on a link in order to navigate to a particular Web page. The packets making up the request are sent to an intranet router, which checks the destination address, and then routes the request to the proper server.

When you type in the URL, the Web browser looks at the URL and then determines which server to contact, which directory to ask for, and what specific document in that directory is the one that you want. It then uses HTTP (Hypertext Transfer Protocol) to contact the Web server and request the document that you're interested in. HTTP is an application level protocol.

The Web server receives requests from browsers using HTTP. Its job is simple: to deliver the page or other object to the browser, using HTTP. It receives the request and sends the requested information back to the Web browser. After it sends the information, the connection is closed. In this way, the intranet's resources can be used most efficiently, since whenever the server isn't sending or receiving data, it's available.

Increasingly, the Web is becoming a true multimedia environment. It allows for animation, video, and other forms of interactivity. It does this in a variety of ways. One way is by using a programming language called Java, which allows intranet programmers to create interactive applications delivered over the Web. Java applets require that Web browsers be able to read the language. Popular browsers like Netscape Navigator are able to do that.

Another way that the Web is becoming a multimedia environment is by the use of an increased amount of sound files. Web browsers by themselves often won't be able to play these kinds of files. Sometimes, home pages contain links to files that the Web browser can't play or display, such as sound and animation files. In that case, you'll need a *helper application*. You configure your Web browser to use the helper application whenever it comes across a sound or animation file that the browser itself can't run or play. A special kind of helper application is known as a *plug-in*. Plug-ins allow the sound, animation, or video to play right inside the Web browser. You don't need the browser to run a separate program, as you need to with helper applications.

The Web is important for intranets because, increasingly, it is a way to allow people within corporations to be able to mine the rich amounts of data found in corporate databases. Before intranets and the Web, it was often difficult to give many people access to this information. The relative ease of publishing and creating forms with HTML makes it easier to give people access to this information. Often, some kind of link needs to be forged between the Web and a corporate database that allows someone on the intranet Web to query a database that doesn't understand HTML. One way to do this is to use the Common Gateway Interface (CGI). With CGI programs or scripts, an intranet programmer can allow someone from the Web to search a database, and then have the information sent back to that person in an HTML page that's easy to read and understand. The data can be sent back with new HTML links that would lead the user to other data, allowing for expanded interactivity with the information.

In some ways, intranet Web servers work the same as their Internet counterparts. Both receive requests specified by the HTTP request from Web browsers, and both send back the resulting pages using the TCP/IP protocol as the actual delivery mechanism. But there are some major differences as well. Inside an intranet, Web pages can be delivered at higher speeds than pages delivered over the Internet. That's because corporations can build high-speed intranets that aren't bedeviled by the traffic problems, bad connections, and low-bandwidth connections common on the Internet. So when someone inside an intranet requests a Web page, that page can be delivered from the server to the browser at a much higher speed—which is significant, considering that many pages are rich with graphics, sounds, and other multimedia files, which can take a long time to deliver over the Internet.

Intranet Web servers can also find ways to deliver information from the Internet to intranet users at high speeds. An intranet Web server can *cache* pages in memory that intranet users commonly request. It is important to realize, however, that pages from the cache are not updated, so technically, the data contained in them may have changed—with serious consequences if the item being retrieved is a stock quote or an inventory figure.

A company with an intranet may want to publish some of its information on the intranet, or allow people on the intranet to buy goods and services through it. In this case, the company will not only have their normal private intranet servers—they'll also have public Internet servers as well. Public information that anyone can see will be on the Internet servers. However, the company will still have intranet servers behind a corporate firewall, protecting vital corporate data from Internet access.

How Intranet Webs Work

The heart of any intranet is the World Wide Web. In many instances a large part of the reason that an intranet was created in the first place is that the Web makes it easy to publish company-wide information and forms by using the Hypertext Markup Language (HTML). The Web allows for the creation of multimedia home pages, which are composed of text, graphics, and multimedia contents such as sound and video. *Hypertext links* let you jump from any place on the Web to any other place on the Web, which means that you can jump either to places inside an intranet or outside on the greater Internet from a home page.

2 When browsers are launched, they will visit a certain location by default. On an intranet, that location may be a departmental Web page or a company-wide Web page. To visit a different location, type in the intranet location you want to visit, or click on a link to the location. The name for any Web location is the URL (uniform resource locator). Your Web browser sends the URL request using HTTP (Hypertext Transfer Protocol), which defines the way in which the Web browser and the Web server communicate with one another.

1 Intranet Webs are based on client/server architecture. Client software—a Web browser—runs on a local computer, and server software runs on a Web intranet host. Client software is available for PCs, Macintoshes, and UNIX workstations. Server software runs on UNIX, Windows NT, and a variety of other operating systems. The client software and server software need not run on the same operating system. To use an intranet Web, first launch your Web browser. If you're directly connected to your intranet, the TCP/IP software you need to run the browser will already be installed on your computer.

3 If the request is for a page found on the intranet, routers send the request to that intranet Web page. A very high-speed connection may be available, since intranets can be built using high-speed wires, and all traffic inside the intranet can be conducted over those wires. Internet connection can be much slower because of the amount of traffic on the Internet, and because there may be a variety of low-speed connections that the request from the intranet will have to traverse. The packets that make up the request are individually routed at the network level of the OSI model to an intranet router, which in turn sends the request to the Web server.

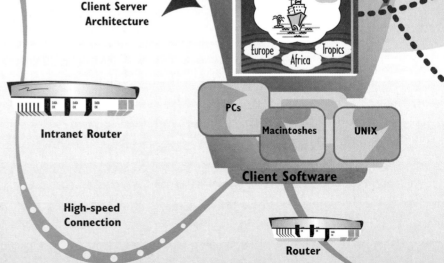

UNIX

Windows NT

Others

Server

Client Server Architecture

URL   http://www.zdnet.com

COMPANY TRAVELS   ZD PRESS

Far East

Europe   Africa   Tropics

PCs

Macintoshes   UNIX

Client Software

Intranet Router

High-speed Connection

Router

Hyperlinked Pages

```
<HTML>
<HEAD>
<B>Company Travels</B>
</HEAD>
ALIGN=RIGHT>
<BODY BACKGROUND="Cruise
ship.gif">
<IMG SRC="logo.gif"
<A HREF="Far_East_
Destinations.HTML"
Far East</A>
<A HREF="Europe_
Destinations.HTML">Europe</A>
<A HREF="Africa_
Destinations.HTML">Africa</A>
<A HREF="Tropical_
Destinations.HTML">Tropics</A>
</BODY></HTML>
```

HTML

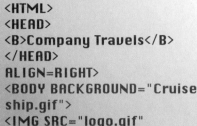

XR Forms Request Page

- *Medical*
- *Tax*
- *Travel & Expenses*
- *401k*

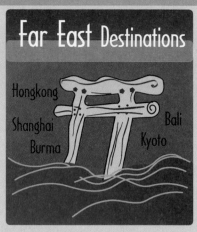

Far East Destinations

Hongkong
Shanghai   Bali
Burma   Kyoto

Classifieds

For Sale   Personals

Wanted   Rentals

Houses   Misc.

Music   Cars

Web Server

Your Help Desk Staff Page

E-mail
Home Page

Training
Sign-up

Weekly
Newsletter

Phone Directory

● Index   ● By Location

Lorem ipsum dolor sit amet, consectetuer adipiscing elit, sed diam nonummy nibh euismod tincidunt ut laoreet dolore magna aliquam erat volutpat. Ut wisi enim ad minim veniam, quis nostrud exerci tation ullamcorper suscipit

RECENT CHANGES

New Faces   Farewells
Promotions
POLITICS
Transfers

4 The Web server receives the request using HTTP. The request is for a specific document. It sends the home page, document, or object back to the Web browser client. The information now is displayed on the computer screen in the Web browser. After the object is sent to the Web browser, the HTTP connection is closed to make more efficient use of network resources.

5 URLs contain several parts. The first part—the "http://"—details what Internet protocol to use. The "www.zdnet.com" segment varies in length and identifies the Web server to be contacted. The final part identifies a specific directory on the server, and a home page, document, or other Internet or intranet object.

URL   **http://www.zdnet.com/logo/index.html**

CHAPTER
7

How the Domain Name System (DNS) Works

THE heart of intranets and the Internet is the Domain Name System (DNS), the way in which computers can contact each other and do things such as exchange electronic mail, or display Web pages. The Internet Protocol (IP) uses Internet address information and the DNS to deliver mail and other information from computer to computer.

You may not realize that every IP address on the Internet is actually a series of four numbers separated by periods (called dots), such as 163.52.128.72. It would be impossible for you to remember these numeric addresses when you wanted to send e-mail or visit a site. Also, because sometimes numeric IP addresses change, you would never be able to know every time those numeric addresses change. The DNS solves these problems.

The DNS creates a hierarchy of domains or groups of computers and it establishes a domain name (also known as an Internet address) for each computer on an intranet or the Internet, using easily recognizable letters and words instead of numbers. Major domains also have the responsibility for maintaining lists and addresses of the domains that are underneath them. That next level of domains is responsible for the following level down and so on.

An Internet address is made up of two major parts separated by an @ (pronounced at) sign. The first part of the address—to the left of the @ sign—is the user name, which usually refers to the person who holds the Internet account, and is often that person's login name. The second part of the address, to the right of the @ sign, is the host name or domain name, which identifies the specific computer where the person has an Internet mail account. Often, the domain name will be the name of the intranet.

The rightmost portion of the domain section of the address identifies the largest domain and kind of organization where the person has his or her address. Common domains in the United States are com for commercial; edu for education; gov for government; mil for military; net for network (companies and groups concerned with the organization of the Internet); and org for organization. Outside the United States, only two letters are used to identify the domains, such as au for Australia; ca for Canada; uk for United Kingdom; and fr for France.

Typically, an intranet will have its own domain, often the name of the company that owns it. Mail to be delivered begins with a request to an intranet nameserver first. If the host receiving the mail is on the intranet, the nameserver will be able to translate the Internet address into the numeric IP address, and so the mail can be delivered. If the host isn't on the intranet, the nameserver may have to contact an Internet nameserver. It does this by contacting an Internet root domain name server, which then tells it which Internet name server to contact. That Internet nameserver will be able to translate the Internet address into the numeric IP address, and again, the mail will be able to be delivered.

How Intranet Domain Name System (DNS) Servers Work

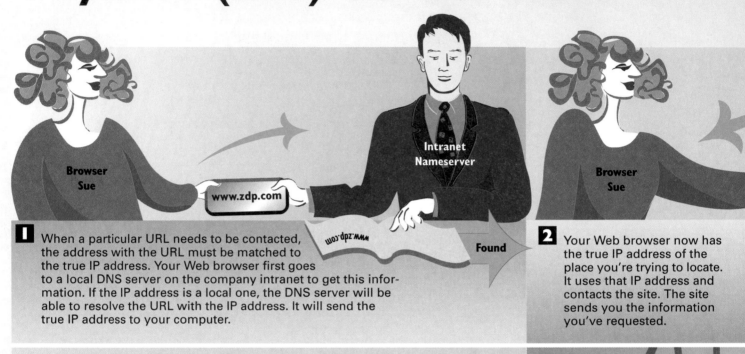

Intranet Nameserver

Browser Sue

www.zdp.com

www.zdp.com

Found

Browser Sue

1 When a particular URL needs to be contacted, the address with the URL must be matched to the true IP address. Your Web browser first goes to a local DNS server on the company intranet to get this information. If the IP address is a local one, the DNS server will be able to resolve the URL with the IP address. It will send the true IP address to your computer.

2 Your Web browser now has the true IP address of the place you're trying to locate. It uses that IP address and contacts the site. The site sends you the information you've requested.

Browser Joe

www.zdnet.com

Intranet Nameserver

NOT Found...Asks

interNic Internet Nameserver

www.zdnet.com

3 If the information you have requested isn't on your intranet—and if your local DNS server doesn't have the IP address—the intranet DNS server must get the information from a DNS server on the Internet. The intranet DNS server contacts what's called the *root domain server*, which is maintained by a group called the InterNIC. The root domain server tells the intranet server which primary nameserver and secondary nameserver has the information about the requested URL.

4 The intranet DNS server now contacts the primary nameserver. If the information cannot be found in the primary nameserver, the intranet DNS server contacts the secondary server. One of those nameservers will have the proper information. It will then pass the information back to the intranet DNS server.

When someone on an intranet wants to contact a location—for example, to visit a Web site—they will type in an address, such as www.metahouse.com. In fact, though, the Internet doesn't truly use these alphanumeric addresses. Instead, it uses IP addresses, which are numerical addresses, in four 8-bit numbers separated by dots, such as 123.5.56.255. A DNS server, also called a nameserver, matches alphanumeric addresses to their IP addresses, and allows you to contact the proper location.

www.zdp.com
129.333.29.8

Intranet
Nameserver

Browser
Sue

Web Site

www.zdp.com
129.333.29.8

Primary
Nameserver

Secondary
Nameserver

Root
Directory

interNic
Internet
Nameserver

www.zdnet.com
129.333.29.8

Browser
Joe

Web
Site

5 The intranet DNS server sends the information back to you. Your Web browser now uses the IP address to contact the proper site.

CHAPTER

8

How Java Works

INTRANETS

are different from the Internet because they are private networks, set off from the rest of the world by firewalls. They also differ in that they often connect disparate corporate networks. And they often access corporate resources and databases that were built with non-Internet technology in mind.

In order to connect disparate networks, and in order to get at data residing on legacy databases and systems, custom programs need to be written. There are many ways that those programs can be created. Many people believe that the Java programming language, created by Sun Microsystems, may eventually become the programming glue that holds intranets together.

The primary reason for Java to be the programming language of choice for intranets is that it is platform-independent. That means that programs written in Java can run on a wide variety of computers, including PCs, Macintoshes, and UNIX workstations. In addition to being platform independent, Java was designed with lots of classes and methods for dealing with sockets, URLs, and other technical pieces of the process.

Java is similar to the C++ computer language that is already used by many programmers, and it is object-oriented so that new applications can be built from pre-existing components, two more reasons that intranet developers may favor the language.

Like many programming languages, Java is a compiled language, so that after it's written, it must be run through a compiler to allow computers to understand it. But in Java, only a single compiled version of the program is created. That single compiled program can run on many different computers, such as PCs, Macintoshes, and SPARC workstations. Other languages require that the completed program be compiled separately for each type of computer, which results in several different versions of the code. This requires a substantial amount of programming work and debugging.

Java is so important to intranet applications that hardware and software companies such as IBM have released special Java add-ons and libraries to allow Java developers to tap into legacy databases, such as IBM mainframes. This may accelerate the move toward Java on intranets.

Java can be used for far more than tapping into databases. It can create interactive multimedia applications as well. A common use of Java is to create a news ticker broadcasting the latest news that people can click on to get more details. This can be used on intranets for presenting company information and news. What happens behind the scenes here is that a file is written, read, and "printed" to the screen. This process also allows people to choose to turn it off. Depending on the applet, the hit on the client resources (like memory) will vary. Basically, though, the larger the applet, the more resources are required. Java can also be used to create programs that help people navigate through an intranet more easily, and more easily "mine" the enormous amounts of data locked up in corporate databases.

How Java Works

Java, a programming language developed by Sun Microsystems, is expected to be one of the cornerstones of building an intranet. Using Java, programmers can tie into corporate data from an intranet, enabling use of legacy systems such as databases. Java can also be used by programmers, editors, and artists to create multimedia programming. Java will also be able to create customized intranet programs for everything from workgroup computing to electronic commerce.

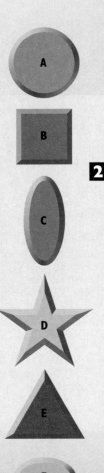

1 Java is similar to the C++ computer language and is *object-oriented*, which means that programs can be created by using many pre-existing components, instead of having to write the entire program from scratch. This will be a great help on intranets, since it will allow corporate programmers to share components and so build customized applications much more quickly.

2 Java is a *compiled language*, which means that after a Java program is written, the program must be run through a *compiler* in order to turn the program into a language that a computer can understand. Java differs from other compiled languages, however. In other compiled languages, computer-specific compilers create different executable binary code for all the different computers that the program can run on. In Java, by contrast, a single compiled version of the program—called Java bytecode—is created by a compiler. Interpreters on different computers—such as a PC, Macintosh, or SPARC workstation—understand the Java bytecode and run the program. In this way, a Java program can be created once, and then used on many different kinds of computers. Java programs designed to run inside a Web browser are called applets. Applets are a subset of Java and for security reasons cannot read from or write to local files, whereas full Java can do so. Java-enabled browsers have Java bytecode interpreters in them.

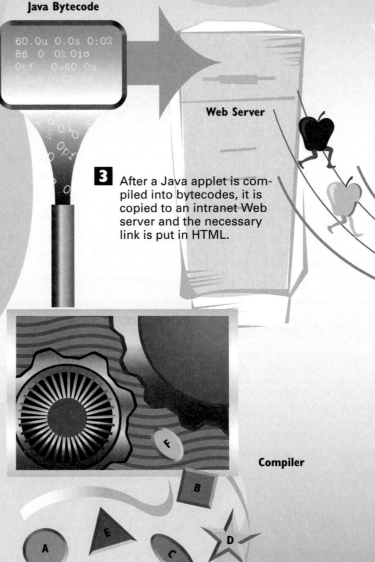

Java Bytecode

60.0u 0.0s 0:02
86 0 0k 0io
0pf 0w60.0u

Web Server

3 After a Java applet is compiled into bytecodes, it is copied to an intranet Web server and the necessary link is put in HTML.

Compiler

CYBERMUSIC SIGNS NEW CEO

Java Corporate News Ticker

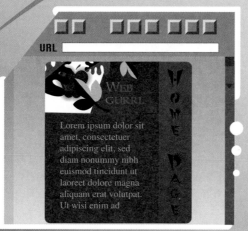

WEB GURRL

Lorem ipsum dolor sit amet, consectetuer adipiscing elit, sed diam nonummy nibh euismod tincidunt ut laoreet dolore magna aliquam erat volutpat. Ut wisi enim ad

HOME PAGE

URL

4 When someone on an intranet visits a home page with a Java applet on it, the applet automatically downloads to their computer. The applet doesn't wait for an invitation. That is why there is so much concern about viruses being embedded in applets. In order to run the Java applet, you will need a Web browser that has a bytecode interpreter that can run Java applets. Many browsers designed for intranets, such as Netscape, have these built into them.

Verification

Write

Read

Java Program

7 The Java applet is run. Applets can query databases by presenting a list of queries or data entry forms to the user. They can assist searching intranet sites by creating more sophisticated searching mechanisms than is possible with HTML. Most important, since the client's CPU cycles are used rather than the server's, all kinds of multimedia, including animation and interactivity, are possible with Java applets.

5 Since Java applets are programs that run on your computer, they could theoretically carry a virus just like any other computer program. To help ensure that no viruses can infect your computer, when a Java applet is downloaded to your computer, the applet first goes through *verification*—a process that checks that the bytecodes can be safely run. However, again, applets cannot read from or write to local files which are usually involved in virus attacks, so this should reduce virus infection risk substantially.

6 After the bytecodes have been verified, the Java interpreter in the browser puts them into a restricted area in your computer's memory and runs them. By putting the applet into this special area of your computer, further care is taken that no virus can harm your computer.

8 Java will have special Application Programming Interfaces (APIs) and other kind of software "hooks" to allow intranet programmers to more easily integrate intranet programs such as Web browsers with existing corporate databases and networks.

CHAPTER

9

How Common Gateway Interface (CGI) Works

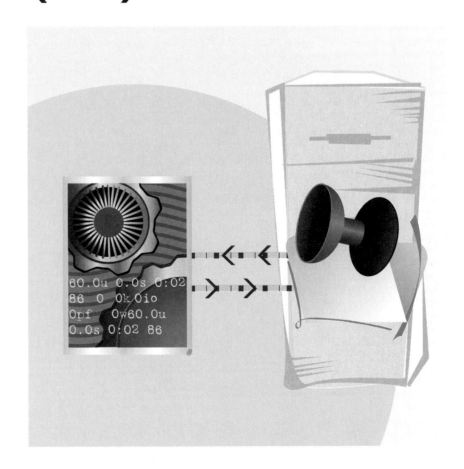

In general, Web software is not particularly database friendly—it often happens that valuable corporate information is not always accessible to many people who need it.

In the earliest days of the Web, it was exceedingly difficult for anyone to gain access to those databases. As technology developed, however, and it became easier to access databases, an increasing number of databases became available, both on the Internet and then later on intranets as well. Web server software was developed to make it easier to access databases for the Web.

There are a number of ways in which someone from an intranet can tap into corporate databases. An exceedingly popular one is called the *Common Gateway Interface* (CGI). CGI allows any executable to run and have its output sent back to the requesting client. Therefore, it allows intranet programmers to write programs and scripts that will allow people on an intranet to use their Web browsers to easily query databases by filling out forms on Web pages—and they will then send those results back in HTML form that the browsers can understand.

Essentially, CGI is an interface that delivers information from the server to your program and from your program back to the requesting client. It is not a programming language. The program does all the processing. CGI only gets data to the program. On an intranet, the data accessed is often from a database of some sort. You've no doubt used CGI many times without knowing it. On the Internet, for example, if you've filled out a form on a Web page in order to register to use a site, and then later received an e-mail notification with a password for you to use, you've probably used CGI. CGI most likely took the information you filled in the form, performed several actions on it (including putting the information in a database), automatically created a password, and then automatically sent you mail.

On your corporate intranet, if you have one, you may well have used CGI programs or scripts as well. If you've queried a corporate database from a Web page and gotten information from it, then there's a good chance that a CGI program or script is what did the work for you.

Intranet programmers can use a variety of technologies to make use of CGI. One of the simplest is to use what's called an *interpreted language.* An interpreted language, such as the popular Perl used on UNIX systems, is often favored because scripts written with them are easy to debug, modify, and maintain.

CGI can also be accessed with more sophisticated computer languages, such as C, C++, or Fortran. When a programmer writes a program in a language such as C to be accessed by CGI, the program must first be *compiled.* That means running it through a program called a compiler that can change the application into a machine-readable language that the computer can understand.

How Common Gateway Interface (CGI) Works

Essentially, CGI is an interface that delivers information from the server to your program and from your program back to the requesting client. It is not a programming language. The program does all the processing. CGI only gets data to the program. CGI is a standard that allows programmers to write programs that can access information servers and databases, and then send the information to users on an intranet. Using CGI, Web-based intranet technologies can communicate with non-TCP/IP resources and databases. Using CGI, an intranet programmer can write an application that searches a database and displays the result in HTML format. CGI is used to allow people to fill out corporate forms on an intranet, and have that information entered into a database.

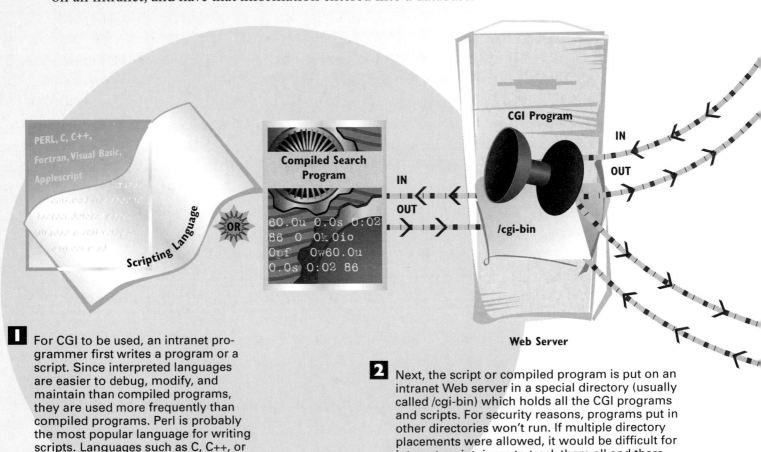

PERL, C, C++, Fortran, Visual Basic, Applescript

Scripting Language

OR

Compiled Search Program

```
60.0u  0.0s  0:02
86   0   0k 0io
0pf    0w60.0u
0.0s  0:02 86
```

IN

OUT

CGI Program

IN

OUT

/cgi-bin

Web Server

1 For CGI to be used, an intranet programmer first writes a program or a script. Since interpreted languages are easier to debug, modify, and maintain than compiled programs, they are used more frequently than compiled programs. Perl is probably the most popular language for writing scripts. Languages such as C, C++, or Fortran can be used to access CGI as well after they have been compiled.

2 Next, the script or compiled program is put on an intranet Web server in a special directory (usually called /cgi-bin) which holds all the CGI programs and scripts. For security reasons, programs put in other directories won't run. If multiple directory placements were allowed, it would be difficult for intranet maintainers to track them all and therefore realize if an unauthorized user posted a rogue CGI program.

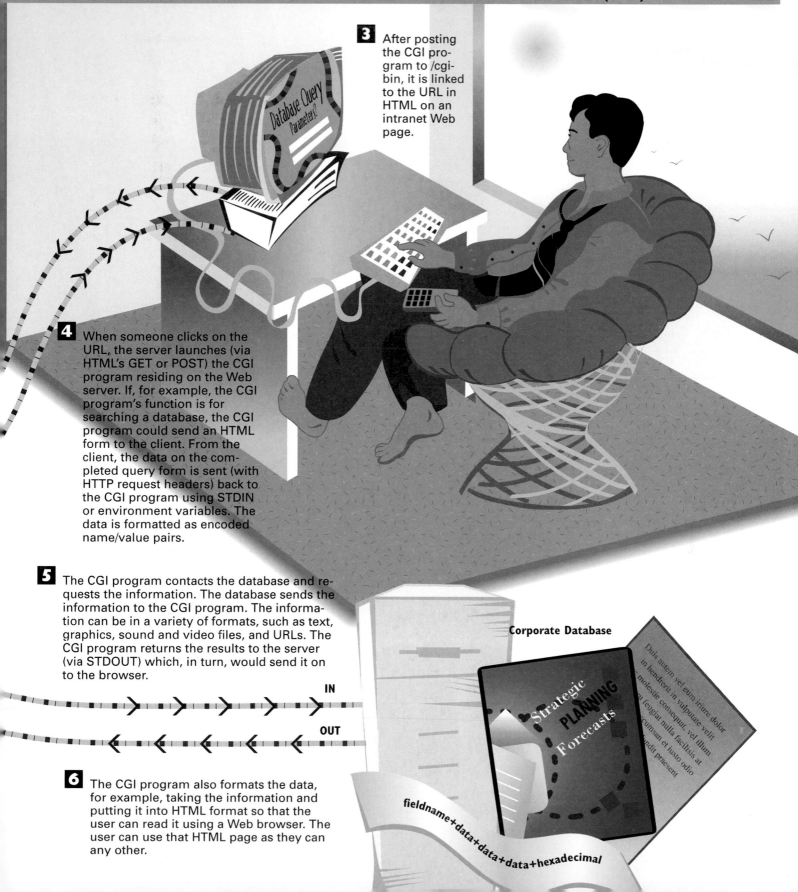

3 After posting the CGI program to /cgi-bin, it is linked to the URL in HTML on an intranet Web page.

4 When someone clicks on the URL, the server launches (via HTML's GET or POST) the CGI program residing on the Web server. If, for example, the CGI program's function is for searching a database, the CGI program could send an HTML form to the client. From the client, the data on the completed query form is sent (with HTTP request headers) back to the CGI program using STDIN or environment variables. The data is formatted as encoded name/value pairs.

5 The CGI program contacts the database and requests the information. The database sends the information to the CGI program. The information can be in a variety of formats, such as text, graphics, sound and video files, and URLs. The CGI program returns the results to the server (via STDOUT) which, in turn, would send it on to the browser.

IN

OUT

Corporate Database

Strategic PLANNING Forecasts

fieldname+data+data+data+hexadecimal

6 The CGI program also formats the data, for example, taking the information and putting it into HTML format so that the user can read it using a Web browser. The user can use that HTML page as they can any other.

CHAPTER

10

Subnetting an Intranet

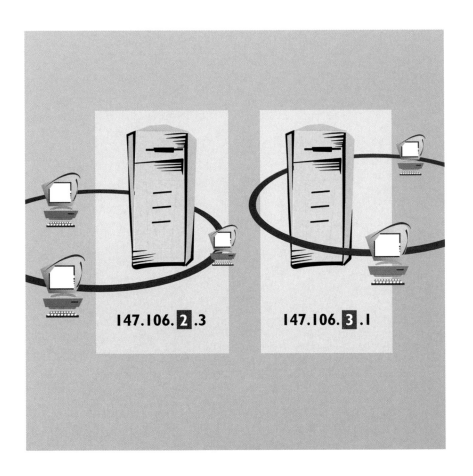

147.106.2.3   147.106.3.1

INTRANETS

come in different sizes. In a small company, an intranet can be composed of only a handful of computers. In a medium-sized business, it may include dozens or hundreds of computers. And in a large corporation, there may be thousands of computers spread across the globe, all connected to a single intranet. When intranets get large, they need to be subdivided into individual *subnets* or *subnetworks.*

To understand how subnetting works, you first need to understand IP addresses. Every IP address is a 32-bit numeric address that uniquely identifies a network and then a specific host on that network. The IP address is divided into two sections: the network section, called the *netid,* and the host section, called the *hostid.*

Each 32-bit IP address is handled differently, according to what *class* of network the address refers to. There are three main classes of network addresses: *Class A, Class B,* and *Class C.* In some classes, more of the 32-bit address space is devoted to the netid, while in others, more of the address space is devoted to the hostid. In a Class A network, the netid is composed of 8 bits, while the hostid is composed of 24 bits. In a Class B network, both the netid and the hostid are composed of 16 bits. In a Class C network, the netid is composed of 24 bits, while the hostid is composed of 8 bits. There's a simple way of knowing what class a network is in. If the first number of the IP address is less than 128, the network is a Class A address. If the first number is from 128 to 191, it's a Class B network. If the first number is from 192 to 223, it's a Class C network. Numbers above 223 are reserved for other purposes. The smaller the netid, the fewer number of networks that can be subnetted, but the larger number of hosts on the network. A Class A rating is best for large networks while a Class C is best for small ones.

To create a subnet, the demarcation line on the IP address is moved between the netid and the hostid, to give the netid more bits to work with and to take away bits from the hostid. To do this, a special number called a *subnet mask* is used.

Subnetting is used when intranets grow over a certain size and they begin to have problems. One problem is management of host IP addresses—making sure that every computer on the network has a proper, up-to-date host address, and that old host addresses are put out of use until needed in the future. In a corporation spread out over several locations—or across the world—it's difficult, if not impossible, to have one person responsible for managing the host addresses at every location and department in the company.

Another problem has to do with a variety of hardware limitations of networks. Dissimilar networks may all be part of an intranet. An intranet may have some sections that are Ethernet, other sections that are Token Ring networks, and conceivably other sections that use different networking technologies altogether. There is no easy way for an intranet router to link these dissimilar networks together and route the information to the proper places.

Another set of problems has to do with the physical limitations of network technology. In some kinds of networks, there are some strict limitations on how far cables can extend in the network. In other words, you can't go over a certain distance of cabling without using repeaters or routers. A "thick" Ethernet cable, for example, can only be extended to 500 meters, while a "thin" Ethernet cable can only go to 300 meters. Routers can be used to link these cables together, so that an intranet can be extended well beyond those distances. But when that is done, each length of wire is essentially considered its own subnetwork.

Yet one more set of problems has to do with the volume of traffic that travels across an intranet. Often in a corporation, in a given department, most of the traffic is intradepartmental traffic—in other words, mail and other data that people within a department send to each another. The volume of traffic outside to other departments is considerably less. What's called for is a way to confine intradepartmental traffic inside the departments, to cut down on the amount of data that needs to be routed and managed across the entire intranet.

Subnetting solves all these problems and more. When an intranet is divided into subnets, one central administrator doesn't have to manage every aspect of the entire intranet. Instead, each subnet can take care of its own administration. That means smaller organizations within the larger organization can take care of problems such as address management and a variety of trouble-shooting chores. If an intranet is subnetted by divisions or departments, it means that each division or department can guide the development of its own network, while adhering to general intranet architecture. Doing this allows departments or divisions more freedom to use technology to pursue their business goals.

Subnets also get around problems that arise when an intranet has within it different kinds of network architecture, such as Ethernet and Token Ring technologies. Normally—if there is no subnetting—a router can't link these different networks together because they don't have their own addresses. However, if each of the different networks is its own subnet—and so has its own network address—routers can then link them together and properly route intranet traffic.

Subnetting can also cut down on the traffic traveling across the intranet and its routers. Since much network traffic may be confined within departments, having each department be its own subnet means that all that traffic need never cross an intranet router and cross the intranet—it will stay within its own subnet.

Subnetting can also increase the security on an intranet. If the payroll department, for example, were on its own subnet, then much of its traffic would not have to travel across an intranet. Having its data traveling across the intranet could mean that someone could conceivably hack into the data to read it. Confining the data to its own subnet makes that much less likely to happen.

Dividing an intranet into subnets can also make the entire intranet more stable. If an intranet is divided in this way, then if one subnet goes down or is often unstable, it won't affect the rest of the intranet.

This all may sound rather confusing. To see how it's done, let's take a look at a network, and see how to use the IP address to create subnets. Let's say we have a Class B network. That network is assigned the address of 130.97.0.0. When a network is given an address, it is assigned the netid numbers—in this case, the 130.97—and it can assign the host numbers (in this case, 0.0) in any way that it chooses.

The 130.97.0.0 network is a single intranet. It's getting too large to manage, though, and we've decided to divide it into two subnets. What we do is fairly straightforward. We take a number from the hostid field and use it to identify each of the subnets. So one subnet gets the address 130.97.1.0, and the other gets the address 130.97.2.0. Individual machines on the first subnet get addresses of 130.97.1.1, 130.97.1.2, and so on. Individual machines on the second subnet get addresses of 130.97.2.1, 130.97.2.2 and so on.

Sounds simple. But we have a problem. The Internet doesn't recognize 130.97.1.0 and 130.97.2.0 as separate networks. It treats them both as 130.97.0.0 since the "1" and "2" that we're using as a netid is only known to the Internet as a hostid. So our intranet router will not be able to route incoming traffic to the proper network.

To solve the problem, a subnet mask is used. A subnet mask is a 32-bit number in IP form used by intranet routers and hosts that will help routers understand how to route information to the proper subnet. To the outside Internet, there is still only one network, but the subnet mask allows routers inside the intranet to send traffic to the proper host.

A subnet mask is a number such as 255.255.255.0 (the built-in default for Class C addresses; the Class B default is 255.255.0.0 and the default for Class A is 255.0.0.0). A router takes the subnet mask and applies that number against the IP number of incoming mail to the network by using it to perform a calculation. Based on the resulting IP number, it will route mail to the proper subnet, and then to a particular computer on the subnet. For consistency, everyone in a particular intranet will use the same subnet mask.

Subnetting an Intranet

When intranets are over a certain size, or are spread over several geographical locations, it becomes difficult to manage them as a single network. To solve the problem, the single intranet can be subdivided into several *subnets*, subsections of an intranet that make them easier to manage. To the outside world, the intranet still looks as if it's a single network.

1 If you're building an intranet and want it to be connected to the Internet, you'll need a unique IP address for your intranet network, which the InterNIC Registration Services will handle. There are three classes of intranet you can have: Class A, Class B, or Class C. Generally, a Class A rating is best for the largest networks, while a Class C is best for the smallest. A Class A network can be composed of 127 networks, and a total of 16,777,214 nodes on the network. A Class B network can be composed of 16,383 networks, and a total of 65,534 nodes. A Class C network can be composed of 2,097,151 networks, and 254 nodes.

2 When an intranet is assigned an address, it is assigned the first two IP numbers of the Internet numeric address (called the *netid* field) and the remaining two numbers (called the *hostid* field) are left blank, so that the intranet itself can assign them, such as 147.106.0.0. The hostid field consists of a number for a subnet and a host number.

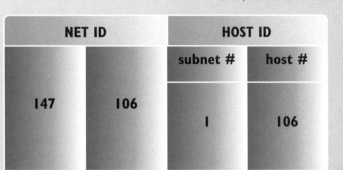

NET ID		HOST ID	
		subnet #	host #
147	106	1	106
first #	second #	third #	fourth #

6 Each computer on each subnet gets its own IP address, as in a normal intranet. The combination of the netid field, the subnet number, and then finally a host number, forms the IP address.

CLASSES		DEFAULT SUBNET MASK			
A	<128	255	0	0	0
B	129–191	255	255	0	0
C	192–223	255	255	255	0

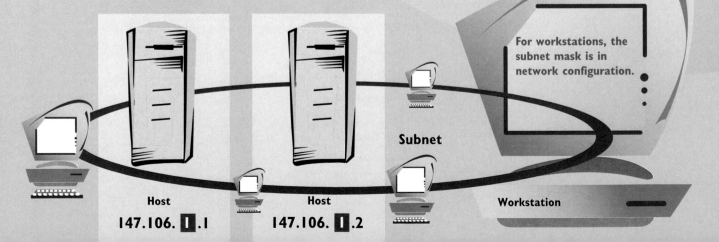

For workstations, the subnet mask is in network configuration.

Subnet

Host
147.106. █ .1

Host
147.106. █ .2

Workstation

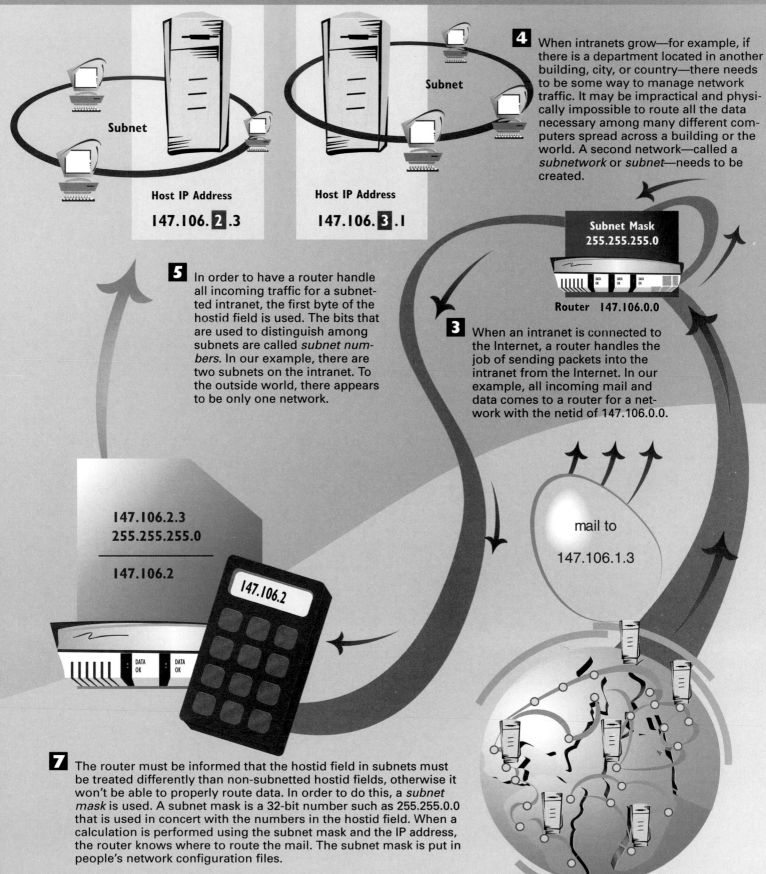

Subnet

Subnet

Host IP Address

147.106.**2**.3

Host IP Address

147.106.**3**.1

4 When intranets grow—for example, if there is a department located in another building, city, or country—there needs to be some way to manage network traffic. It may be impractical and physically impossible to route all the data necessary among many different computers spread across a building or the world. A second network—called a *subnetwork* or *subnet*—needs to be created.

Subnet Mask
255.255.255.0

Router 147.106.0.0

5 In order to have a router handle all incoming traffic for a subnetted intranet, the first byte of the hostid field is used. The bits that are used to distinguish among subnets are called *subnet numbers*. In our example, there are two subnets on the intranet. To the outside world, there appears to be only one network.

3 When an intranet is connected to the Internet, a router handles the job of sending packets into the intranet from the Internet. In our example, all incoming mail and data comes to a router for a network with the netid of 147.106.0.0.

147.106.2.3
255.255.255.0
_____
147.106.2

147.106.2

mail to

147.106.1.3

7 The router must be informed that the hostid field in subnets must be treated differently than non-subnetted hostid fields, otherwise it won't be able to properly route data. In order to do this, a *subnet mask* is used. A subnet mask is a 32-bit number such as 255.255.0.0 that is used in concert with the numbers in the hostid field. When a calculation is performed using the subnet mask and the IP address, the router knows where to route the mail. The subnet mask is put in people's network configuration files.

CHAPTER

11

How Converting IPX Networks to an Intranet Works

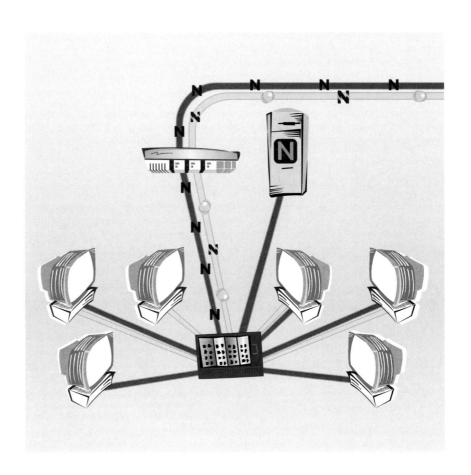

IT'S

rare that an entire intranet will be built completely from scratch. It is more likely that an existing network, such as a Novell NetWare network, will be converted to an intranet. At a corporation there can be many networks already in existence before an intranet comes in, often connected in a company-wide Wide Area Network (WAN). There may be a variety of different network technologies connected to the WAN. One way of converting a network to an intranet is to take it piece by piece and convert individual department LANs to an intranet, and then build from there.

Often, the single most important factor in convincing a corporation to start an intranet is that people within the company will gain access to the Internet and its resources. So the first step in creating the intranet will often be giving easy access to the Internet from an existing corporate network. It's much faster for people to get at the Internet over a network instead of having to dial in via modem—and it also saves money in the long run. But when that Internet access is provided, it's also important that all the existing network services be maintained as well.

A simple solution is to have people run software needed both for the existing network as well as for the Internet. Let's take a NetWare network as an example. In order to use NetWare and get access to its services such as electronic mail and others, computers on the network need to run the IPX (Internet Packet Exchange) protocol. Don't be confused about the name—IPX doesn't allow access to the Internet, but instead to a NetWare network's resources.

When people want access to the Internet as well, they can run a *TCP/IP stack*—software that will allow them to access the Internet. The TCP/IP stack and IPX will both be running simultaneously on their computers. When they need to access a NetWare resource, IPX allows them to do it. When they want to access the Internet, TCP/IP does the job. The problem with this is that it is not as simple as it sounds because the protocol stacks take up considerable memory and sometimes there is not enough memory left to start applications without unloading one of the protocols.

Internet requests go via TCP/IP to an intranet router, which is connected to an Internet Service Provider via a Channel Service Unit/Data Service Unit (CSU/DSU). Especially in large companies with many people on a network, this connection will be made via a leased high-speed digital line, such as a T1 line. There needs to be a CSU/DSU and a router on the other end, and the requests travel through them in reverse order, that is into the CSU/DSU and then to the router. The CSU/DSU units are used to assure quality digital signals over digital phone lines.

In this kind of setup, people can access an intranet as well as the Internet. In this way, a company can slowly build up an intranet while keeping an existing Novell network. People on the network will be able to access intranet resources since they're running TCP/IP stacks, and NetWare resources, since they're running IPX.

How Converting IPX to an Intranet Works

Most intranets aren't built from scratch—many are existing networks, such as Novell NetWare, that have to be converted into an intranet. Often, the first step in moving toward an intranet is to give Internet access to users on an existing network. At some later point, intranet technology can then be brought inside the network itself and it can be turned into an intranet. This illustration shows that first step: how an existing network, such as a NetWare-based one, can be given access to the Internet, yet still keep access to the NetWare architecture.

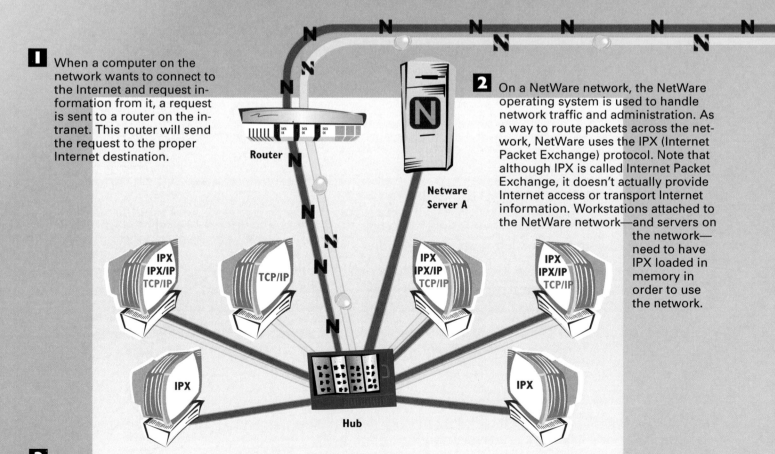

1 When a computer on the network wants to connect to the Internet and request information from it, a request is sent to a router on the intranet. This router will send the request to the proper Internet destination.

Router

2 On a NetWare network, the NetWare operating system is used to handle network traffic and administration. As a way to route packets across the network, NetWare uses the IPX (Internet Packet Exchange) protocol. Note that although IPX is called Internet Packet Exchange, it doesn't actually provide Internet access or transport Internet information. Workstations attached to the NetWare network—and servers on the network—need to have IPX loaded in memory in order to use the network.

Netware Server A

IPX
IPX/IP
TCP/IP

TCP/IP

IPX
IPX/IP
TCP/IP

IPX
IPX/IP
TCP/IP

IPX

IPX

Hub

3 In order for workstations on the Novell network to gain access to the Internet or intranet, they need to run the TCP/IP protocols that form the basis of the Internet. To do that, a *TCP/IP stack* must be installed on each computer that will allow it to access the Internet. That means that each computer will have both IPX and a TCP/IP stack installed on it, to allow it to access the Internet as well as the Ethernet network. Basically, this results in "RAM cram" and is one of the biggest headaches for anyone trying to run both protocol stacks.

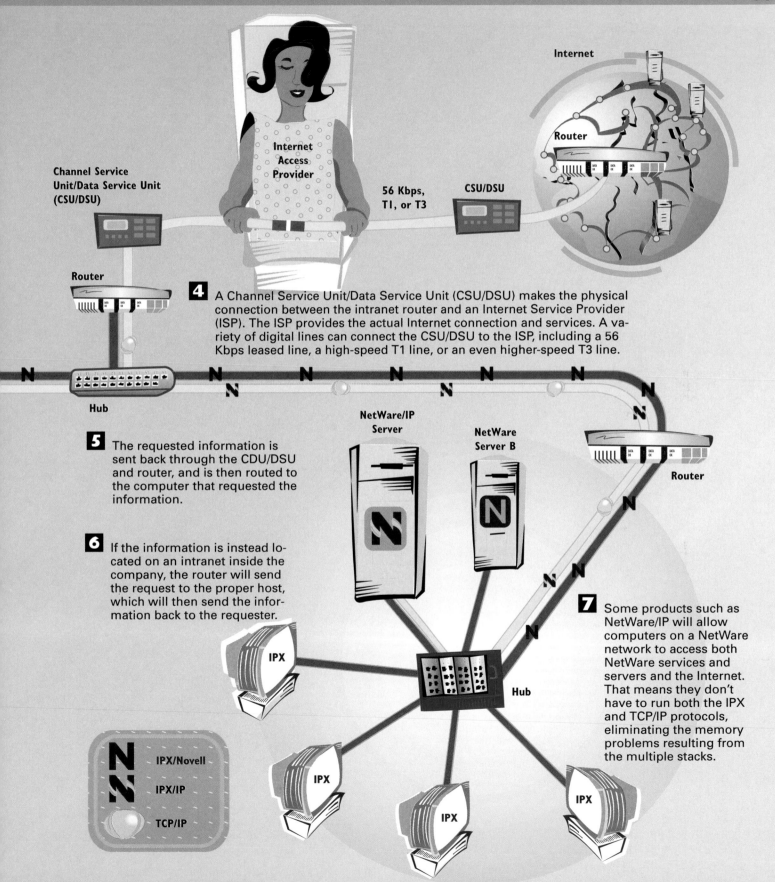

Internet

Router

Internet Access Provider

Channel Service Unit/Data Service Unit (CSU/DSU)

56 Kbps, T1, or T3

CSU/DSU

Router

Hub

4 A Channel Service Unit/Data Service Unit (CSU/DSU) makes the physical connection between the intranet router and an Internet Service Provider (ISP). The ISP provides the actual Internet connection and services. A variety of digital lines can connect the CSU/DSU to the ISP, including a 56 Kbps leased line, a high-speed T1 line, or an even higher-speed T3 line.

NetWare/IP Server

NetWare Server B

Router

5 The requested information is sent back through the CDU/DSU and router, and is then routed to the computer that requested the information.

6 If the information is instead located on an intranet inside the company, the router will send the request to the proper host, which will then send the information back to the requester.

IPX

Hub

7 Some products such as NetWare/IP will allow computers on a NetWare network to access both NetWare services and servers and the Internet. That means they don't have to run both the IPX and TCP/IP protocols, eliminating the memory problems resulting from the multiple stacks.

IPX/Novell

IPX/IP

TCP/IP

IPX

IPX

IPX

IPX

P A R T

SECURITY AND INTRANETS

I**T'S** a dangerous world out there, and the Internet is full of people who are often bent on, at the minimum, mischief, and at a maximum, destruction. The trouble doesn't come only from external threats. Most companies have information within the organization that requires restricted access, and some of the same security techniques used to defend against external threats offer considerable internal security, too. Intranets can be exploited and are vulnerable to damage, including data theft, unauthorized use of the intranet's resources, and damage to intranet hardware and software.

Those in the know on the Internet can examine the packets as they make their way across the Internet. This is called *packet sniffing*. In packet sniffing, a tap into a router or other hardware on the intranet allows the capture, examination, and replay of every packet that passes through. There are a number of things intruders can do based on examining those packets. They can steal any information, confidential or not. And they can also use the information they find there to help them break further into an intranet. It's difficult, if not impossible, to detect someone who is packet sniffing, because packet sniffing is essentially a passive act: An unauthorized user simply watches the data as it passes, and doesn't do any harm to the data.

Another popular technique to gain unauthorized access is called *IP spoofing* or just *spoofing*. In IP spoofing, an intruder is able to alter the IP packets sent to an intranet, changing them so that it appears he or she is a trusted user of the intranet. The IP address in the packet's headers appears that they are coming from inside the intranet itself, when in fact they are coming from outside the intranet.

Perhaps the most popular way of breaking into intranets, however, is to break in with user passwords. There are a number of ways to get around password security. The simplest is merely to guess passwords. Many people create security problems when they use passwords that are combinations of their first and last names or initials. People can also write programs that dial into intranets, and try sending thousands of user names and passwords until they find a combination that lets them in. This is often referred to as the brute force approach. Password files can be downloaded, and then cracked allowing someone to log in as if they were a legitimate user.

Other dangers to intranets are viruses, destructive programs that damage computer hardware and software. Viruses can spread via infected disks or software downloaded from the Internet; some viruses can hide in document macros.

In Chapter 12, we'll see the components of security system, from filtering routers to proxy servers and password systems and how they fit together to protect an intranet.

In Chapter 13, we'll explore filtering routers. Filtering routers form the core of intranet security, and the core of intranet firewalls. They evaluate every IP packet coming into and going out of the intranet and they won't allow certain packets to pass through.

Chapter 14 examines the front line of defense for many intranets—firewalls. Firewalls are combinations of hardware and software that allow people from inside the intranet to make use of Internet resources, but block people from the Internet from coming inside the intranet. We'll take a close look at one of the most secure—the filtered subnet architecture.

Chapter 15 takes a detailed look at another vital part of firewall security: proxy servers. When proxy servers are used, intranet users don't directly contact Internet resources, such as Web servers or FTP sites. Instead, the users contact the proxy server, which evaluates the request and then, if acceptable, contacts the Internet resource. The proxy also receives and passes the information back to the user.

In Chapter 16, we'll cover bastion hosts, the servers that sit in a firewall and are the main point of contact between an intranet and the Internet. By having all intranet-to-Internet traffic go through this single server, better security can be maintained, and all traffic can be watched so that if an attack takes place, it's easier to uncover and defend against.

In Chapter 17 we look at encryption. Encryption is vital not only for intranet security, but also for doing any kind of financial transaction on intranets or the Internet. Encryption garbles data so that the only person who can read it is the intended recipient.

In Chapter 18, we will look at password and authentication systems. Password systems control access to the intranet. These systems may use encryption as a way to ensure the integrity of passwords. We'll also look at authentication systems that use a combination of encryption and passwords to assure only authorized users are allowed access to the intranet.

Chapter 19 covers virus scanning software. The server version of such software examines data coming into an intranet, ensuring that intranets won't get viruses brought in from the Internet.

Chapter 20 describes a what happens when people inside the intranet visit inappropriate sites, such as those with sexual content. We'll look at the way that intranets can block anyone inside them from visiting those sites by using server-based site blocking software.

Chapter 21 examines monitoring software. These programs can analyze many aspects of intranet use, from detailing which sites are visited to looking at hourly traffic.

Finally, in Chapter 22 we'll cover how companies can communicate without having anyone snoop on confidential information. Virtual Secure Private Networks (VSPNs) allow intranets to use encryption to send data between them over the public Internet, and yet have no one be able to read or use that data except those on the intended intranet.

CHAPTER

12

Overview of an Intranet Security System

IF you think that you're completely safe from external threats, think again. Consider this: A government study found that the United States Pentagon's computers are attacked by hackers some 250,000 times a year—and that about 160,000 of those times the attacks are successful. In the successful attacks, data and software are read, stolen, modified, or destroyed. The attacks have cost the government hundreds of millions of dollars.

If the Pentagon can be broken into, so can you. Intranets are vulnerable because of the openness of Internet technology. Look at it this way: There's a door between your intranet and the Internet that lets people inside an intranet go out onto the Internet to get information. That same door can let intruders from the Internet into your intranet.

In addition to unauthorized external access that leads to attacks and theft, there are other security issues to worry about. It's not just people from outside the intranet who can pose security risks. People within the corporation on the intranet can pose problems as well. There is data within a company that requires restricted access, such as personnel records. Malicious mischief is not restricted only to people outside a company.

Computer viruses can be brought in to the intranet with an innocent looking program picked up on the Internet. It can then infect the other computers on the intranet, damaging millions of dollars worth of hardware and software.

There are ways to combat these problems. Any intranet needs to have a comprehensive security system in place. In addition to considering the nature of the threats that require defensive measures, you must evaluate factors such as the size of the intranet and/or company, the value or confidentiality of the data, and how important an uninterrupted, operational intranet is to the company. Technology changes all the time, so the system needs to be constantly monitored and updated.

Security systems are generically referred to as *firewalls*. Firewalls are hardware/software combinations that allow people from inside an intranet to access data on the Internet, but keep intruders from getting onto the intranet. In fact, firewalls are only one part of a comprehensive intranet security system.

Routers play a major role in firewalls—and are important in any security system. Routers are the technology that lets people on the intranet connect to the Internet, and allows data from the Internet to get to users on the intranet. Because all data going to and from the Internet passes through routers, they're a logical place to put security measures. A variety of security measures can be used in concert with routers. The primary one is called *filtering* and is accomplished by *filtering routers*. What filtering routers do is quite simple. They examine every packet coming into and going out of an intranet. Based on a set of rules that a system administrator has established, the router will let some packets in (pass) and will keep other packets out (drop). For example, packets coming from specific users or specific networks can be blocked. Access to entire Internet resources, such as FTP, can be blocked if, for example, a system administrator fears a virus infection if file transfers were allowed.

Proxy servers are another important tool in the fight for intranet security. They allow people on an intranet to get to Internet resources, but the proxy servers act as a kind of go-between. In a system set up with a proxy server, this process can be invisible to the user making the request. The proxy server evaluates the request against an authorization database, and if the request is acceptable, the proxy contacts the Internet. The returning page also passes through the proxy server from the Internet and passes it to the person who requested it. In this way, the proxy server can keep a record of all transactions, and provides a trail to track any kind of attacks. Additionally, the proxy server can be used as a way to keep the intranet shielded from the Internet, because the only IP address going out to the Internet is that of the proxy server, so anyone trying to capture IP addresses for a spoofing attack (pretending to be a legitimate client) can't "see" the originating IP addresses.

Another kind of server important for intranet security is a *bastion server*. A bastion server is configured especially to resist attacks. Frequently, it is put on its own subnetwork, known as a perimeter network. That way, if the bastion server is attacked and broken into, the intranet is still shielded—the only part compromised is the bastion server.

Encryption and authentication systems are used to prevent unauthorized access to an intranet. Encryption can be used to protect data and passwords. Encryption depends on the use of secret and/or public keys. User names and passwords can be compromised fairly easily, allowing someone to masquerade as a legitimate user. Authentication systems expand on the basic "something you know" security provided by passwords to one that checks that there is "something you have" that is uniquely in your possession, a token of some sort. Encrypted digital signatures are created with keys that also are uniquely in your possession so they can't be altered without such tampering being discovered. Encrypted digital signatures help authenticate the sender of a message and protect against message tampering.

Viruses are a major concern to anyone running an intranet. While the threat of viruses is undoubtedly overblown by the news media, the truth is that viruses are a problem and a potential danger. One way to solve the problem is to use traditional virus scanning and eradication software. This software runs on each user's computer, and allows people to check their computers for viruses, and to kill the virus if at all possible. But doing things that way depends on each user actually running the most up-to-date virus checkers, which doesn't always happen. A better solution is to run virus-checking software specifically designed for intranets. It runs on a server, and as files are sent to the intranet it checks them for viruses. If they're virus-free, it lets them through. If they appear to contain viruses, it blocks them.

There is software that can block users from accessing objectionable sites, such as sites with violent or sexual content. On an intranet a server-based software that does this examines outgoing requests, such as the URL name and words contained in the header of the file. The software has a database of objectionable URLs and objectionable words. When it comes across a site that has an objectionable URL or objectionable word, it won't allow that request to be sent. It will also inform the user that the site is blocked. Since there are so many sites on the Internet, and so many more new ones being created each day, the database can be updated monthly. That way, even new sites will be blocked.

Traffic monitoring is another method to maintain a secure intranet. This is software that sits on a server, and monitors all traffic between the Internet and the intranet. It can also monitor all traffic on the intranet itself. The intranet administrator can set rules and decide what kind of traffic to track. The nature of the traffic is the area of concern when trying to assure yourself that only authorized users and services are involved.

Overview of an Intranet Security System

Any intranet is vulnerable to attack by people intent on destruction or on stealing corporate data. The open nature of the Internet and TCP/IP protocols expose a corporation to attack. Intranets require a variety of security measures, including hardware and software combinations that provide control of traffic; encryption and passwords to validate users; and software tools to prevent and cure viruses, block objectionable sites, and monitor traffic.

The generic term for a line of defense against intruders is a *firewall*. A firewall is a hardware/software combination that controls the type of services allowed to or from the intranet.

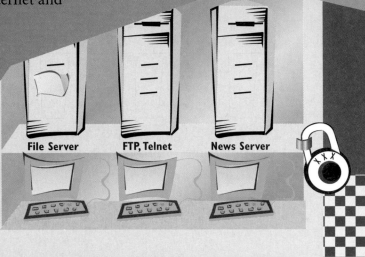

File Server   FTP, Telnet   News Server

COMPUTER OPERATIONS

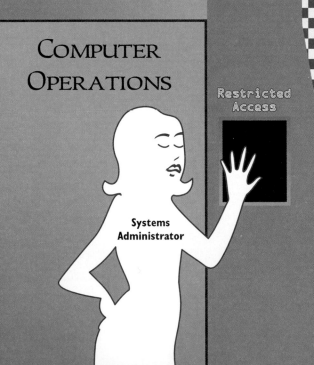

Restricted Access

Systems Administrator

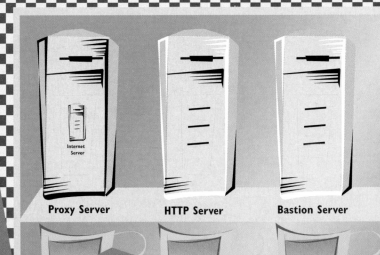

Proxy Server   HTTP Server   Bastion Server

Internet Server

Proxy servers are another common tool used in building a firewall. A proxy server allows system administrators to track all traffic coming in and out of an intranet.

A *bastion server* firewall is configured to withstand and prevent unauthorized access or services. It is typically segmented from the rest of the intranet in its own subnet or *perimeter network*. In this way, if the server is broken into, the rest of the intranet won't be compromised.

Authentication systems are an important part of any intranet security scheme. Authentication systems are used to ensure that anyone trying to log into the intranet or any of its resources is the person they claim to be. Authentication systems typically use user names, passwords, and encryption systems.

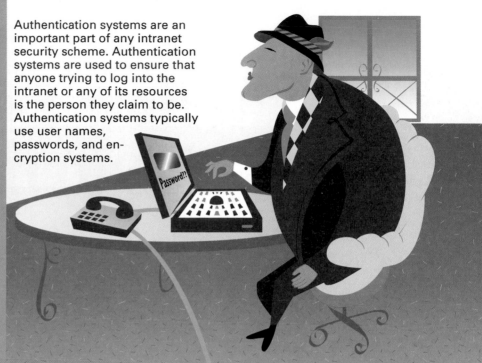

E-Mail Server   **Gateway Server**

Virus Checking Server   **Site Blocking Server**

Server-based virus-checking software can check every file coming into the intranet to make sure that it's virus-free.

Server-based site-blocking software can bar people on an intranet from getting objectionable material. Monitoring software tracks where people have gone and what services they have used, such as HTTP for Web access.

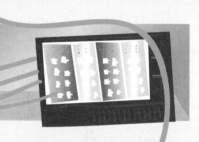

Firewall

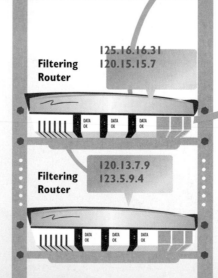

Filtering Router   125.16.16.31 120.15.15.7

DATA OK   DATA OK   DATA OK

Filtering Router   120.13.7.9 123.5.9.4

DATA OK   DATA OK   DATA OK

One way of ensuring that the wrong people or erroneous data can't get into the intranet is to use a *filtering router*. This is a special kind of router that examines the IP address and header information in every packet coming into the network, and allows in only those packets that have addresses or other data, like e-mail, that the system administrator has decided should be allowed into the intranet.

CHAPTER 13

How Filtering Routers Work

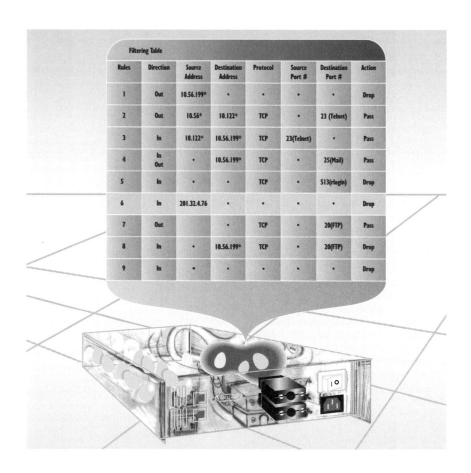

Filtering Table

Rules	Direction	Source Address	Destination Address	Protocol	Source Port #	Destination Port #	Action
1	Out	10.56.199*	*	*	*	*	Drop
2	Out	10.56*	10.122*	TCP	*	23 (Telnet)	Pass
3	In	10.122*	10.56.199*	TCP	23(Telnet)	*	Pass
4	In Out	*	10.56.199*	TCP	*	25(Mail)	Pass
5	In	*	*	TCP	*	513(rlogin)	Drop
6	In	201.32.4.76	*	*	*	*	Drop
7	Out	*	*	TCP	*	20(FTP)	Pass
8	In	*	10.56.199*	TCP	*	20(FTP)	Drop
9	In	*	*	*	*	*	Drop

OFTEN, routers are the first line of defense against unauthorized access to an intranet. The only way that anyone outside the intranet can get to the intranet is through a router, so it makes sense that the router will be the first place to put security rules into place. Routers can also be used within intranets to prevent internal security breaches.

Routers examine every packet coming into and going out of an intranet and decide where to send those packets so that they can be delivered to the proper address. They can control the type and direction of traffic permitted and essentially can also decide whether packets should even be delivered. In other words, they can block certain packets from coming into or going out of an intranet.

When routers are used in this way—to protect an intranet by blocking certain packets—they are called *filtering routers* or *screening routers.*

An intranet administrator establishes a filtering table that contains many rules about which packets are allowed to pass and which are to be dropped. Each packet coming into and going out of an intranet has a number of layers of information in it. These layers contain the data being sent and information about the kind of Internet resource being used (FTP, Telnet, and so forth), the source address and destination address of the packet, and other information. Filtering routers use the information in those layers to evaluate which rules in the filtering table apply to each packet. When packets pass through the router, the router examines the packets, looks at the filtering table, and then decides which action to take. The * wild card can be used at the end of IP addresses, for example, to apply rules to entire subnets or servers.

Rules can differ for incoming packets and outgoing packets. This means people inside the intranet can be given different levels of access to services and data, and prevent people from outside the intranet from getting at intranet resources and data.

For example, a filtering router can allow people from inside an intranet to use Telnet, but not allow anyone outside the intranet to Telnet into the intranet. It can block specific source addresses from accessing the intranet. A filtering router distinguishes between input and output ports traffic. Even if someone hacked into the IP header and forged an address to try to make it look as if they were a legitimate user, the router would recognize the address as an internal one coming in from the output port—a condition that could only be an attack and so the router would drop the packet.

How Filtering Routers Work

Filtering routers, sometimes called screening routers, are the first line of defense against attacks on an intranet. Filtering routers examine every packet moving between networks on an intranet as well as from the Internet. An intranet administrator establishes the rules the routers use to make decisions about which packets should be passed or dropped.

1 Different rules can be set up for incoming packets and outgoing packets so that intranet users can be given access to Internet services, while anyone on the Internet could be banned from accessing certain intranet services and data.

Filtering Table

Rules	Direction	Source Address	Destination Address	Protocol	Source Port #	Destination Port #	Action
1	Out	10.56.199*	•	•	•	•	Drop
2	Out	10.56*	10.122*	TCP	•	23 (Telnet)	Pass
3	In	10.122*	10.56.199*	TCP	23(Telnet)	•	Pass
4	In Out	•	10.56.199*	TCP	•	25(Mail)	Pass
5	In	•	•	TCP	•	513(rlogin)	Drop
6	In	201.32.4.76	•	•	•	•	Drop
7	Out		•	TCP	•	20(FTP)	Pass
8	In	•	10.56.199*	TCP	•	20(FTP)	Drop
9	In	•	•	•	•	•	Drop

2 Filtering routers can keep logs about filtering activity. Commonly, they track packets not allowed to pass between the Internet and the intranet, which would indicate an intranet has been under attack.

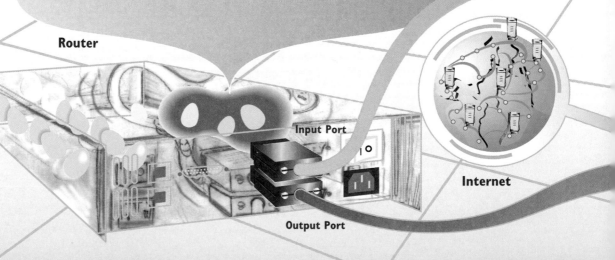

Router

Input Port

Output Port

Internet

Transportation Packet

Application Packet

DATA

4 Source addresses are read from the IP header and compared to the source address listings in the filtering tables. Certain addresses may be known to be dangerous and including them in the table allows the router to drop that traffic.

Rule 3
10.122.3.4 telecommuter (pass)

Rule 4
Traffic to log on E-mail server (pass)

Rule 5
FTP allowed out from Finance (pass)

Rule 5
rlogin request (drop)

Rule 6
Specifically blocked IP (drop)

Rule 9
FTP from Engineering to Finance (drop)

6 A filtering router can allow users to have access to services like Telnet and FTP, while restricting Internet use of these services to access the intranet. This same technique can be used to prevent internal users from accessing restricted data on an intranet. For example, it can allow finance members outgoing use of FTP while dropping FTP requests from the engineering department into the finance department.

7 Certain kinds of services are more dangerous than others. For example, FTP is used to download files but may bring files containing a virus. Telnet and the *rlogin* command (like Telnet but with a greater risk for security break-ins) are banned by rules in the filtering table that evaluate this type of service by the source or destination port number. Telnet addresses port 23, and rlogin port 513.

Rule 4
E-mail (pass)

Rule 8
FTP not allowed in to Financial
(drop)

Rule 8
10.56.199 spoofing
(dropped because via output port)

3 The router examines the data in the IP header which wraps the data and the transport layer header information. That means that any given packet will have data in it, as well as two sets of headers—one from the transport layer, and one from the Internet layer. Filtering routers examine all these data and headers to decide whether to let packets pass.

5 Routers can have different rules for subnets since they may require different levels of security. A subnet that contained highly private financial or competitive information might have many restrictions. An engineering subnet may have few restrictions on incoming or outgoing activities.

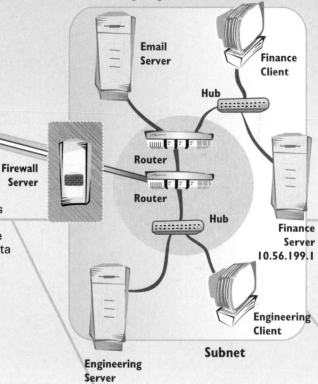

Email Server

Finance Client

Hub

Router

Firewall Server

Router

Hub

Finance Server 10.56.199.1

Engineering Client

Subnet

Engineering Server 10.56.254.1

8 *Address spoofing* is a common method of attack. In address spoofing, someone from outside the intranet forges a source address so that it looks to a router as if the source address is really someone from inside the intranet. The spoofer hopes to trick the filtering router into allowing greater access to the intranet than would be allowed an external originating address. Once the router was convinced that the spoofer was already inside the intranet, private files potentially could be sent outside the intranet.

9 Filtering routers have a way of handling address spoofing. A rule can be established that tells the router to look at the source address in every incoming—but not outgoing—IP header. If the source address is internal, but the packet is coming from outside the intranet, the router would drop the packet.

14

How Firewalls Work

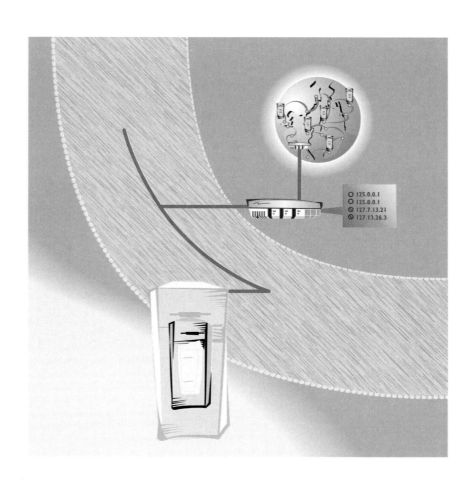

ALL intranets are vulnerable to attack. Their underlying TCP/IP architecture is identical to that of the Internet. Since the Internet was built for maximum openness and communication, there are countless techniques that can be used to attack intranets. Attacks can involve the theft of vital company information and even cash. Attacks can destroy or deny a company's computing resources and services. Attackers can break in or pose as a company employee to use the company's intranet resources.

Firewalls are hardware and software combinations that block intruders from access to an intranet while still allowing people on the intranet to access the resources of the Internet. Depending on how secure a site needs to be, and on how much time, money, and resources can be spent on a firewall, there are many kinds that can be built. Most of them, though, are built using only a few elements. Servers and routers are the primary components of firewalls.

Most firewalls use some kind of *packet filtering*. In packet filtering, a *screening router* or *filtering router* looks at every packet of data traveling between an intranet and the Internet. See Chapter 13 for more information on filtering.

Proxy servers on an intranet are used when someone from the intranet wants to access a server on the Internet. A request from the user's computer is sent to the proxy server instead of directly to the Internet. The proxy server contacts the server on the Internet, receives the information from the Internet, and then sends the information to the requester on the intranet. By acting as a go-between like this, proxy servers can filter traffic and maintain security as well as log all traffic between the Internet and the network.

Bastion hosts are heavily fortified servers that handle all incoming requests from the Internet, such as FTP requests. A single bastion host handling incoming requests makes it easier to maintain security and track attacks. In the event of a break in, only that single host has been compromised, instead of the entire network. In some firewalls, multiple bastion hosts can be used, one for each different kind of intranet service request.

How Firewalls Work

Firewalls protect intranets from any attacks launched against them from the Internet. They are designed to protect an intranet from unauthorized access to corporate information, and damaging or denying computer resources and services. They are also designed to stop people on the intranet from accessing Internet services that can be dangerous, such as FTP.

1 Intranet computers are allowed access to the Internet only after passing through a firewall. Requests have to pass through an *internal screening router*, also called an *internal filtering router* or *choke router*. This router prevents packet traffic from being sniffed remotely. A choke router examines all packets for information such as the source and destination of the packet.

E-mail

Internal Network

2 The router compares the information it finds to rules in a *filtering table*, and passes or drops the packets based on those rules. For example, some services, such as rlogin, may not be allowed to run. The router also might not allow any packets to be sent to specific suspicious Internet locations. A router can also block every packet traveling between the Internet and the internal network, except for e-mail. System administrators set the rules for determining which packets to allow in and which to block.

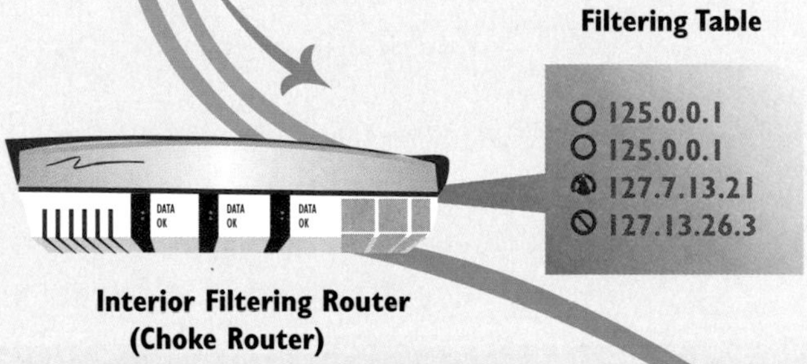

Filtering Table

○ 125.0.0.1
○ 125.0.0.1
⊕ 127.7.13.21
⊘ 127.13.26.3

DATA OK   DATA OK   DATA OK

**Interior Filtering Router
(Choke Router)**

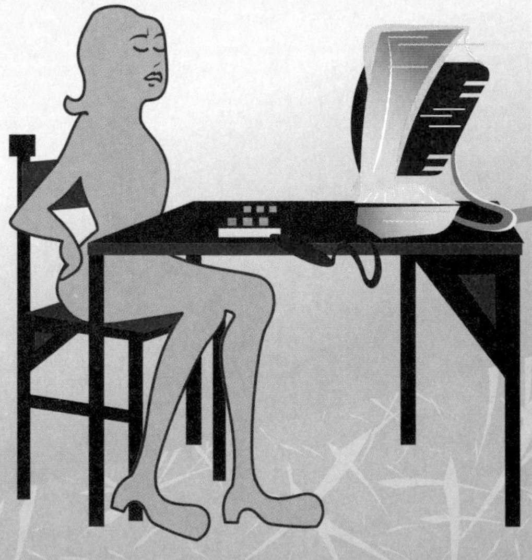

3 When an intranet is protected by a firewall, the usual internal intranet services are available—such as e-mail, access to corporate databases and Web services, and the use of groupware.

6 A bastion host is the main point of contact for connections coming in from the Internet for all services such as e-mail, FTP access, and any other data and requests. The bastion host services all those requests—people on the intranet contact only this one server, and they don't directly contact any other intranet servers. In this way, intranet servers are protected from attack. Bastion hosts can also be set up as proxy servers. See Chapter 15 for more information about proxy servers and Chapter 16 for more information about bastion hosts.

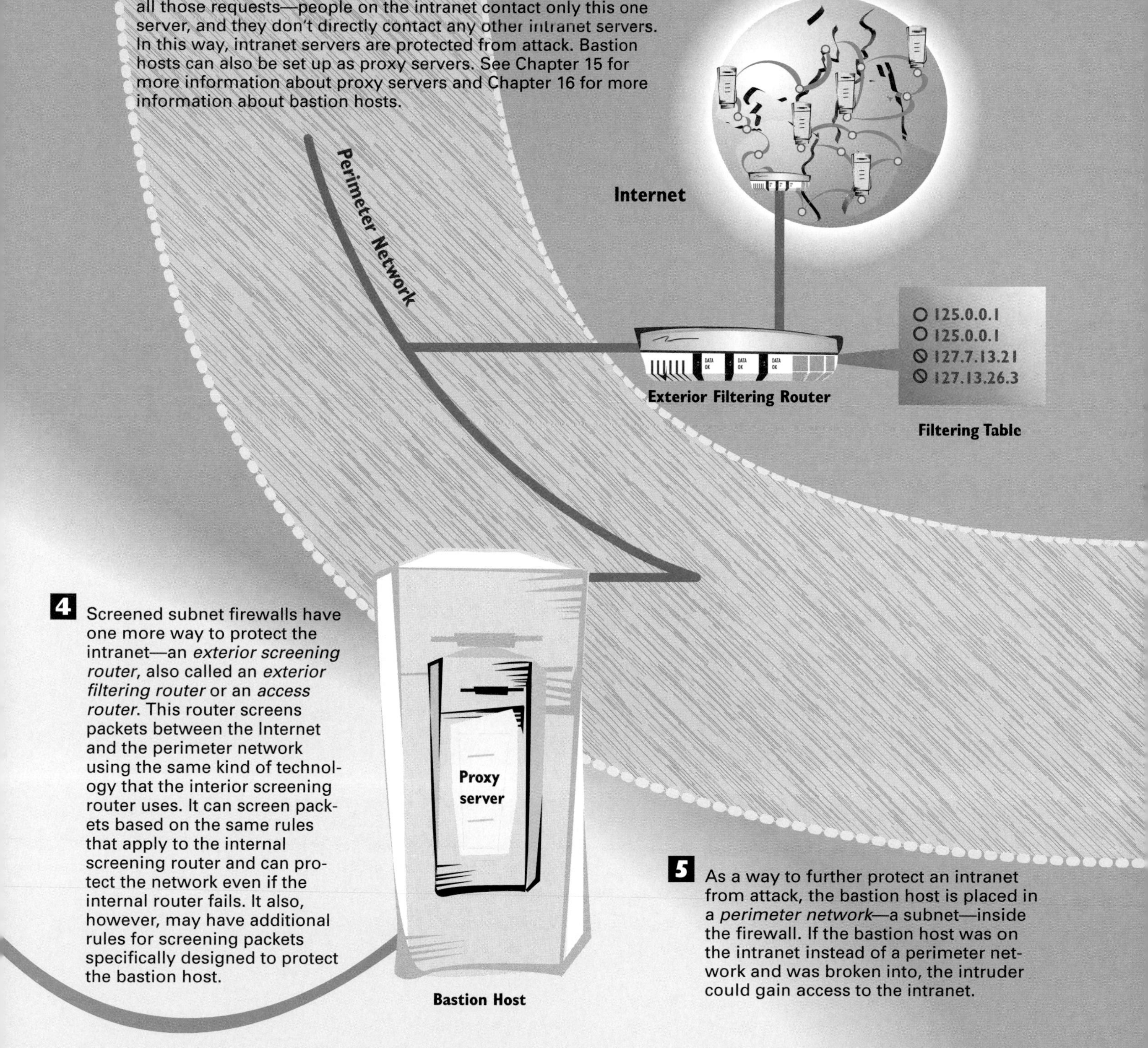

Perimeter Network

Internet

Exterior Filtering Router

○ 125.0.0.1
○ 125.0.0.1
⊘ 127.7.13.21
⊘ 127.13.26.3

Filtering Table

4 Screened subnet firewalls have one more way to protect the intranet—an *exterior screening router*, also called an *exterior filtering router* or an *access router*. This router screens packets between the Internet and the perimeter network using the same kind of technology that the interior screening router uses. It can screen packets based on the same rules that apply to the internal screening router and can protect the network even if the internal router fails. It also, however, may have additional rules for screening packets specifically designed to protect the bastion host.

Proxy
server

Bastion Host

5 As a way to further protect an intranet from attack, the bastion host is placed in a *perimeter network*—a subnet—inside the firewall. If the bastion host was on the intranet instead of a perimeter network and was broken into, the intruder could gain access to the intranet.

CHAPTER

15 How Proxy Servers Work

Proxy Server Software

FTP Proxy Server

Telnet Proxy Server

Web Proxy Server

THERE are certain risks associated with allowing people from inside an intranet to directly contact Internet servers and resources. An intranet user might obtain a file from the Internet that could damage the files on their computer and the entire intranet. Additionally, when intranet users are allowed unfettered access to the Internet, it is difficult for intranet administrators to guard against intruders who attempt to take over an intranet computer or server.

A common way to block this kind of access is to use *proxy servers.* These servers sit inside a firewall, frequently on a *bastion host* (see Chapter 16 for more on how bastion hosts work). They balance the two functions of providing intranet users with easy access to the Internet and keeping the network secure. When someone inside the intranet wants to contact the Internet to get information or a resource—for example, to visit a Web page—they don't actually contact the Internet directly. Instead, they contact a proxy server inside an intranet firewall, and the proxy server contacts the Internet (in this instance, a Web server). The Web server sends the proxy server the page, and the proxy server then sends that page to the requester on the intranet.

Proxy servers can log all actions they take so that intranet administrators can check for attacks. Proxy servers offer other benefits as well. They can cache Internet Web pages in their memory, so that when someone on the intranet wants to get back to a Web page they've accessed before, the Web page will be delivered directly from the proxy server, and the requester won't have to go out across the Internet. Since intranet connections are often made at higher speeds than Internet connections, that means quicker response and faster viewing of Web pages and other Internet resources. However, this would not be an acceptable response for time-sensitive items like stock quotes, because the cached Web pages are not the most current version.

There may be multiple proxy servers on a single intranet. There may be separate proxy servers for the Web, Telnet, FTP, and other Internet services. Often on an intranet, some services will require a proxy server, while others will not. For example, this includes anything involving Telnet or FTP, because they involve file transferring, and they would be likely to be on a proxy server. When a new Internet resource is first made available, such as streaming multimedia files, proxy servers usually can't be used because proxy server technology has not yet been developed for it. The intranet administrator will have to decide whether to block those services completely or let them be used until proxy software catches up to the new technology.

Sometimes special proxy client software has to be used in concert with proxy services. This can be a problem because not all operating systems have proxy clients for all Internet services. Other possible problems include nonstandard client software, which can be difficult to use. A better approach is to use standard, off-the-shelf software such as Netscape Navigator, and use a configuration screen that tells the software where the proxy server can be found. The software and server will then take care of the rest.

How Proxy Servers Work

An integral part of many intranet security systems is a *proxy server*. A proxy server is software and a server that sits in a firewall and acts as a go-between among computers on an intranet and the Internet. Proxy servers often run on bastion hosts. (See Chapter 16 for more information on bastion hosts.) Only the proxy server—instead of the many individual computers on the intranet—interact with the Internet, so security can be maintained because the server can be kept more secure than can hundreds of individual intranet computers. Intranet administrators can set up proxy servers to be used for many services, such as FTP, the Web, and Telnet. Intranet administrators decide which Internet services must go through a proxy server, and which do not have to. Specific proxy server software is required for each different kind of Internet service.

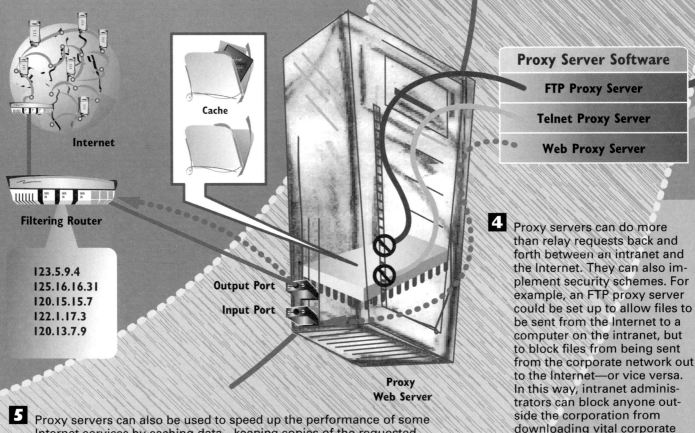

Internet

Cache

Proxy Server Software

FTP Proxy Server

Telnet Proxy Server

Web Proxy Server

Filtering Router

123.5.9.4
125.16.16.31
120.15.15.7
122.1.17.3
120.13.7.9

Output Port

Input Port

Proxy
Web Server

4 Proxy servers can do more than relay requests back and forth between an intranet and the Internet. They can also implement security schemes. For example, an FTP proxy server could be set up to allow files to be sent from the Internet to a computer on the intranet, but to block files from being sent from the corporate network out to the Internet—or vice versa. In this way, intranet administrators can block anyone outside the corporation from downloading vital corporate data. Or they can stop intranet users from downloading files which may contain viruses.

5 Proxy servers can also be used to speed up the performance of some Internet services by caching data—keeping copies of the requested data. For example, a Web proxy server could cache many Web pages, so that whenever someone from the intranet wanted to get one of those Web pages, they could get it directly from the proxy server across high-speed intranet lines, instead of having to go out across the Internet and get the page at a lower speed from Internet lines.

1 When a computer on the intranet makes a request out to the Internet—such as to retrieve a Web page from a Web server—the internal computer actually contacts the proxy server, which in turn contacts the Internet server. The Internet server sends the Web page to the proxy server, which then forwards the page to the computer on the intranet.

123.5.9.4
125.16.16.31
120.15.15.7
122.1.17.3
120.13.7.9

Filtering Router

FTP
Request denied.

2 Proxy servers log all traffic between the Internet and the intranet. For example, a Telnet proxy server could track every single keystroke hit in every Telnet session on the intranet—and could also track how the external server on the Internet reacts to those keystrokes. Proxy servers can log every IP address, date and time of access, URL, number of bytes downloaded, and so on. This information can be used to analyze any attacks launched against the network. It can also help intranet administrators build better access and services for employees.

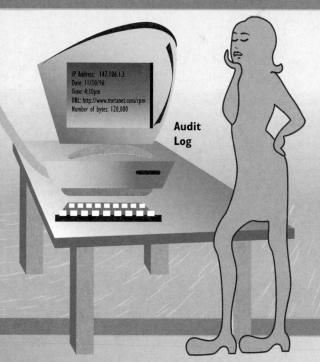

IP Address: 147.106.1.3
Date: 11/30/96
Time: 4:30pm
URL: http://www.metanet.com/rpm
Number of bytes: 120,000

Audit Log

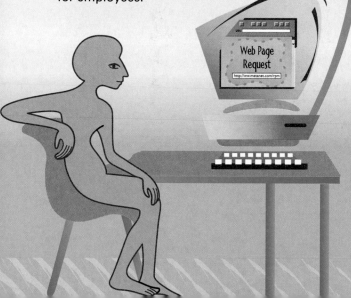

Web Page Request
http://www.metanet.com/rpm

3 Some proxy servers must work with special proxy clients. A more popular approach is to use off-the-shelf clients such as Netscape with proxy servers. When such an off-the-shelf package is used, it must be specially configured to work with proxy servers from a configuration menu. Then the intranet employee uses the client software as usual. The client software knows to go out to a proxy server to get the data, instead of to the Internet.

CHAPTER

16

How Bastion Hosts Work

ONE of the best ways to protect an intranet from attack is to put a heavily fortified *bastion host* or *bastion server* in a firewall. Having a bastion host means that all access to an intranet from the Internet will be required to come through the bastion host. By concentrating all access in a single server, or a small group of servers, it's much easier to protect the entire intranet.

The bastion host does not provide intranet services itself. When it receives a request from the Internet for an intranet service, the host passes the request to the appropriate server. Subsequently, it takes the response and passes it back to the Internet.

Proxy server programs can also run on bastion hosts. That is, when someone on the intranet wants to get at an Internet resource, they first contact the proxy server on the bastion host, and the bastion host then relays the request to the Internet server. The Internet server sends the information to the proxy server on the bastion host, which in turn passes the information back to the user on the intranet.

Several means are taken to ensure that the bastion host is as secure as possible—and also to make sure that if the host is hacked into, intranet security won't be compromised.

To make the bastion host secure, it is stripped of all but the most basic services. A typical network server provides login, file, print, and other services, including access to additional servers. On a bastion host, those services have been prohibited. Since there are no user accounts, it's difficult for someone to break in using passwords. Since it has few services available, even if someone did break in, there wouldn't be much they could do with it.

For even more security, bastion hosts can be put on a private subnet (often referred to as a *perimeter network*), further isolating the host so that if someone breaks into it, they can only get access to that subnet, not to the rest of the intranet. A filtering router reviews packets coming from the private subnet, making sure that only authorized incoming requests pass through to the intranet.

Even more security measures can protect the server and intranet, sending alerts to intranet administrators if someone is trying to break in. The bastion host can log all access to it, and keep a secure backup of that log on a physically separate machine connected by the serial port so no one can gain access to the log remotely. System administrators can examine the log for signs of break-ins. Even more powerful are monitoring programs that watch the log and sound an alarm if it detects someone has been trying to break into the server. Auditing software can also constantly check the server software to see if it has been altered in any way—a possible sign that an intruder has successfully attacked it and taken control of its resources.

How Bastion Hosts Work

A bastion host (also called a bastion server) is one of the main defenses in an intranet firewall. It's a heavily fortified server that sits inside the firewall, and it is the main point of contact between the intranet and the Internet. By having an isolated, heavily defended server as the main point of contact, the rest of the intranet resources can be shielded from attacks starting on the Internet.

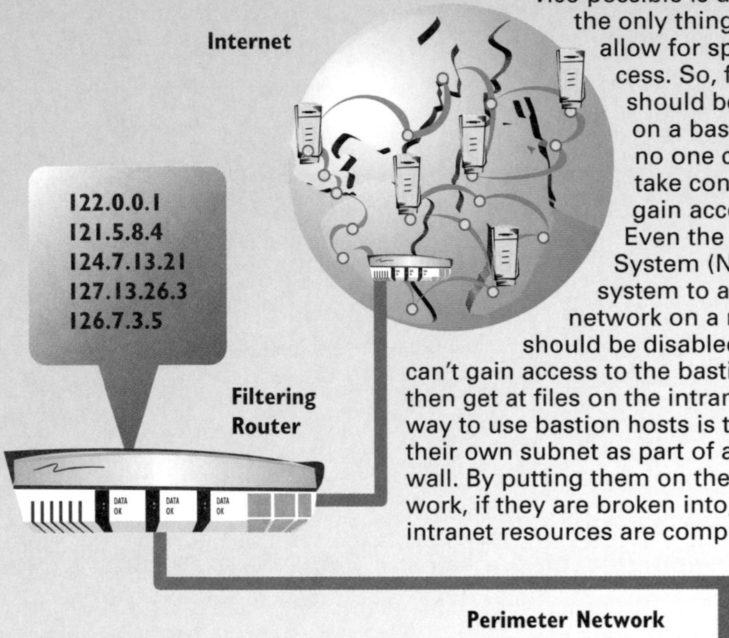

Internet

122.0.0.1
121.5.8.4
124.7.13.21
127.13.26.3
126.7.3.5

Filtering Router

Bastion hosts are built so that every network service possible is disabled on them—the only thing the server does is allow for specified Internet access. So, for example, there should be no user accounts on a bastion server, so that no one can log into it and take control of it and then gain access to the intranet. Even the Network File System (NFS), which allows a system to access files across a network on a remote system, should be disabled, so that intruders can't gain access to the bastion server and then get at files on the intranet. The safest way to use bastion hosts is to put them on their own subnet as part of an intranet firewall. By putting them on their own network, if they are broken into, no other intranet resources are compromised.

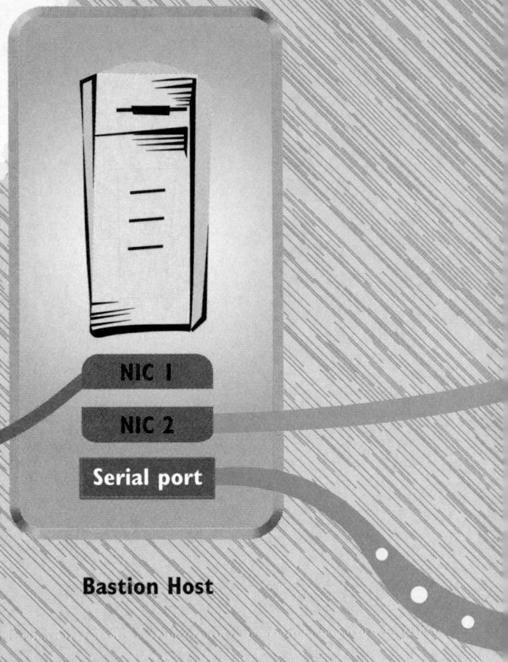

NIC 1
NIC 2
Serial port

Bastion Host

Perimeter Network

Bastion servers log all activity so that intranet administrators can tell if the intranet has been attacked. They often keep two copies of system logs for security reasons: In case one log is destroyed or tampered with, the other log is always available as a backup. One way to keep a secure copy of the log is to connect the bastion server via a serial port to a dedicated computer, whose only purpose is to keep track of the secure backup log.

Automated monitors are even more sophisticated programs than auditing software. Automated monitors regularly check the bastion server's system logs, and send an alarm if it finds a suspicious pattern. For example, an alarm might be sent if someone attempted more than three unsuccessful logins.

SERVER.EXE
37128 bytes

Victim Machine

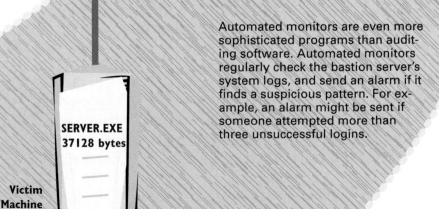

Some bastion servers include auditing programs, which actively check to see whether an attack has been launched against them. There are a variety of ways to do auditing. One way to audit is to use a checksum program, which checks to see whether any software on the bastion server has been changed by an unauthorized person. A checksum program calculates a number based on the size of an executable program on the server. It then regularly calculates the checksum to see if it has changed. If it has changed, someone has altered the software, which could signal an attack.

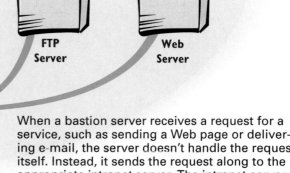

FTP Server

Web Server

123.5.9.4
125.16.16.31
120.15.15.7
122.1.17.3
120.13.7.9

Hub

When a bastion server receives a request for a service, such as sending a Web page or delivering e-mail, the server doesn't handle the request itself. Instead, it sends the request along to the appropriate intranet server. The intranet server handles the request, and then sends the information back to the bastion server. The bastion server now sends the requested information to the requester on the Internet.

Interior Filtering Router (Choke Router)

Placing a filtering router between the bastion host and the intranet provides additional security. The filtering router checks all packets between the Internet and the intranet, dropping unauthorized traffic.

Log.txt
Login: hack
Denied
Login: imposter
Denied
Login: enemy
Denied

Warning!
ALARM
Admin
PC

Serial Connection

There can be more than one bastion host in a firewall. Each bastion host can handle one or more Internet services for the intranet. Sometimes, a bastion host can be used as a victim machine. This is a server that is stripped bare of almost all services except one specific Internet service. Victim machines can be used to provide Internet services that are hard to handle using proxying or a filtering router, or whose security concerns are not yet known. The services are put on the victim machine instead of a bastion host with other services. That way, if the server is broken into, other bastion hosts won't be affected.

17

How Encryption Works

ENCRYPTION

works to protect against many threats to the security of an intranet. There is vulnerability during data transmission when people capture data sent across an intranet, or from the intranet through the Internet. This is a particular problem when transmitting sensitive information. Data is also vulnerable to a variety of threats while stored, including unauthorized access and theft.

When information and data is *encrypted*, it is altered so that to anyone other than the intended recipient it will look like meaningless garble. Encrypted information needs to be *decrypted* in order to view it and understand it—that is, turned back to the original message by the recipient, and only by the recipient.

There are several terms you'll need to understand in the encryption process: keys, algorithm, hash function, message digest, and digital fingerprint.

The heart of understanding how cryptosystems work is to understand the concept of *keys*. There are two basic kinds of encryption: *secret-key (symmetric)* and *public-key (asymmetric) cryptography*. Keys are secret values that are used by computers in concert with complex mathematical formulas called algorithms to encrypt and decrypt messages. The idea behind keys is that if someone encrypts a message with a key, only someone with a matching key will be able to decrypt it. Key size is the critical characteristic of encryption systems. Size is counted in bits. DES (Data Encryption Standard) is the most common secret key system. Both the sender and the receiver need to have copies of the same secret key. DES is used by the U.S. government and relies on a 56-bit key. This is the minimum size for effectiveness. DES performs 16 sequential calculations of substitutions on separate halves of the message to derive the encrypted result. DES is a symmetric process, linear calculation, and results in one secret key.

RSA encryption, named after the MIT professors who developed it in 1977 (Ronald Rivest, Adi Shamir, and Leonard Adleman), differs from DES in both technique to derive the result and because RSA uses key pairs instead of one key. The key pairs of RSA are derived by multiplying two large (each a few hundred bits long) prime numbers (factorization) and additional mathematical calculations. The RSA algorithm is the best-known public-key system. In public-key cryptography, a pair of keys are involved: a *public key* and a *private key*. Every person has both a public key and a private key. An individual's public key is made freely available, while the private key is exclusively known to each individual. If the public key is used to encrypt a message, only the companion private key can decrypt the message. If someone wanted to send a message to you, for example, he or she would encrypt it with your public key. Only you, with your private key, would be able to decrypt the message and read it. Your public key could not decrypt it. This means that once the message is encrypted, not even the sender can decrypt the message. Conversely, messages encrypted with private keys can only be decrypted with the matching public key. This ensures the authenticity of the sender to the recipient: Only someone with the private key code can encrypt a message that can be decrypted with that public key.

You may have heard about the Clipper chip and the Skipjack method to program a secret key. Skipjack uses an 80-bit key, so would be tougher to crack than DES. The controversy over the Clipper chip is not about the effectiveness of Skipjack, rather it is the fact that the chip contains a "back-door" that would allow others (theoretically only specifically authorized government agents) to get at the secret key, completely defeating the reasons people use encryption, privacy, and security.

PGP (Pretty Good Privacy) is an encryption program that uses a 128-bit key, and furthermore, it uses the RSA algorithm to encrypt the encryption of the 128-bit key. This means that PGP has 2^{128} possible keys. PGP as an implementation with RSA, uses key pairs, also known as public and private keys.

When a message is run through an encryption algorithm (like RSA) it can also call a hash function. Algorithms are essentially the mathematical method used to generate the keys. The hash function is used as a method to ensure that a message hasn't been altered. For example, if a sent message was 500 words long, but arrived as a message 501 words long, you could tell something had changed in transit. Word count by itself is not sufficient for ensuring that a message hasn't been altered since you could have multiple changes that have a net result of 500 words, and there would be no way to tell that the 500 words contained different words than the original. Hash functions on messages, therefore, are more complex. For example, it might use the number of words and the number of letters as components in the calculation. Because the message is the basis for the algorithm's calculation the result is unique to the message.

This process produces a number known as the message digest. For the purposes of this explanation, think of it as the value of the word count result, 500. The message digest (the 500 value) is then encrypted apart from the message itself, with a sender's private key. Because only the sender has access to this private key, the result is a "digital fingerprint"—a unique number that only the originator with a private key can create and which can only be decrypted with the companion public key.

Next, a new, random key is generated to encrypt the actual message and the digital signature. The recipient will need a copy of this random key in order to decrypt the message. This random key is the only key in the world that can decrypt the message and it is solely in the possession of the sender. This means the random key must now be sent, maintaining its secrecy, to the recipient, so the message can be decrypted. To allow for secure sending of the random key, it too is encrypted, this time with the recipient's public key. The encrypted random key is referred to as the digital envelope. Only the recipient will be able to decrypt the random key since it was encrypted with his or her public key—and so only his or her private key can decrypt it.

The result of this process is an encrypted confidential message, an encrypted signature, and the encrypted digital envelope. When the recipient gets the message, he or she decrypts the digital envelope with the private key, which results in the random key used to encrypt the message. The recipient then uses the random key to decrypt the actual message. However, at this stage there is no way to check that the message hasn't been altered en route—or that the message is authentic; that is, sent by the person it claims to be sent by. The recipient now uses the sender's public key to decrypt his or her encrypted digital signature. The recipient then gets the message digest—the message's "digital fingerprint."

By running the digital fingerprint message through the same algorithm—the hash function—a new message digest is generated. If authentic, this new message digest should match the original message digest precisely. If they don't match, either someone else composed the message, or the message was altered by someone after it was written.

In the process described above, a public-key system was crucial to the flow. Private key (or secret key) cryptosystems are not feasible to be used widely on the Internet or intranets for things such as electronic commerce. For a company to conduct business over the Internet or intranets with a private key system would mean creating millions of different private keys—one for each person who wanted to do business—and then figuring out some way to send those private keys securely over the Internet, which is not really possible. In secret key cryptography, only one key is used to encrypt and decrypt messages. With a public-key system, a business only needs to create a single public/private key combination. The business would post the public key for anyone to use to encrypt information—but only the business itself, with the private key, would be able to decrypt the data.

How Encryption Works

One means of securing an intranet is to use encryption—altering data so that only someone with access to specific decryption codes can understand the information. Encryption is used for storing and sending passwords to make sure that no snoopers can understand them. Encryption is used as well when data is sent between intranets on Very Secure Private Networks (VSPNs). Encryption is also used to conduct commerce on the Internet to protect credit card information during transmission.

Algorithm

Hash Function

Message Digest

Digital Fingerprint

1 *Keys* are the heart of encryption. Keys are complex mathematical formulas (algorithms), that are used to encrypt and decrypt messages. If someone encrypts a message, only someone with the proper key will be able to decrypt the message. There are two basic key systems, secret-key and public-key cryptography.

2 An algorithm is used to perform a hash function. This process produces a message digest unique to the message. The message digest is encrypted with the sender's private key which results in a digital fingerprint.

Symmetric

DES

**Secret-Key
1 Key**

3 Data Encryption Standard (DES) is a secret-key (symmetric) system; there is no public key component. Both the sender and the receiver know the secret code word. This method is not feasible for conducting business over the Internet.

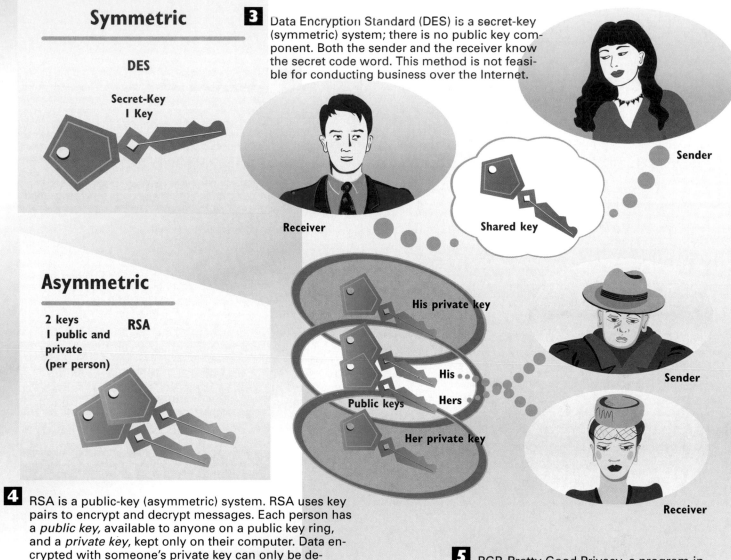

Sender

Receiver

Shared key

Asymmetric

**2 keys
1 public and
private
(per person)**

RSA

His private key

His

Hers

Public keys

Her private key

Sender

Receiver

4 RSA is a public-key (asymmetric) system. RSA uses key pairs to encrypt and decrypt messages. Each person has a *public key,* available to anyone on a public key ring, and a *private key*, kept only on their computer. Data encrypted with someone's private key can only be decrypted with their public key; and data encrypted with their public key can only be decrypted with their private key. Therefore, RSA requires an exchange of public keys; this can be done without a need for secrecy since the public key is useless without the companion private key.

5 PGP, Pretty Good Privacy, a program invented by Philip Zimmermann, is a popular method used to encrypt data. It uses MD5 (message-digest 5) and RSA cryptosystems to generate the key pairs. PGP is a popular program that can run on UNIX, DOS, and Macintosh platforms. It offers some variations of functionality, like compression, that other cryptosystems do not. Multiple key pairs can be generated and placed on public and private key rings.

PGP

(Pretty Good Privacy)

Multiple keys

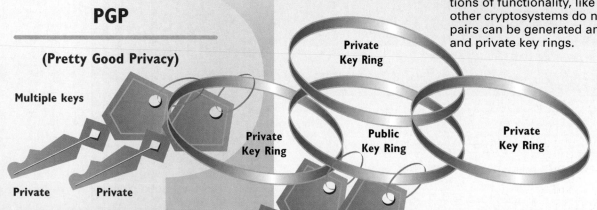

**Private
Key Ring**

**Private
Key Ring**

**Public
Key Ring**

**Private
Key Ring**

Private   **Private**

How Cryptosystems Work

Because of the open nature of the Internet, it is easy for people to intercept messages that travel across it—making it difficult to send confidential messages or financial data, such as credit card information. To solve the problem, cryptosystems have been developed. A popular one, called RSA, uses keys to encrypt and decrypt messages so that only the sender and receiver can understand the messages. The system requires that each person have a public key that is made available to anyone, and a private key that they keep only on their computer. Data encrypted with someone's private key can only be decrypted with their private key. This illustration is an example of how a public-key system works. In it, Gabriel and Mia want to exchange a confidential message. They have already exchanged public keys.

GABRIEL'S COMPUTER

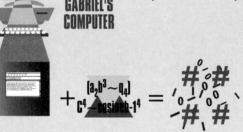

$$+ \frac{(a_2 b^3 \sim q_4)}{c^4 \sim \cos n b \cdot 1^4} = \#$$

Gabriel wants to send a confidential message over the Internet to Mia. Mia will need some way to decrypt the message—as well as a way to guarantee that the message has been actually sent by Gabriel, and not by an imposter. First, Gabriel runs his message through an algorithm called a *hash function*. This produces a number known as the *message digest*. The message digest acts as a sort of "digital fingerprint" that Mia will use to ensure that no one has altered the message.

Gabriel now uses his private key to encrypt the message disgest. This produces a unique digital signature that only he, with his private key, could have created.

GABRIEL'S PRIVATE + # =

+ **RANDOM KEY** =

+ **RANDOM KEY** = **ENCRYPTED**

Gabriel generates a new random key. He uses this key to encrypt his original message and his digital signature. Mia will need a copy of this random key in order to decrypt Gabriel's message. This random key is the only key in the world that can decrypt the message—and at this point only Gabriel has the key.

Gabriel encrypts this new random key with Mia's public key. This encrypted random key is referred to as the *digital envelope*. Only Mia will be able to decrypt the random key since it was encrypted with her public key—and so only her private key can decrypt it.

RANDOM KEY + **PUBLIC** = **RANDOM KEY ENCRYPTED**

Gabriel sends a message over the Internet to Mia that is composed of several parts: the encrypted confidential message, the encrypted digital signature, and the encrypted digtal envelope.

ENCRYPTED   ENCRYPTED   ENCRYPTED

 + **PRIVATE**  = RANDOM KEY

Mia gets the message. She decrypts the digital envelope with her private key—and out of it gets the random key that Gabriel used to encrypt the message.

Original Message

$[a_2 b^3 \sim q_4]$
$c^4 \sim cosineb\text{-}1^4$
Hash Function

Message Digest

Digital Signature

PUBLIC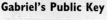
Gabriel's Public Key

Mia uses the random key to decrypt Gabriel's message. She can now read the confidential message that he sent her. She can't yet be sure, however, that the message hasn't been altered en route—or that the message was in fact sent by Gabriel.

RANDOM KEY +  DECRYPTED =

PRIVATE
Gabriel's Private Key

PUBLIC
Mia's Public Key

PRIVATE
Mia's Private Key

She now uses Gabriel's public key to decrypt his encrypted digital signature. When she does this, she gets his message digest—the message's "digital fingerprint."

PUBLIC + 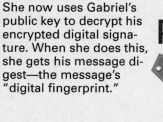 DECRYPTED =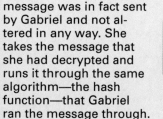

 RANDOM KEY
Random Key

Encrypted Message

Mia will use this message digest to see whether the message was in fact sent by Gabriel and not altered in any way. She takes the message that she had decrypted and runs it through the same algorithm—the hash function—that Gabriel ran the message through. This will produce a new message digest

 + $[a_2 b^3 \sim q_4]$ $c^4 \sim cosineb\text{-}1^4$ =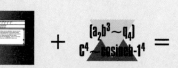

Encrypted Digital Signature

Encrypted Random Key (Digital Envelope)

Mia compares the message digest that she calculated to the one that she got out of Gabriel's digital signature. If the two match precisely, she can be sure that Gabriel signed the message that it was not altered after he composed it. If they don't match, then she knows that either he didn't compose the messsage or that someone altered the message after he wrote it.

 + $[a_2 b^3 \sim q_4]$ $c^4 \sim cosineb\text{-}1^4$ =

PUBLIC + =

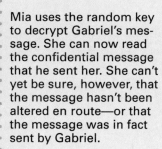 

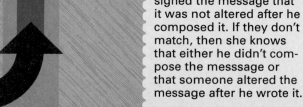
INTERNET

CHAPTER

18

How Passwords and Authentication Systems Work

WHAT'S the most effective way to gain unauthorized access to an intranet? If you guessed high-tech wizardry, programming beyond the mere ken of mortals, or some kind of mastery of and insight into the innermost workings of TCP/IP, you would be wrong. Most attacks occur because an unauthorized person has managed to discover an authorized person's user name and password. One cumbersome way to address this problem is to require that users log in through a firewall with one password, and then require additional, different passwords to access various resources. However, making it hard for users to use passwords is counterproductive and leads to increased vulnerability. The passwords of systems administrators or superusers require special care, since if these passwords were compromised, the intruder would have full access to an intranet and all its corporate riches.

New servers often come with standard default passwords. However, it is really the fault of the systems administrators who fail to change the defaults. Similarly, care must be taken when, due to necessary technical work being done, technicians require root access or load custom utilities. Sometimes the default passwords are changed, and you think you are safe, but at some point during a disaster recovery process old users and/or passwords are loaded back in place.

Passwords can be discovered through brute force. Programs can be written (or bought) that generate thousands of passwords. This is often referred to as a "dictionary" password checker program. Administrators can purchase such programs to help find weak passwords, and can customize them to include additional terms. Brute force is more effective when passwords are short, so systems administrators may require certain minimum lengths for passwords and password phrases.

Unauthorized access is an internal as well as external threat. No one would intentionally allow all internal users access to their company's financial system, such as a check-writing program, even though as employees they would be authorized users for other parts of the intranet. Secure passwords are probably more critical for protection from internal threats than external threats. Insiders already have access to the names of fellow employees, their departments, and would know the conventions of the user name format.

In an effort to use passwords they can remember, people create passwords that can be fairly easily guessed. Many people, for example, use passwords made up of some combination of their first and last names or their initials. Other popular passwords include the names of children, birth dates or anniversary dates, license numbers of cars, and other familiar things. Again, internal threats are the greater risk because of insider familiarity with colleagues' habits and physical access to cubicles (where the poster of the cobra is so prominently displayed).

Social engineering is another technique that can easily break the security of passwords. A remote access caller who contacts the help desk late at night with a tale of woe about "a big report due the next morning and I can't get in under my usual password, and so please just change it to something to get me in for this emergency" is using social engineering to crack the security of the password system. People don't want to mistrust their colleagues and are reluctant to sound paranoid or foolish by refusing access to co-workers. Workers also often need to provide others with access to something that would normally be off-limits, while workers are on vacation, for example. In such cases intruders don't have to guess passwords, they are told the passwords. The real problems from this can come later, when authorized users fail to change their password upon returning from vacation or when, unknown to them, a third party has been told the password for some purpose while they were gone.

Most systems require that passwords be changed periodically so that even if passwords are discovered or given out, there is only a limited window of vulnerability. People, of course, might (and often do) try to circumvent this by changing their password and then changing it right back again. However, this can be prevented by systems requiring that when users change their passwords they must choose a password that they have not used before.

The logical extension of this "never before used" password requirement is the single-use password. There are several methods of generating these passwords, including software and hardware methods. The software method still requires a truly secret password but it is used to generate a number of one-time variations that are used without encryption. The software method is still fundamentally a "something you know" type of protection. Hardware solutions add a "something you have" component, a physical device that generates single use passwords. Smart cards are a hardware solution. They are credit card-sized devices that work with special readers to respond to authorization requests.

Authentication systems work with password systems to make sure the users are who they say they are. Depending on the kind of password system used in authentication systems, the password files containing the master list of all passwords on an intranet can be plain text or encrypted.

In one system called the Password Authentication Protocol (PAP), the password file is encrypted. When someone logs onto the intranet, a server asks them for their user name and password. The user's response is not encrypted at the workstation and so goes over the wire in clear text. When the server receives the password from the user, it encrypts it using the same encryption scheme that was used to encrypt the password in the password file. The server then compares the two encrypted passwords. If they match, it knows to let the person in.

While the password file itself is particularly secure since it's encrypted, the PAP system is vulnerable in another way. Since the password isn't encrypted until the server encrypts it, this method is vulnerable to packet sniffing attacks. Packet sniffing is a form of eavesdropping on the traffic over the wire. Since the passwords travel in clear text, someone capturing traffic could steal all passwords transmitted across the intranet. Even encrypted passwords traveling the wire are vulnerable to eavesdropping when they are captured and replayed, convincing the server that they are authorized users. This is another reason why single-use passwords provide more security.

The Challenge Handshake Authentication Protocol (CHAP), *a challenge-response* system, does not completely eliminate sending clear text over the wire to solve the problem. Furthermore, the table of passwords on the server is not encrypted. What happens is this: When someone types in a user name, the server generates a random key and sends the key (also in clear text) to the user. The user uses the key to encrypt his or her password and sends the encrypted password back to the server. The server checks the password table for the key it assigned, and encrypts the password. The server then compares the encrypted password from the user with the encrypted password it created. If they match, the user is allowed in.

CHAP performs an additional check to authenticate the user, that is, it attempts to verify that the person in an ongoing session is the person originally authorized. CHAP continuously sends different challenges to the user throughout the session, not just at the beginning. This authentication process solves problems with unattended-but-logged-in workstations. This system also solves the problem of password theft by packet sniffing, since the password sent between user and server is encrypted. However, the password file itself is vulnerable, since it's not encrypted.

Extensive systems have been devised that combine encryption, password technology, and authentication to make sure that no unauthorized person can gain access to intranets.

One particularly secure authentication system is called Kerberos. Kerberos is named after the mythological three-headed dog who guarded the gates of Hades in Greek mythology. (The dog is also called Cerberus, sometimes spelled Kerberos.) Developed at the Massachusetts Institute of Technology, the Kerberos system requires that all computers, servers, and workstations be running the Kerberos software. When anyone wants to get onto the network, they have to type in a password and user name. They are then given an encrypted token by the system. In order to use any network resource, that encrypted token is required. This stops any intruders from accessing any intranet resources unless they first go through password authentication.

How Passwords Work

Password Authentication Protocol

One of an intranet's first lines of defense is to use password protection. A variety of security techniques, including encryption, helps ensure that passwords are kept secure. It is also necessary to require that passwords are changed frequently, are not easily guessed or common dictionary words, and are not simply given out. Authentication is the additional step of verifying that the person providing the password is the person authorized to do so.

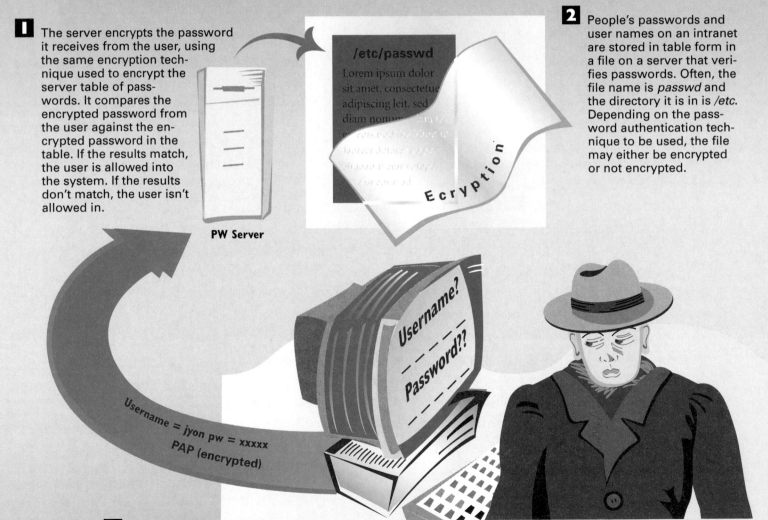

1 The server encrypts the password it receives from the user, using the same encryption technique used to encrypt the server table of passwords. It compares the encrypted password from the user against the encrypted password in the table. If the results match, the user is allowed into the system. If the results don't match, the user isn't allowed in.

PW Server

/etc/passwd

Lorem ipsum dolor sit amet, consectetue adipiscing leit, sed diam nonum...

Ecryption

2 People's passwords and user names on an intranet are stored in table form in a file on a server that verifies passwords. Often, the file name is *passwd* and the directory it is in is */etc*. Depending on the password authentication technique to be used, the file may either be encrypted or not encrypted.

Username = jyon pw = xxxxx
PAP (encrypted)

Username?
Password??

3 One method of authenticating a user is through the Password Authentication Protocol (PAP). PAP doesn't mandate encryption, but the table of passwords on the server is usually encrypted. When someone wants to log into the network or a password-protected network resource, they are asked for a user name and password. The user name and password are then sent to the server.

Challenge Handshake Authentication Protocol

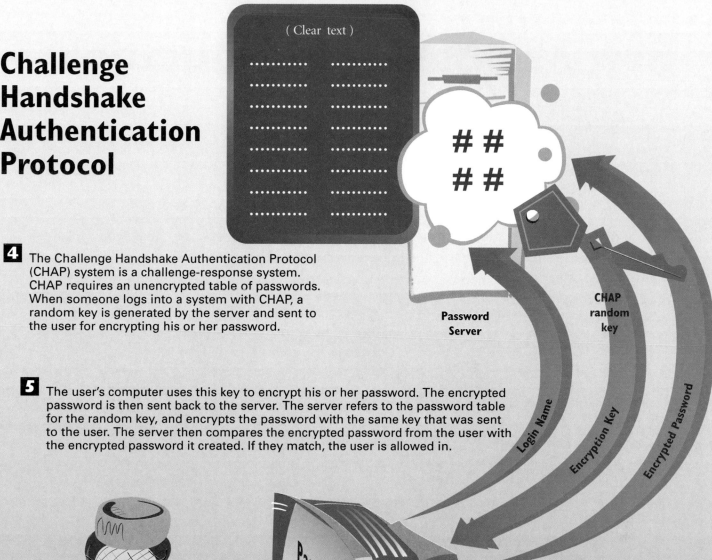

Password Table

(Clear text)

# # # #

4 The Challenge Handshake Authentication Protocol (CHAP) system is a challenge-response system. CHAP requires an unencrypted table of passwords. When someone logs into a system with CHAP, a random key is generated by the server and sent to the user for encrypting his or her password.

Password Server

CHAP random key

5 The user's computer uses this key to encrypt his or her password. The encrypted password is then sent back to the server. The server refers to the password table for the random key, and encrypts the password with the same key that was sent to the user. The server then compares the encrypted password from the user with the encrypted password it created. If they match, the user is allowed in.

Login Name

Encryption Key

Encrypted Password

Password?

_ _ _ _

6 The key difference with CHAP is that *the server continues to challenge the user's computer throughout the session.* Additionally, different challenges are sent that must be encrypted and returned by the computer, without human intervention. This way CHAP limits your window of vulnerability. A session cannot be hijacked, since a hijacker would be dropped once his computer failed to respond correctly to the periodically occurring challenges.

7 No matter which kind of password system is used—and whether the password table is encrypted or not—it's important to protect the password table. The file must be protected against FTP access and there should be very restricted access to the file so that only the administrator or someone under the administrator's control can gain access to it.

How Additional Authentication Systems Work

Various methods and devices provide additional security barriers to prevent unauthorized access. Devices supplement the "something you know" of login names and passwords with the requirement that remote users also provide "something you have." Many intranets allow people from remote locations to dial in to the intranet and use its resources. In order to get onto the network, a user name and password are required. Authentication systems are built to make sure that people logging into an intranet really are who they claim to be. This is especially important for remote access since none of the physical security necessary to enter a company's headquarters is available to screen dial-in users.

A call-back system is one way to ensure that only people who are supposed to dial in are allowed in. In a call-back system, after a user logs in with a user name and password, the system hangs up and calls back to a predetermined phone number. That way, no one can pose as an employee since it will call only specific phone numbers. This works for telecommuters who consistently work from their home, but is not practical for a roving sales force who never know the numbers in advance.

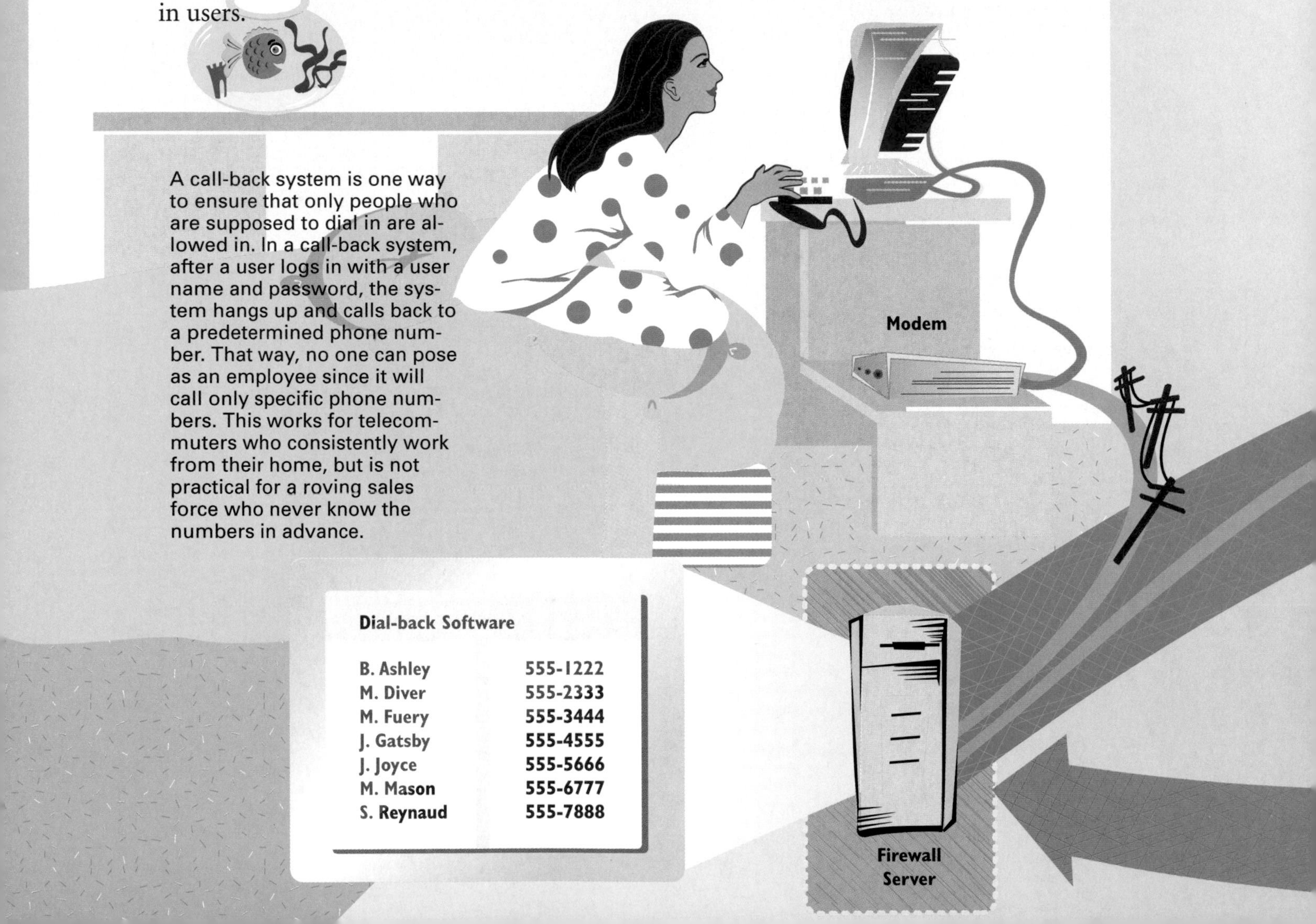

Modem

Dial-back Software

B. Ashley	555-1222
M. Diver	555-2333
M. Fuery	555-3444
J. Gatsby	555-4555
J. Joyce	555-5666
M. Mason	555-6777
S. Reynaud	555-7888

Firewall Server

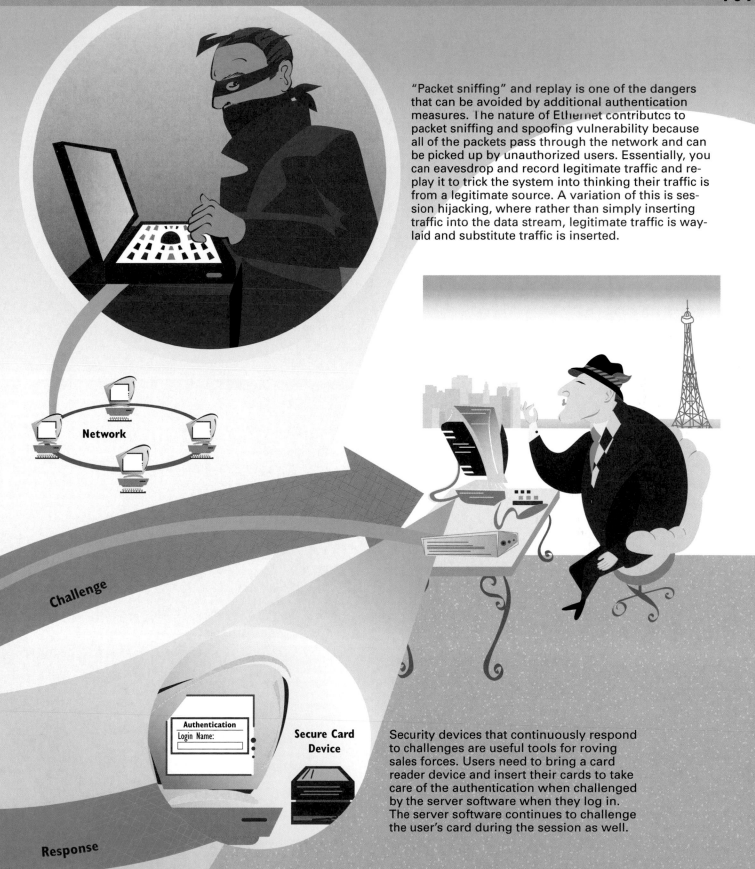

"Packet sniffing" and replay is one of the dangers that can be avoided by additional authentication measures. The nature of Ethernet contributes to packet sniffing and spoofing vulnerability because all of the packets pass through the network and can be picked up by unauthorized users. Essentially, you can eavesdrop and record legitimate traffic and replay it to trick the system into thinking their traffic is from a legitimate source. A variation of this is session hijacking, where rather than simply inserting traffic into the data stream, legitimate traffic is waylaid and substitute traffic is inserted.

Network

Challenge

Authentication
Login Name:

Secure Card
Device

Response

Security devices that continuously respond to challenges are useful tools for roving sales forces. Users need to bring a card reader device and insert their cards to take care of the authentication when challenged by the server software when they log in. The server software continues to challenge the user's card during the session as well.

CHAPTER

19

Virus Protection and Hostile Applets

THE most publicized dangers to an intranet are computer viruses. While the danger is not as extreme as portrayed in the press, nonetheless, the danger is real. Viruses are malicious programs that can cause many different kinds of damage, such as deleting data files, erasing programs, or destroying everything on a hard disk. Not every virus causes damage; some simply flash annoying messages on your screen. Still, any virus attack must be taken very seriously. There's no way of knowing when one has been created out of malicious intent or whether the perpetrator thought it was merely a harmless prank. In most cases, a virus causes real damage.

Viruses pose particular dangers to an intranet. On an intranet all computers are connected to one another, and that means that viruses can quickly spread from one networked computer to another. For example, let's say someone on an intranet gets a virus from a program they've gotten from the Internet via an FTP transfer. That virus will infect that person's computer. Before it does damage, however, and before the person knows an infection has occurred, the file might be shared with someone else by sending it via intranet e-mail. That person in turn might send it to yet someone else, who in turn shares it with another person. In a very short time, hundreds or thousands of computers can be infected. A virus can spread very much like an epidemic spreads.

An even greater danger to an intranet is a virus that infects a network server. The consequences of this can be disastrous. The virus could destroy the server software or its data. This could bring the entire intranet to its knees if the server is one that is vital to the functioning of the intranet. It is even more dangerous if the virus gets loose on a server that hosts corporate databases. The virus could conceivably destroy the entire database.

Other threats to intranets are special viruses called *worms*. Worms are viruses that have been designed to attack not just individual computers, but an entire network — an intranet, for example. Below, you'll find out more information about worms.

The term virus refers to many different kinds of programs. They usually attack four parts of a computer: its executable program files, its file-directory system that tracks the location of all of a computer's files (and without which, a computer won't work), its boot and system areas that are needed in order to start your computer, and its data files. Viruses usually are found in executable files, such as programs. For many years, it had been thought that viruses could not infect data files. Recently, new "macro" viruses have been written that hide inside a data file. The data file itself is not the culprit, but when something triggers the macro (which is, essentially, a little program file), the virus is let loose to do its damage.

Even more ominous for intranets, viruses can also hide themselves inside Java applets or be Java applets—applications written in a programming language that is expected to be used to build the next generation of interactive Internet and intranet applications. When a Java applet runs on your computer, an executable program is downloaded from an Internet or intranet server to your computer. When that program is on your computer, it runs and your Web browser shows the results of its running—for example, you'll see a news ticker flashing across your screen.

The developers of languages such as Java have done much work to try and make sure that viruses can't infect programs written in the languages. In Java, for example, when the applet downloads to your computer, before it is executed it is put into protected memory so that if it has a virus, it can't infect any part of your computer. Java applets also cannot read from or write to local drives. Some Java developers will tell you that because of security measures like that, there's no way that a virus from a Java applet could infect your computer.

However, other people maintain that there are many security holes in Java through which a variety of viruses can slip through. These people claim that some of these holes will do things such as lock up a keyboard and a mouse, or do more dangerous things, such as allowing a cracker to use Java as a way to circumvent firewall security and slip a virus into an intranet undetected. These kinds of Java applets are often called *hostile applets*. In fact, some of these hostile applets have been publicly posted on the Internet, with warnings about them, as a way to alert people that Java has dangerous holes in it.

As these hostile applets are made public, those who create the Java language—and other similar Internet programming languages—attempt to plug the holes. That's what happened when a team of computer scientists at Princeton University discovered a serious security flaw that could allow crackers to use Java to attack intranets. Pictured later in this chapter is an illustration of how such an attack could be made. The security flaw has since been patched, but people using older versions of Netscape are vulnerable to it.

Java, as yet, is not a great threat to intranets. It is still not in sufficiently widespread use, and there have yet to be documented attacks spread through using it. Of more immediate concern are several kinds of viruses. *Trojan horses* are programs that disguise themselves as normal, helpful programs, but do damage to your computer, its data, or your hard disk. For example, someone may download a file that claims to be a financial calculator. When the program was run, it would do calculations. But in the background, it would be doing damage to your computer. The theoretical Java security flaw that the Princeton researchers uncovered was a kind of Trojan horse.

Other viruses are called *worms*. These viruses are relatively rare, but they are of great concern to those on an intranet. That's because they have been specifically designed to infect networks. They travel between networked computers, replicating themselves along the way. They can attack the networked computers or the network itself. They can also chew up an enormous amount of network resources as they replicate and run. That's what the most infamous worm of all did. It was an Internet worm released on November 2, 1988. It copied itself onto many Internet host computers, and eventually brought huge sections of the Internet to a halt.

The most common viruses hide themselves inside other programs. Many of them can hide in any kind of program. You get this kind of virus by running a program that has the virus inside it. When the program is run, the virus is let loose, and it travels throughout your computer, infecting other program files. Depending on the kind of virus it is, it can attack certain sections of your computer, such as the boot sector, which could damage all your programs and data. Or it could attack other sections of your hard disk. If you don't check regularly for viruses, you may only find out about the infection after it's too late and the damage has been done.

Antiviral software has long been used on individual computers. A *scanner* checks to see if your computer has any files that have been infected, while an *eradication program* will wipe the virus from your hard disk. Since viruses pose such a danger to intranets, it is also best to protect against viruses by putting a virus scanner on a server inside a firewall, where that scanner can check every file coming into the intranet for known viruses. This does not eliminate the need for client software to cover such cases as a virus that may travel in a diskette from an external source.

Such a scanner typically doesn't check every single packet coming in, since many types of packets won't be able to have viruses in them. Instead, the scanner checks only those packets sent with certain Internet protocols, such as for e-mail, FTP, and the Web, that may indicate that a binary file is being transferred into the intranet. It looks at only those files, using packet filtering technology similar to that used by filtering routers. It then scans those files for viruses, letting in those files that are virus-free, and stopping any infected files from entering the intranet.

How Intranet Virus Scanning Software Works

Viruses are a major security risk for intranets. They can damage data, occupy and consume resources, and disrupt operations. Program files were the major source of trouble in the past, but new "macro" viruses can hide in data files and launch, for example, when a macro in a word processing program is run. Server-based and client-based virus-scanning software both have roles that help protect the intranet.

1 A virus hides inside a legitimate program. Until you run the infected program, the virus remains dormant. When you run the infected program, the virus springs into action. Sometimes, the first thing it will do is infect other programs on your hard disk by copying itself into them.

2 Some viruses place messages called *v-markers* or *virus markers* inside programs that they infect, and they help manage the viruses' activities. Each virus has a specific virus marker associated with it. If a virus encounters one of these markers in another program, it knows that the program is already infected, and so doesn't replicate itself there. When a virus cannot find any more unmarked files on a computer, that can signal to the virus that there are no more files to be infected. At this point, the virus may begin to damage the computer and its data. Viruses can corrupt program or data files so that they work oddly, not at all, or cause damage when they run. They can destroy all the files on your computer, change the system files that your computer needs when it is turned on, and cause other types of damage.

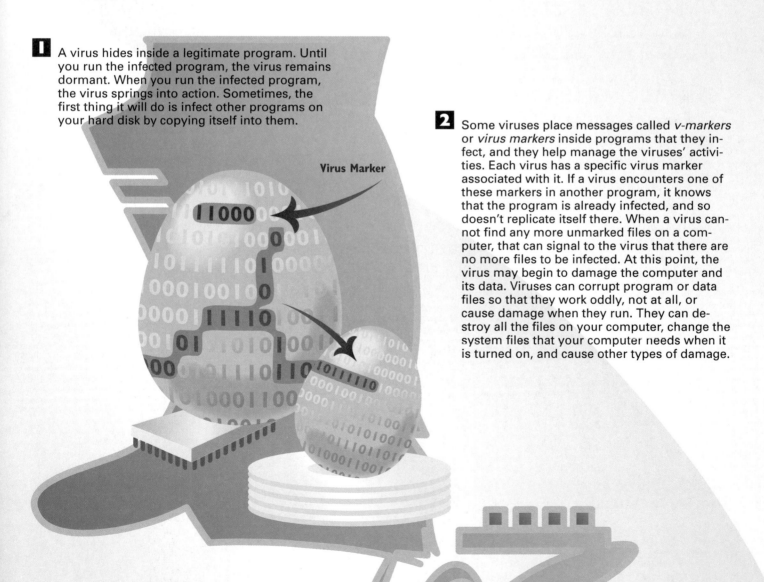

Virus Marker

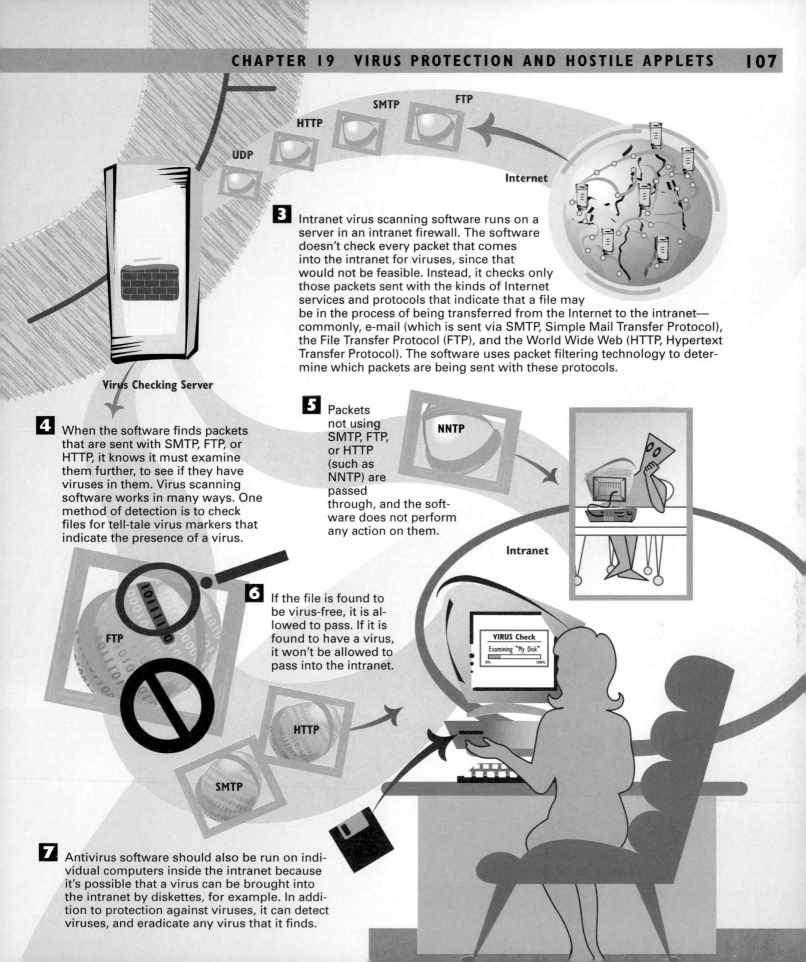

Internet

Virus Checking Server

3 Intranet virus scanning software runs on a server in an intranet firewall. The software doesn't check every packet that comes into the intranet for viruses, since that would not be feasible. Instead, it checks only those packets sent with the kinds of Internet services and protocols that indicate that a file may be in the process of being transferred from the Internet to the intranet—commonly, e-mail (which is sent via SMTP, Simple Mail Transfer Protocol), the File Transfer Protocol (FTP), and the World Wide Web (HTTP, Hypertext Transfer Protocol). The software uses packet filtering technology to determine which packets are being sent with these protocols.

4 When the software finds packets that are sent with SMTP, FTP, or HTTP, it knows it must examine them further, to see if they have viruses in them. Virus scanning software works in many ways. One method of detection is to check files for tell-tale virus markers that indicate the presence of a virus.

5 Packets not using SMTP, FTP, or HTTP (such as NNTP) are passed through, and the software does not perform any action on them.

Intranet

6 If the file is found to be virus-free, it is allowed to pass. If it is found to have a virus, it won't be allowed to pass into the intranet.

VIRUS Check
Examining "My Disk"
0%   100%

7 Antivirus software should also be run on individual computers inside the intranet because it's possible that a virus can be brought into the intranet by diskettes, for example. In addition to protection against viruses, it can detect viruses, and eradicate any virus that it finds.

How a "Hostile" Java Applet Can Attack an Intranet

The Java programming language can create interactive, multimedia applications (called applets) that can greatly extend the power of the World Wide Web on intranets and the Internet. However, some people believe that it can theoretically be used to attack an intranet. Here is an example of such an attack, which computer scientists at Princeton University discovered was possible due to holes in the Java protection scheme. Since then, this particular hole was covered up, but only if people use specific versions of Netscape which contain the fix. Many computer scientists say that other security holes still exist in Java.

1 The cracker begins by targeting a specific pair of computers on an intranet, stooge.victim.com, and target.victim.com. One of the computers will be used by the cracker as a jumping off point to attack the other. The cracker knows their IP addresses, 123.123.122.1 for stooge.victim.com, and 123.123.122.2 for target.victim.com.

7 The Java applet is now connected to the target computer, target.victim.com (123.123.122.2), and can make full use of the intranet's resources, as if it were a trusted computer inside the intranet. That's because the connection was made from inside the intranet, directly from another intranet computer—the attack was made from within the firewall. Using the applet, the cracker can now make a direct connection to 123.123.122.2, as if inside the intranet. A cracker can then probe the intranet's security weaknesses by using a security-probing program like the particularly powerful one called SATAN, and then attack not just the target computer, but the entire intranet.

Firewall

2 The cracker's computer's name is www.hackit.com, and its IP address is 114.12.12.12. There is also a "bogus" machine name—a computer that does not exist, but looks to the rest of the Internet as if it does. The bogus machine is called bogus.hackit.com. The cracker creates a DNS mapping from this bogus machine to a pair of IP addresses: the cracker's, 114.12.12.12; and the machine targeted for attack, 123.123.122.2. When a DNS server looks up the bogus machine name to see its IP address, it will see these two IP addresses. Note that the cracker hasn't yet used Java; what has been done so far has commonly been done by crackers on the Internet since well before Java was released.

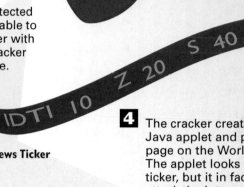

www.hackit.com

3 The intranet that the cracker has targeted is protected by a firewall. Normally, he or she would not be able to break through the firewall to attack the computer with the IP address 123.122.122.2. With a hole the cracker discovered in Java, however, now it can be done.

News Ticker

www.bogus.hackit.com

Downloads

4 The cracker creates a "hostile" Java applet and posts it on a page on the World Wide Web. The applet looks as if it's a news ticker, but it in fact is designed to attack the intranet. The cracker sends out an e-mail note to the target intranet, disguised as a press release, inviting people to visit a free news site on the Internet. Stooge.victim.com browses the Internet to the site and comes across the Java applet on www.hackit.com. The applet will download.

5 The applet appears to be a news ticker, so stooge.victim.com reads the news ticker. In fact, the applet has begun to attack the computer and the intranet.

DNS Server

www.bogus.hackit.com DNS mapping 123.123.122.2 114.12.12.12

6 The applet tries to make a connection to the "bogus" computer created by the cracker, bogus.hackit.com. In order to make the connection, Java uses the DNS mapping created by the cracker. It finds the mapping of 123.123.122.2 and 114.12.12.12 for the name bogus.hackit.com. As a security measure, Java only lets applets contact the server on which they were launched, and no other server. In this case, that server is 114.12.12.12, so Java allows the connection since it sees it in the entry. However, since the first number in the entry is 123.123.122.2, it actually makes the connection to that computer, not to 114.12.12.12.

CHAPTER

20

How Site Blocking Works

INSIDE

INSIDE an intranet, it's easy to control the kinds of pages, information, pictures, and other data that people are accessing. The corporation controls what gets posted and what doesn't, and so nothing can get posted that the company believes would be objectionable. That's far from true out on the Internet, however. Objectionable content makes up a very small part of what's available on the Internet, and to find the objectionable content you have to do a bit of digging. Still, anyone who wants to find it can certainly get access to it.

Congress, among others, has tried to ban certain kinds of content—such as pornography—from being available on the Internet. The real answer to the problem, though, doesn't lie in legislation, because even if such laws are held constitutional, anyone who truly understands the Internet and its technology also recognizes that the laws are unenforceable. The real answer lies with technology itself: software that will allow people such as parents and intranet administrators to block access to those sites. A number of companies make and sell software that allows site blocking.

Many problems can occur if people from inside an intranet are visiting pornographic or objectionable sites on the intranet. And in any event, companies would not want employees viewing those kinds of sites on company time, using company hardware, software, and network resources.

To block objectionable sites on an intranet, the answer is not to put site-blocking software on each individual computer on the network. It would be too unwieldy and expensive to do that. Instead, server-based site-blocking software is used. Site-blocking software on a proxy server examines the URLs sent to it and decides whether or not to retrieve the requested page by reviewing databases that list objectionable sites and words.

One group working on the issue is PICS (Platform for Internet Content Selection). They are trying to develop industry standards for technology that would allow the content of all sites and documents on the Internet to be rated according to its sexual and violent content. They would also create standards that would allow software to be developed that would be able to block sites based on those ratings.

Not all intranets need site-blocking software. However, intranet administrators may want to know what kind of sites people on the intranet are visiting. They can use server-based software that can keep logs of what kinds of sites people are visiting on the Internet. This will help not only to decide whether site-blocking software is needed, but also to know when more server resources are needed for the intranet.

Blocking Objectionable Sites from an Intranet

Since intranets allow access to the Internet, intranet users can visit objectionable sites on the Internet—sites with sexual, violent, or other kinds of distasteful content. This illustration shows how server-based blocking software might work, based on the SurfWatch product that can be used to block sites on individual computers.

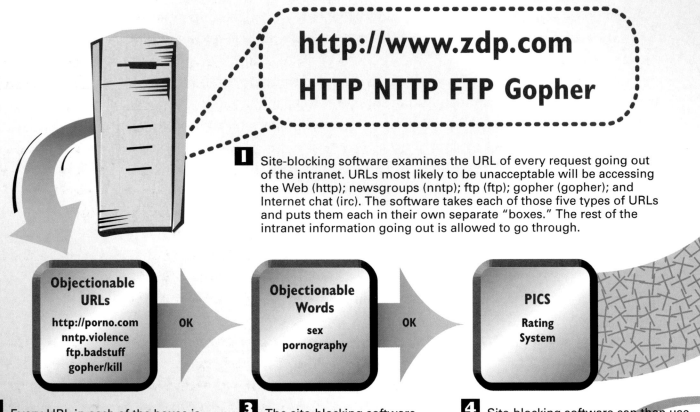

http://www.zdp.com

HTTP NTTP FTP Gopher

1 Site-blocking software examines the URL of every request going out of the intranet. URLs most likely to be unacceptable will be accessing the Web (http); newsgroups (nntp); ftp (ftp); gopher (gopher); and Internet chat (irc). The software takes each of those five types of URLs and puts them each in their own separate "boxes." The rest of the intranet information going out is allowed to go through.

Objectionable URLs

http://porno.com
nntp.violence
ftp.badstuff
gopher/kill

OK

Objectionable Words

sex
pornography

OK

PICS

Rating System

2 Every URL in each of the boxes is checked against a database of the URLs of objectionable sites. If the blocking software finds that any of the URLs are from objectionable sites, it won't allow that information to be passed on to the intranet. Products like SurfWatch check thousands of sites, and list several thousand in their database that have been found to be objectionable.

3 The site-blocking software next checks the URL against a database of words (such as "sex") that may indicate that the material being requested may be objectionable. If the blocking software finds a matching pattern, it won't allow that information to be passed on to the intranet.

4 Site-blocking software can then use a third method of checking for objectionable sites, a rating system called PICS (Platform for Internet Content Selection). If site-blocking software finds, based on the rating system, that the URL is for a site that may contain objectionable material, it won't allow access to that site. Rules about passing or dropping can be configured to control access to unrated sites.

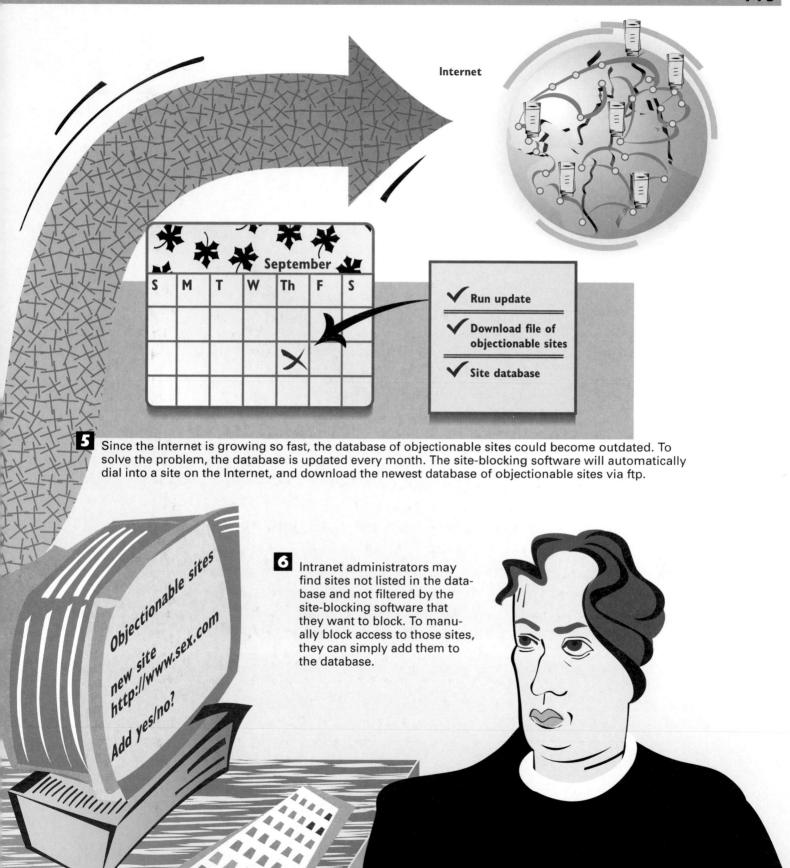

Internet

September

S	M	T	W	Th	F	S
				✗		

✓ **Run update**

✓ **Download file of objectionable sites**

✓ **Site database**

5 Since the Internet is growing so fast, the database of objectionable sites could become outdated. To solve the problem, the database is updated every month. The site-blocking software will automatically dial into a site on the Internet, and download the newest database of objectionable sites via ftp.

Objectionable sites

new site
http://www.sex.com

Add yes/no?

6 Intranet administrators may find sites not listed in the database and not filtered by the site-blocking software that they want to block. To manually block access to those sites, they can simply add them to the database.

21

How Intranet Monitoring Software Works

IN the last chapter, we saw how network administrators can block intranet users from visiting objectionable sites on the intranet using server software. But in many cases, intranet administrators want to do much more than simply block users from visiting objectionable sites. They may also want to track the overall usage of the Internet from inside the intranet, and be able to see in exquisite detail exactly how the Internet is being used—for example, to see the times of the greatest access, or which departments and subnets make the greatest use of the Internet. And they may want to track not only how people on the intranet are accessing the Internet, they may also want to see how they are using the intranet itself.

All that can be done—and a lot more—using intranet monitoring software. This is software that sits on a server, and monitors all traffic between the Internet and the intranet. It can also monitor all traffic on the intranet itself.

The software works by examining every IP packet coming into and going out of the intranet. It looks into both the IP header and at the data itself. The intranet administrator decides what kind of traffic to track. For example, access to intranet and Internet Web servers; FTP (File Transfer Protocol) usage; access to newsgroups; use of e-mail; and Telnet could all be tracked using this software. The monitoring software can then log all that traffic in extraordinary detail. It can track the destination address as well as the originating address; the amount of data transferred; the time of day; and many other pieces of data. All that data is automatically put into a database that intranet administrators can use to create reports of just about any type.

This information can help intranet administrators in many ways. It can help them know when new bandwidth needs to be ordered or new servers need to be installed. And it can also tell them if inappropriate sites are often visited.

Some monitoring software goes beyond merely tracking usage, and allows administrators to set access rules for the entire corporation or for individual departments. For example, it will allow network administrators to lock out certain sites from the entire corporation, such as those that have pornographic material on them. And it can let them decide on a department-by-department basis what kind of Internet access should be allowed.

While this type of software is certainly helpful to intranet administrators, some intranet users may be leery of it. They may think that it has a "Big Brother" feel to it, that intranet administrators are violating their privacy, or watching in detail how they use their computers. While that is a possibility, when used correctly the software can help to make sure that the network is functioning at top efficiency, and not to snoop into other people's lives.

How Intranet Monitoring Software Works

Server software is available to allow for extensive monitoring of how intranet users access the Internet. Administrators may find it useful to know, in general, what kinds of sites are being visited, and may even want to track what sites individual users are visiting. It is possible to do much more detailed analysis as well, including how much individual users access the Internet, what hours are most heavily trafficked, and much more. The software can also customize how people are allowed to access the Internet and/or the intranet. All outgoing and incoming traffic must pass through the monitoring machine.

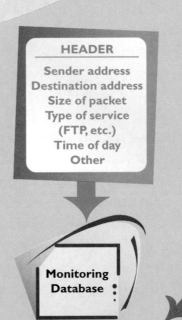

CHECK
Telnet
NNTP
HTTP
FTP
SMTP

PASS
UDP with Streaming Audio

Monitoring Machine

Serial Connection

Firewall

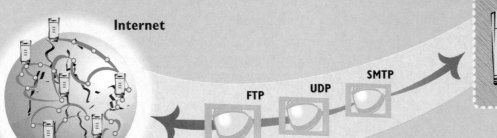

Internet

FTP   UDP   SMTP

1 The software uses packet filtering, much like filtering routers (see Chapter 13). Both look at the data in the header of every IP packet coming in and going out of the intranet, and every packet traveling across the intranet. However, they differ significantly in that filtering routers make decisions about passing or dropping packets. Monitoring software simply lets the packets pass through, and tracks information about packets. Data such as the sender and destination address; size of the packet; type of Internet service involved (such as the Web or FTP) and time of day is captured to a database.

HEADER
Sender address
Destination address
Size of packet
Type of service
(FTP, etc.)
Time of day
Other

Monitoring Database

2 While all packets must pass through the server, the software does not necessarily put information about every packet into the database. For example, information about HTTP packets (World Wide Web), file transfer protocol packets (FTP), e-mail packets (SMTP), newsgroup packets (NNTP), and Telnet packets might be tracked, while streaming audio packets might be ignored.

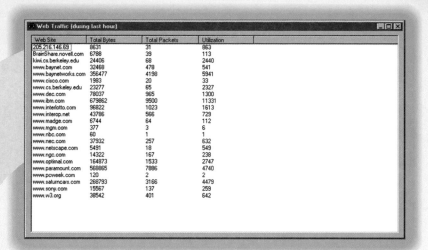

User Traffic

3 Software included with the server program allows network administrators to view and analyze intranet and Internet traffic to a remarkable degree. It can show the total amount of network traffic by the day and the hour, for example, and show in any hour which Internet sites were being accessed and how much data was being transferred. It can even show what sites individual users on the intranet were visiting, and the most popular sites visited in graph form.

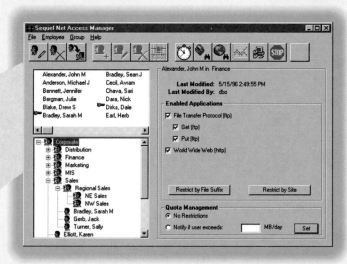

Access Manager

4 Some software goes beyond analysis, and allows intranet administrators to change the kind of Internet access allowed to intranet users, based on traffic, usage, and other factors. For example, an intranet administrator could allow only certain departments access to some Internet resources.

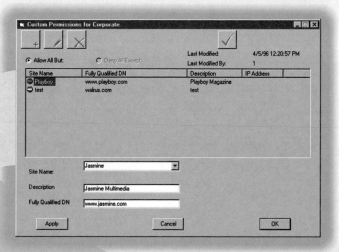

Custom Permissions

5 The software could also allow intranet administrators to ban certain sites from being visited by the entire intranet. For example, if there are pornographic sites that analysis has shown intranet users are visiting, the administrator could set rules that would ban anyone from visiting those sites. The packet filtering software would then not allow in any packets from those sites.

CHAPTER

22

How Virtual Secure Private Networks Work

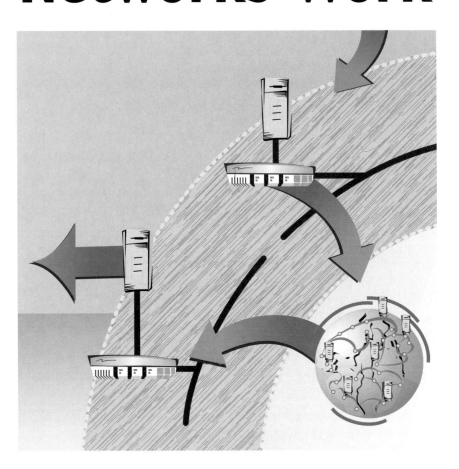

AN intranet by itself may help a company make better use of its computing resources, allow for better intra-company communications, and allow for the company to present a better face to the world. But for many corporations, that isn't enough. Many companies also need to do business directly with other business partners, such as subcontractors, or companies from whom they're buying goods and services.

Intranets can help there as well. They can allow companies to do business directly with each other over the Internet — and to do so securely. The technology that allows this to be done is called Virtual Secure Private Networks (VSPNs) or Virtual Private Networks (VPNs). In essence, the technology allows two companies with intranets to create a "virtual" link between them across the Internet that is as secure as if they were connected via a private connection. VSPN technology can also be used to create a "virtual" intranet for a company that can link branch offices together over the Internet, while at the same time ensuring that the data that passes between them can't be seen by anyone except people in the "virtual" intranet.

These VSPNs can save corporations a substantial amount of money, both for communicating with business partners and for hooking together branch offices. Today, businesses commonly spend significant amounts of money every month leasing private lines that no one else can use. The data sent along these private lines cannot be seen by anyone else; they are used by the company only. Because of that, they are secure from prying eyes. If, however, there were a way to link company's intranets over the Internet, there would be no need to pay for leased lines—all the traffic could be handled over the Internet. In addition to saving money on lines, the creation of secure links from intranet to intranet would also allow companies to communicate more effectively electronically, leading to more efficiency and even more in savings.

VSPNs use a combination of routing technology, encryption technology, and a technique called tunneling. When someone from one intranet wants to send information to another intranet via a VSPN, VSPN server software recognizes that the destination is a VSPN, and so knows to handle the data differently than if it is being sent to an unsecured site on the Internet. Using powerful encryption technology, the software encrypts the IP packets so that no one will be able to read it. It then places those IP packets inside an IP "envelope" or "wrapper." That envelope is essentially a normal IP packet, so it gets delivered as does any other data, via routers. No one can read what is inside the wrapper, though, because it has been encrypted. When packets are sent this way over the Internet, it is called tunneling.

On the receiving intranet, the VSPN software throws away the wrapper, and then decrypts the data inside of it. The data is then delivered over the intranet via intranet routers.

How Virtual Secure Private Networks Work

1 When someone on an intranet wants to send private data to another company via a VSPN, they don't do anything different than when they send public data—they merely send the data as they would to any location on the Internet. As with any data sent through an intranet, it is broken up into TCP/IP packets.

2 All packets sent out from the intranet go through a special VSPN server. The server examines each IP packet to see whether the packet is bound for another VSPN intranet, or instead to the Internet. It determines whether it's bound for another VSPN by examining the IP addresses in the packet headers. It checks the destination address against a database of VSPN addresses. If the packet doesn't match a VSPN address in the database, it means that the packet is bound for the general Internet, not a VSPN, and so the VSPN software takes no further action. The packet is sent to its destination as a normal packet, via routers.

Decrypter

7 The packet is sent to an intranet router, which delivers it to its final destination. It can be used as any normal TCP/IP packet.

To Final Destination

6 The packet is delivered to the destination VSPN, where the VSPN server examines the packet. It checks the IP address of the sender. If the address is not in the database of other VSPN intranets, it simply sends the packet along to an intranet router to deliver it. If the address is in the database, it strips off the IP wrapper, and decrypts the original TCP/IP packet. The packet is now in its original form.

A Virtual Secure Private Network (VSPN) or Virtual Private Network (VPN) allows business partners, each of whom has an intranet, to send secure communications to each other over the Internet, and know that no one else will be able to read the data. In essence, it creates a private, secure channel between intranets, even though the data sent between them travels over the public Internet. This means that companies will not have to lease expensive lines between them to send data over a secure link. The technology can also be used to allow a company to link branch offices with each other, without having to lease expensive lines, and know that the data can only be read by people on the VSPN.

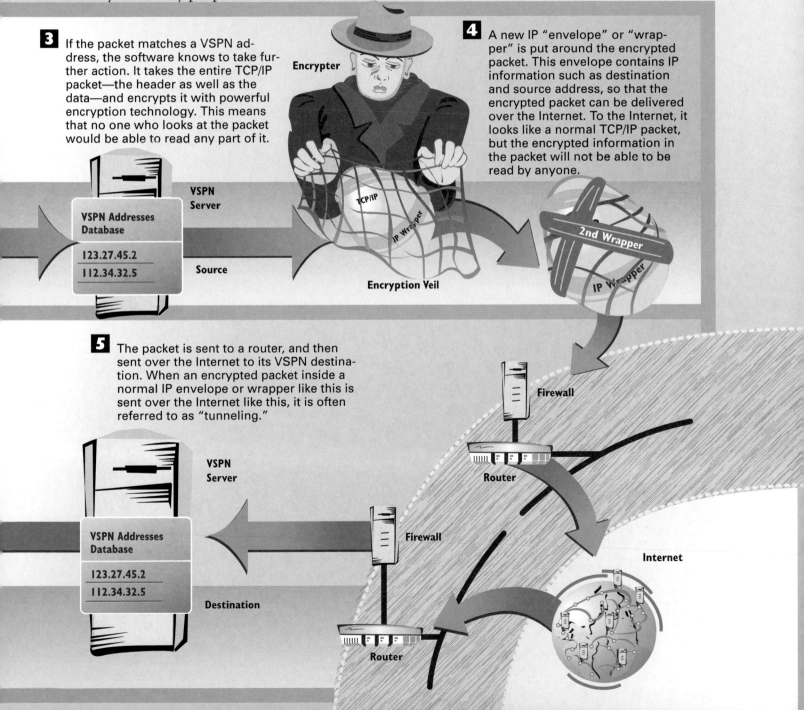

3 If the packet matches a VSPN address, the software knows to take further action. It takes the entire TCP/IP packet—the header as well as the data—and encrypts it with powerful encryption technology. This means that no one who looks at the packet would be able to read any part of it.

4 A new IP "envelope" or "wrapper" is put around the encrypted packet. This envelope contains IP information such as destination and source address, so that the encrypted packet can be delivered over the Internet. To the Internet, it looks like a normal TCP/IP packet, but the encrypted information in the packet will not be able to be read by anyone.

Encrypter

VSPN Server

VSPN Addresses Database

123.27.45.2

112.34.32.5

Source

TCP/IP

IP Wrapper

Encryption Veil

2nd Wrapper

IP Wrapper

5 The packet is sent to a router, and then sent over the Internet to its VSPN destination. When an encrypted packet inside a normal IP envelope or wrapper like this is sent over the Internet like this, it is often referred to as "tunneling."

VSPN Server

VSPN Addresses Database

123.27.45.2

112.34.32.5

Destination

Firewall

Router

Firewall

Internet

Router

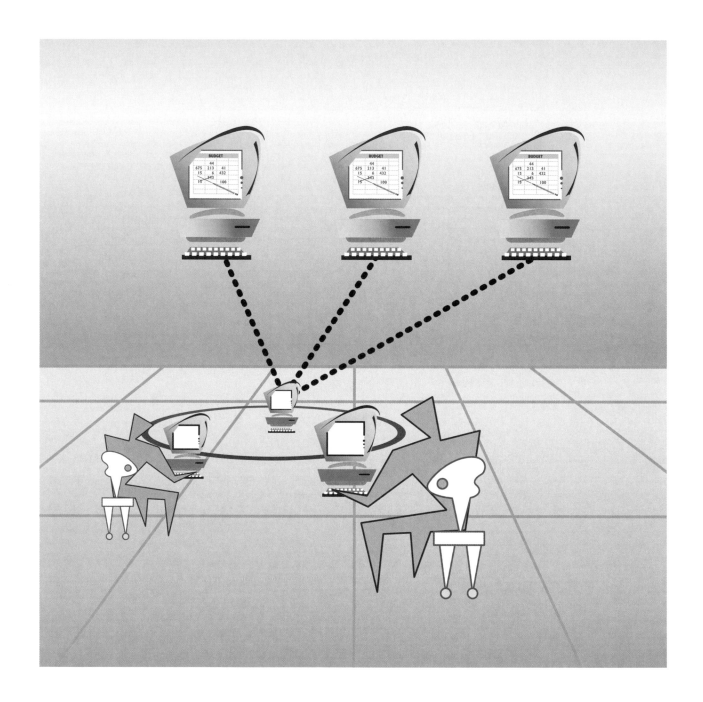

P A R T

3

INTRANETS AND GROUPWARE

MANY people believe that only with groupware will the full potential of any intranet be realized. Groupware is a somewhat broad and even vague term that covers many different kinds of intranet software that range from video-conferencing to whiteboard applications, discussion software, document management software, work flow software, and many others. The point of groupware is simple, though: to enable people to work more closely together. It lets people work together on documents; allows them to create common databases that anyone can tap into and use; permits free-wheeling brainstorming sessions; and allows people to see each other in meetings that are held across the country or across the world. Especially in corporations where people do any travel, or work at odd or off-hours, it can help create a sense of community that other-wise would be impossible. In essence, groupware can create a virtual community of people working closely together, whether they are physically located near one another or not.

Most intranet workgroup software builds on the simplest component: a Web browser, generally either Netscape Navigator or Microsoft Internet Explorer. Both Microsoft and Netscape have added intranet features directly into their browsers, such as the ability to see what is on other people's computer screens across an intranet, the ability to participate in "virtual meetings" via an intranet, and the ability to participate in in-tranet-wide discussions and to send and receive electronic mail.

More sophisticated groupware products often require special servers and server soft-ware. As with most everything else on intranets, groupware is generally based on a client/server model. Servers run special software that enables groupware applications; users on the intranet run client software—generally an off-the-shelf Web browser—to use the groupware applications.

In Chapter 23 we'll take the broadest possible look at how groupware works and is applied on intranets. We'll see how all the parts of groupware on an intranet fit together to make it possible for people to collaborate more easily. We'll examine how discussion software, videoconferencing, whiteboard applications, and document management soft-ware fit together. It's the best chapter to get the bird's-eye view of how intranet workgroup software flows together.

In Chapter 24 we'll take a detailed look at one of the simplest, yet most powerful pieces of workgroup software. Discussion software has its roots in the very earliest days of the Internet, in the newsgroup discussions that have long been the core of the Internet. Before the World Wide Web, multimedia, Java and similar technologies, there were news-groups, which for many people were the primary reason for using the Internet. Intranet discussion software takes the basic idea of newsgroups and extends it further. Using dis-cussion software, people can exchange ideas, publicly brainstorm, post notices, or share their ideas in other ways. What makes these discussions especially powerful is that the newest generation of software allows them also to incorporate other intranet resources. For example, a discussion can include links to intranet Web locations so that from within a discussion anyone can immediately jump out to the Web. And with the use of programming tools, discussions can even include links to corporate databases. So, for example, a discussion about marketing plans could include links to Web locations that have marketing plans for the next two years, and also links to databases so that people could find out how much money is being spent on marketing projects.

Chapter 25 covers how videoconferencing systems work. Videoconferencing can prove to be an enormous time and money saver for corporations. With it, people can hold face-to-face meetings without ever leaving their offices. Anyone who grew up with TV shows like the *Jetsons* will recognize in videoconferencing the realization of the long-held dream of video telephone. On an intranet, however, phone technology is not used at all. Instead, videoconferencing is accomplished using computers only, in concert with video cameras and audio hardware and software. The technology uses data compression, intranet servers, TCP/IP, and related data packet transport. There are many videoconferencing systems available. We'll look at one of the original ones, called CU-See-Me.

In Chapter 26, we'll take a look at whiteboard technology. A *whiteboard* is software that allows people to see what is on each other's computer screens while they are attached to an intranet, to mark up each other's work, and to talk to each other while they do so. This would enable, for example, several people from across the country to work together on a corporate budget, marking up areas of concern so that others could see them. In whiteboard applications, people can see several other peoples' screens simultaneously. In the future, even more powerful whiteboard technology will allow people not just to mark up each others' computer screens, but also to work simultaneously on the data, even if they don't have the application that created it on their own hard disk. As with videoconferencing, there are many different whiteboard technologies available. We'll look at the one that works in concert with CU-See-Me.

Finally, in Chapter 27 we'll examine intranet group document management systems. These are systems that let groups work cooperatively on the same or related documents. Document management systems allow people to "check out" documents from a library, so that no one else can work on the document while it's in their hands. Only when they check it back in can someone else work on it. The software also creates an audit trail, so that anyone can see who has worked on the document and what they've done to it. Related software, called work flow software, manages how documents move from person to person. For example, this software could help when a corporation creates a company newsletter, making sure that only people with the proper rights can work on it, and ensuring that the newsletter is signed off at the highest levels before it is released to the public.

CHAPTER

23

A Global View of Groupware

INTRANET

hardware and underlying communications protocols by themselves are of no great use to anyone. The most powerful servers, fiber-optic cables, T-1 communication lines, ISDN modems, or streaming multimedia can't do anything by themselves. They're only important because they allow people to communicate, share information, and work better together.

While many intranet technologies allow people to work better together—including just about every intranet technology, including even the World Wide Web—the most important set of intranet software for allowing people to better communicate and cooperate is called workgroup software. Workgroup software lets people share files and information; work better together in teams; cooperate more easily on projects; and in general work together in ways never before possible.

You'll never find an exact definition of what workgroup software is. In general, it's something of a fuzzy term. It encompasses many different kinds of technologies, everything ranging from advanced videoconferencing to simple chat technology. To some people, Internet newsgroups are a form of groupware, while to other people, only more sophisticated technologies qualify under that definition.

However, in general, workgroup software is software that goes beyond simple messaging like newsgroups and allows people to work together as a group in more complicated ways. The key is that it allows people to go beyond simply communicating, and lets them work together on documents.

One thing to keep in mind about groupware is that groupware did not come into being with the intranet. There is nothing in the TCP/IP architecture underlying intranets that made groupware possible. In fact, groupware has been around for years. In corporations where there is a significant amount of sophisticated design, and a complicated manufacturing process—such as in companies that build airplanes, for example—workgroup software has long been used in concert with Computer Aided Design/Computer Aided Manufacturing (CAD/CAM) software. With groupware and CAD/CAM software, for example, different designers and engineers are able to work on different parts of an overall design at the same time—and they are able to see the results of other people's work, since what other people do will be reflected in what they see in their part of the design. CAD/CAM systems like this tended to be used not on personal computers, but instead on workstations.

The first major workgroup software for personal computers was Lotus Notes, which combines electronic mail, discussion software, workflow software and database technology. While Notes was designed for personal computers instead of workstations, it wasn't designed for intranets, and worked instead on Netware networks. However, in more recent times, intranet-based features have been added.

Intranet-based groupware does both what Notes and CAD/CAM can do, and more. While it's true that the TCP/IP protocols that underlay intranets by themselves didn't make groupware possible, it's also true that their widespread acceptance has helped spread the use of groupware. Once companies began to see how Internet technologies such as newsgroups allowed people to communicate better on the Internet, they began to look at their corporations and see how similar technologies could help companies work together as a whole.

One of the most basic pieces of workgroup software is messaging software—programs that allow people to publicly participate in group discussions. Group discussion software has its roots in newsgroups, and in discussion software that is found on online services such as CompuServe. One key to messaging software is that it be *threaded*. Threaded messaging means that people can read and respond to individual subject areas of a discussion. For example, in a message area devoted to corporate finances, there may be one thread concerning research-and-development finances, another concerning engineering finances, another about marketing finances, and so on. Good discussion software will allow people to easily follow each of those different threads.

Some messaging software goes beyond that, however. There's nothing about TCP/IP and intranet technology that in particular that enables people to use threaded messaging. However, what makes intranet messaging software especially useful is the way that it integrates with other Internet and intranet technologies. For example, some discussion software will allow the use of Hypertext Markup Language (HTML) embedded inside messages. This means that from within a discussion, someone could embed a link to a Web page or other intranet resource. When powerful programming tools like Java or ActiveX are added to this mix, even more interactive and multimedia possibilities are added, and the true power of mixing discussions with intranet technology can be seen.

An often overlooked workgroup technology is electronic mail. As with discussion software, it too can make use of other intranet technologies. Some intranet e-mail software can read HTML files, so links to Web pages and other intranet documents can be included in e-mail. And e-mail can be integrated with discussion software, so that in a discussion, people have the option of responding to notes either in public discussions or by private e-mail, depending on which link they click on.

Yet another means of communicating over intranets which has its roots in older Internet technology is desktop chat. On the Internet, this kind of chat is called Internet Relay Chat, or IRC. It allows someone from one computer to type messages on a keyboard, and have that message instantly appear on someone else's computer. Intranets can let people do the same thing. While this kind of communication isn't useful for complicated discussions, it can be very good for quick conversations.

A more sophisticated workgroup application is desktop videoconferencing. It requires that everyone involved have computer-linked video cameras (which have become quite inexpensive) and hardware and software that allows computers to send and receive voice and sound. While sitting at computers, people can see each other and speak to each other. Some videoconferencing software is server based, which means that it requires that people involved must log into a server in order to participate in a videoconference with others. Still other videoconferencing software lets people connect directly with other people on an intranet without having to go through a server — all they'll need to know is someone's IP address.

A related technology is called *whiteboard* software. Whiteboard software lets people see what is on someone else's computer on an intranet, while sitting at their own computer. Even more important than just letting people see what is on the computer is that whiteboard software allows people to use their mouse to highlight parts of the screen, write on the screen, and otherwise mark it up. That means that people on the same intranet—even if they're on opposite sides of the country from each other—can comment on each other's work easily.

Document management and workflow software is useful for intranets for companies that have complicated work procedures, or where many people must cooperatively put together a single document. In intranet document management software, a document can be "locked" so that only one person at a time can use it, and so people can't overwrite each others' work. It can also give different people different kinds of rights to a particular document, so that some people may only be able to read documents, while others are able to actually work on them, edit them, and otherwise change them. And the most powerful document management software allows many different people to work on different parts of the same document simultaneously.

Similar to document management is workflow management software. This kind of groupware manages not just individual documents, but the entire workflow of an organization. For example, intranet workflow management software would allow procedures for filing expense reports to be easily computerized, so that the report could be sent automatically up the chain of people who had to approve it and act on it without having to resort to paper or mail.

It's important to note that no one intranet is likely to have all these kinds of workgroup applications. And no single piece of software will allow for all these kinds of cooperative computing. Rather, most intranets will take a mix-and-match kind of approach. In fact, in some companies, different subnets or departments on an intranet may have different kinds of workgroup applications. The point is that intranet administrators can choose whichever workgroup application best suits the company.

A Global View of Groupware

One of the most important reasons that companies put in an intranet is to better enable people to work together. The most powerful kind of software to let people work together falls under the broad heading of *groupware*. Groupware lets people videoconference, share documents, participate in discussions and work together in other ways. Pictured here are some examples of how groupware works together in an intranet.

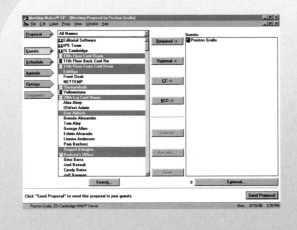

A popular workgroup use of intranets will be *whiteboard* applications. In a whiteboard application, two or more people can see what is on each others' computer screens across the intranet, and they can talk about what they see. Additionally, they can mark up what they see on each others screens.

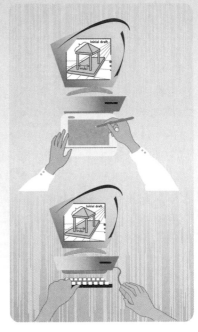

Discussion software allows people from within a corporation to exchange work and ideas. Included in the software are links to other intranet resources, so that from within a discussion, people can link out to a Web page on the Internet or intranet, or can even link into intranet databases. Additionally, software can replicate intranet discussions onto Internet news groups so that from one discussion area, people from an intranet can hold discussions with people from within their company or people out on the Internet.

With intranet groupware, videoconferencing can finally be a corporate reality. Desktop conferencing software allows two or more people to see each other and talk to each other on their computer screens, as long as they have cameras connected to their computers and sound-equipped computers. Since intranets can be built using very high-bandwidth connections, it's possible to have a videoconference across an intranet, while it can be much more difficult to do it across an Internet because of the lower bandwidth of the Internet.

Document and workflow management software allows intranet administrators to create systems that track and control access to documents through every aspect of their creation, for example, allowing only one person at a time to check a document out of a library. They can provide a "version history" of every document so that anyone can see who has worked on it, and what changes that person made. And they can give certain people the right to "lock" the document so that no further changes are allowed to be made.

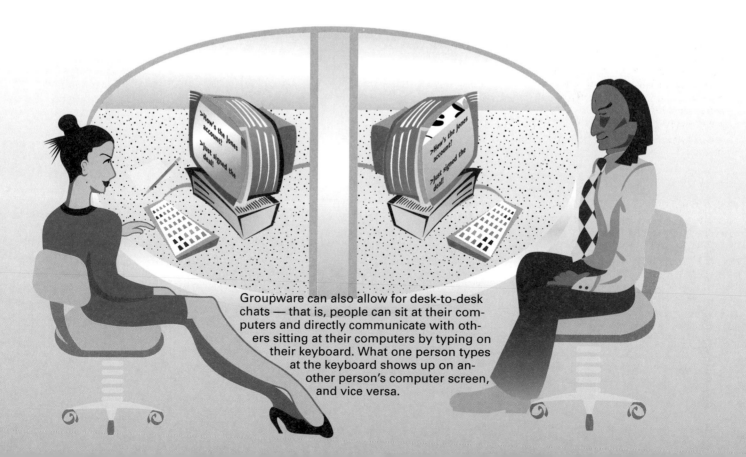

Groupware can also allow for desk-to-desk chats — that is, people can sit at their computers and directly communicate with others sitting at their computers by typing on their keyboard. What one person types at the keyboard shows up on another person's computer screen, and vice versa.

C H A P T E R

24

How Intranet Discussion Software Works

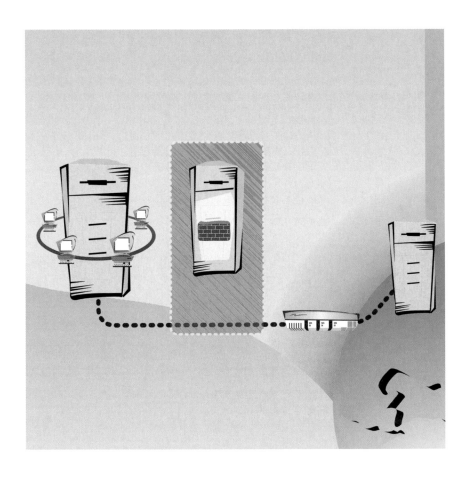

ONE of the greatest time savers on an intranet is discussion software—software that allows people to share their ideas in public and private discussions. These discussions are not held live. Instead, people come in, post or respond to messages, and then other people at another time do the same. The best of this discussion software does more than simply allow people to have discussions: It can also link those discussions to other intranet resources, such as Web pages or even databases.

Intranet discussion software has its roots in Internet newsgroups, which allows people from all over the globe to participate in public discussions. In fact, intranets may use newsgroup technology as the basis of their discussion software. Newsgroup discussions are server-based, and work on a client/server model. The discussions themselves are on the server, while client software is used to access the server to read the discussions and respond to them. Many kinds of clients are used to participate in discussions. Newsgroup servers all over the world replicate the discussions they each hold, so that people from anywhere on the globe can participate by logging into a local server.

Intranet discussion software works in similar ways. It also works on a client/server model. The discussions themselves are hosted on servers, and client software is needed to read and participate in those discussions. Unlike newsgroups, however, most intranet discussion software requires that special client software be used—you won't be able to use just any discussion client. Intranets will often standardize on certain discussion software that's designed for specific server software.

Intranet discussion servers, like their Internet newsgroup server counterparts, replicate their discussions so that people across an entire intranet can participate. A server may host all discussions in a particular department or division; that server then replicates its discussions at pre-set intervals with discussions in other departments and divisions, so that everyone can participate in all discussions.

The most powerful discussion software goes beyond mere talk. It will, for example, allow someone to place a link to a Web page in a discussion. Then, when anyone in the discussion clicks on the link, a Web browser is launched, and the site is visited. This makes it easy for people to get feedback on sites they're designing, or access information contained in those sites. Similarly, programming tools like Java can be used to link discussions to intranet resources such as databases, so that in discussions people can access corporate data and comment on it.

Some discussion software also lets intranet administrators set security levels for different discussions. Certain discussions may be open to the entire company, while others are password-protected so that only certain people can see them. Some discussions can even allow everyone to read them, but only certain people to participate.

Discussion software allows people to instantly communicate, builds a sense of community, and lets people brainstorm in ways never before possible.

Using Intranet Discussion Software

Intranet-based discussion software allows people across an intranet—no matter where they are located—to participate in collaborative discussions. This discussion software offers far more than the newsgroups on the Internet offers. It allows links to Web pages and corporate resources such as databases; gives intranet administrators tools to create private discussions and to moderate discussions; and enables intranet programmers to add features using programming languages such as Java.

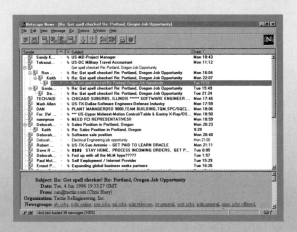

Message threads are a basic and fundamental part of discussion software. Message threads are focused discussions about a single portion of a larger topic. For example, a discussion about marketing plans may have separate threads for marketing plans for last year, this year, and next year.

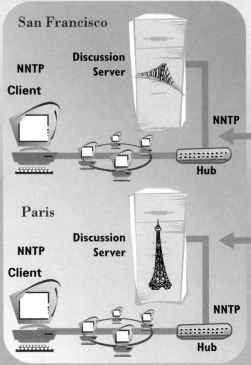

Discussion software is hosted on intranet discussion servers. These servers handle the processing of all messages. When someone reads a message, they're reading it from a server, and when they respond to a message, they're sending it to the server.

Replication

Discussion software can link thousands of employees on a global intranet. Because of the distances involved and the computing resources required, it would be impossible for a single server to host all the discussions. Instead, each server handles a specified group of people. Each server replicates the discussions it hosts on all other servers on the network, so that everyone on the intranet can participate with discussions with each other by interacting with their own local server.

Intranet Discussion Server Replica

Intranet discussion software can be integrated with Internet newsgroup discussions. The intranet discussion servers can replicate Internet newsgroup discussions on them, which means that intranet users can participate in Internet discussions from their own discussion software and server, without having to go out to the Internet.

Discussion Firewall

Some discussion software allows intranet administrators to set up a "discussion firewall." This firewall would allow people inside the intranet to see Internet newsgroup discussions. When they respond to them, however, those responses will only be able to be read by people inside the intranet. The response won't be allowed to go out to the Internet.

Newsgroup Discussion Server

Administrator

Tools:
JAVA

Moderator=
Admin

PW Protect
Y/N

Public
Y/N

Private
Members
Y/N

Discussion software gives intranet administrators a great deal of control over discussions. It allows for administrators to moderate discussions, and weed out inappropriate messages, as well as password-protect certain discussions. So, for example, there can be public discussions set up as well as private discussions.

Discussion software can include programming tools, or it can allow developers to use programming tools such as Java to customize the software and better integrate it into the intranet. For example, a Java applet can be built into discussion software that will allow people to query a database and get results directly from a discussion. This, for example, would allow someone to place real-time information about corporate sales, that changes as the data changes, directly into a sales discussion area.

**Discussion
Server**

Current Sales
$779,158

Sales this year
$779,158

What do you think?

Some intranet discussion software will read HTML and allow for links to other intranet and Internet resources, in particular, the World Wide Web. For example, a link to a specific Web site can be put into a message. Whenever someone clicks on that link, a Web browser will be launched, and the site will be visited.

**Web
Server**

HTML Link

Phone Directory

● Index   ● By Location

Internet

25
How Intranet Videoconferencing Software Works

INTRANETS

are all about communication. And there is often no better way to communicate than in face-to-face encounters. However, intranets are also about communication outside of physical boundaries like buildings, companies, states, and countries. Often, of course, face-to-face meetings are not practical, due to time limits or budget constraints. In a corporation with branch offices, for example, it can be very expensive and a waste of resources to fly people from all over the country to a single location for a one-hour meeting. With intranet videoconferencing software, however, people can hold face-to-face meetings even though they are located on the other side of the continent from each other. It allows people to see each other and talk to each other while seated at their computers.

Videoconferencing requires a few simple hardware components: a video camera, a microphone, and a sound card for each participating computer. The cost of this hardware has dropped dramatically so that it's quite affordable—and most new computers now come equipped for sound.

There are many different software programs available for videoconferencing on intranets. Microsoft and Netscape, among others, are pushing videoconferencing systems. The longest-standing videoconferencing system on the Internet—CU-See-Me—also has intranet-based videoconferencing. It has been around longer than any other IP-based videoconferencing product, and that's what we'll look at in this chapter.

CU-See-Me videoconferencing works on a client/server model, like many other intranet applications. The CU-See-Me client runs on a local computer, and it can run on many different kinds, including PCs and Macs. When someone wants to join a videoconference, they log onto what's called a *reflector*—which is really just another name for videoconferencing server software sitting on an intranet server.

Reflectors can handle multiple videoconferences. Videoconferences can be on an ad hoc basis, with people logging in when they want, or they can be scheduled ahead of time. When someone joins a conference, they will see and hear everyone else in the conference—and every person in the conference will be able to see and hear them.

The reflector software is of special benefit to intranet administrators. It allows for security, so that administrators can block unauthorized users from participating in videoconferences. Administrators can restrict access to particular users for specific conferences by using passwords.

The software also allows for load balancing. When intranet use is high overall, for example, it can devote less bandwidth to videoconferencing, to free intranet resources. When use is low, it can devote more bandwidth to videoconferencing.

The videoconferencing software can be used to broadcast information as well. The head of your company, for example, could make announcements live by video to every desktop computer so everyone in the corporation can watch and listen to the announcement simultaneously.

How CU-See-Me Intranet Videoconferencing Works

There are a variety of software programs available that enable people to engage in videoconferences on intranets. One of the earliest and most popular Internet videoconferencing software, CU-See-Me, has also been built to handle intranet videoconferencing. CU-See-Me allows people with desktop computers to have live videoconferences with individuals and groups anywhere across the intranet. Anyone can do videoconferencing with software and hardware that is quite inexpensive.

Intranet Reflector Server

1 CU-See-Me videoconferencing works on a client/server model. People run the CU-See-Me client on their computer to log into a special server called a *reflector*. A reflector can host many simultaneous live videoconferences. When you log into a reflector, you can join any conference that exists. When logged into a reflector, a signal goes out regularly from your computer to the reflector, telling others logged in that you are available for a videoconference.

packet received,
packet received,
packet received,

2 The video data is sent using UDP (User Datagram Protocol). Unlike TCP, the UDP does not check for data integrity, nor therefore, does it ask for bad packets to be resent; it just acknowledges the receipt of the data. The result is that UDP provides for a more uninterrupted data transfer and so it provides smoother transfer and is more efficient than TCP when sending video data.

3 You need a video camera, a microphone, and a sound card on your computer. The camera converts your video image into digital data. The CU-See-Me software then compresses and encodes that data, enabling it to be sent across the Internet or intranet. If the data wasn't compressed and encoded, it would be too large to be sent. CU-See-Me also saves bandwidth by sending only the part of the image that has changed. So, for example, if someone's head moves, it will transmit only the moving head, and not the background, which hasn't changed. The person who wants to see your image also has to have the CU-See-Me software. The software decodes the video image, and displays it as video on the person's screen.

4 The reflector software contains many tools that intranet administrators can use to better control videoconferencing. It allows administrators to control the intranet bandwidth devoted to videoconferencing, both to ensure the highest-possible video quality, and also to make sure that the rest of the intranet is given the proper resources. It allows administrators to configure specific conferences at specific times, and also enables security measures such as password-protecting the server, so that only authorized users can log in, or so that only specific intranet users can log into specific conferences. Reflectors can also automatically adjust the rate of video transmission to the amount of traffic on the intranet, sending lower-quality video when traffic is congested, and higher-quality video when traffic is lighter.

Videoconference
Bandwidth ____

Scheduled Conferences:
Markering
8AM EST
NY Paris

Password protect server
during conference?
Yes

5 People on an intranet can participate in videoconferences with people on the Internet (provided the firewall doesn't block the packets). To join an Internet conference, people log into an Internet reflector and participate as they would normally. If they can have a direct connection, they can participate in a videoconference by using the Internet person's IP address.

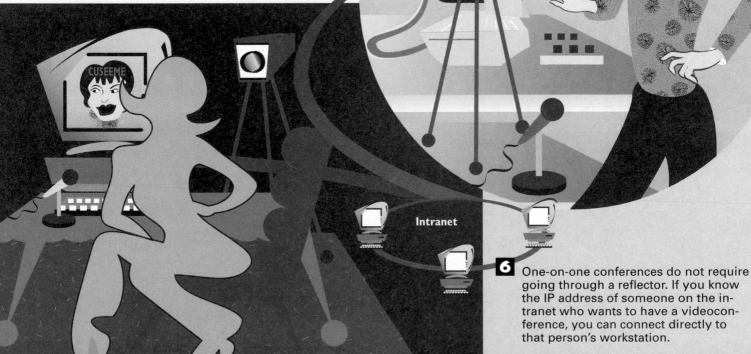

Intranet

6 One-on-one conferences do not require going through a reflector. If you know the IP address of someone on the intranet who wants to have a videoconference, you can connect directly to that person's workstation.

CHAPTER

26

How Intranet Whiteboard Applications Work

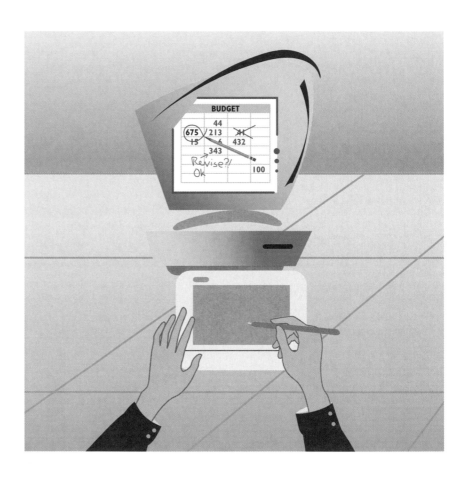

INCREASINGLY, people's work is done not with pen and paper—it's done with computers. That means that one traditional way that people collaborate—by sitting down with pen and pencil and marking up each other's work—is no longer possible.

Online mark-up started with word processing programs offering simple "strikeout" and "redline" styles. Changes, however, were done sequentially, one person at a time. This often caused great delays in document production. It was also difficult to make annotations in documents, although "comment" styles were possible. Another difficulty was keeping track of who made which changes or remarks. This was improved upon by the introduction of color coding revisions by authors. Despite these advances, it was still cumbersome and time consuming for a group to work online on documents. Furthermore, while these features rapidly become common in word processing, other applications like spreadsheets didn't offer similar controls. One other problem was that all the people working on the document usually needed to have the same version of the software to work collaboratively at all.

True document collaborative possibilities emerged when someone recognized that whiteboards—a board on which special markers are used that can easily be wiped off—provided the concept that could help move online mark-up into the realm of the actually useful. These whiteboards are not physical objects set up in rooms. Instead, the whiteboard software resides on the client's desktop. Every computer screen has the ability to become a whiteboard. In addition to writing on a blank whiteboard, people can "write" directly to the documents by writing on their computer screens.

What they write is immediately visible to the other people viewing the document on their screens. People can mark up the budget by circling or otherwise marking items, each using a different color to help identify the author. Different programs also provide a variety of tools, such as erasers and spray cans. Participants can also discuss the comments as they make them.

The next generation of whiteboard applications will allow participants not only to mark up what is on each other's screens, but also to actually change the data as well. Presently, only the originator of the document conference can physically change the data. In the future, however, no doubt there will be controls that allow or restrict the changes that people participating in a whiteboard session can make. Participants will be able to talk about a budget, change the figures on the spot, and perform a "what-if" analysis. Moreover, participants will be able to do this even if they do not have the software for the file on the whiteboard. For example, if they were working on an Excel spreadsheet, they would not have to have Excel on their own computer.

How Intranet Whiteboard Applications Work

A *whiteboard application* refers to software which allows people to simultaneously view and annotate a document on their computer screens. Each participant would have a different color assigned so that the authorship of changes is easily visible. The participants in a whiteboard conference can also talk to each other while they are circling or otherwise pointing to the section of the document they reference in the discussion. Document conferencing by whiteboard applications allows for truly collaborative working. There are a number of companies developing this type of software. This illustration is based on how the CU-See-Me whiteboard works.

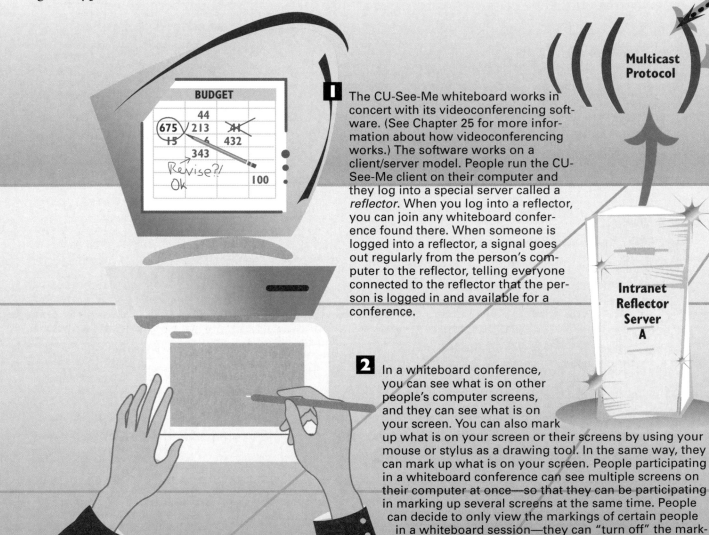

1 The CU-See-Me whiteboard works in concert with its videoconferencing software. (See Chapter 25 for more information about how videoconferencing works.) The software works on a client/server model. People run the CU-See-Me client on their computer and they log into a special server called a *reflector*. When you log into a reflector, you can join any whiteboard conference found there. When someone is logged into a reflector, a signal goes out regularly from the person's computer to the reflector, telling everyone connected to the reflector that the person is logged in and available for a conference.

2 In a whiteboard conference, you can see what is on other people's computer screens, and they can see what is on your screen. You can also mark up what is on your screen or their screens by using your mouse or stylus as a drawing tool. In the same way, they can mark up what is on your screen. People participating in a whiteboard conference can see multiple screens on their computer at once—so that they can be participating in marking up several screens at the same time. People can decide to only view the markings of certain people in a whiteboard session—they can "turn off" the markings of some people.

Multicast Protocol

Intranet Reflector Server A

BUDGET

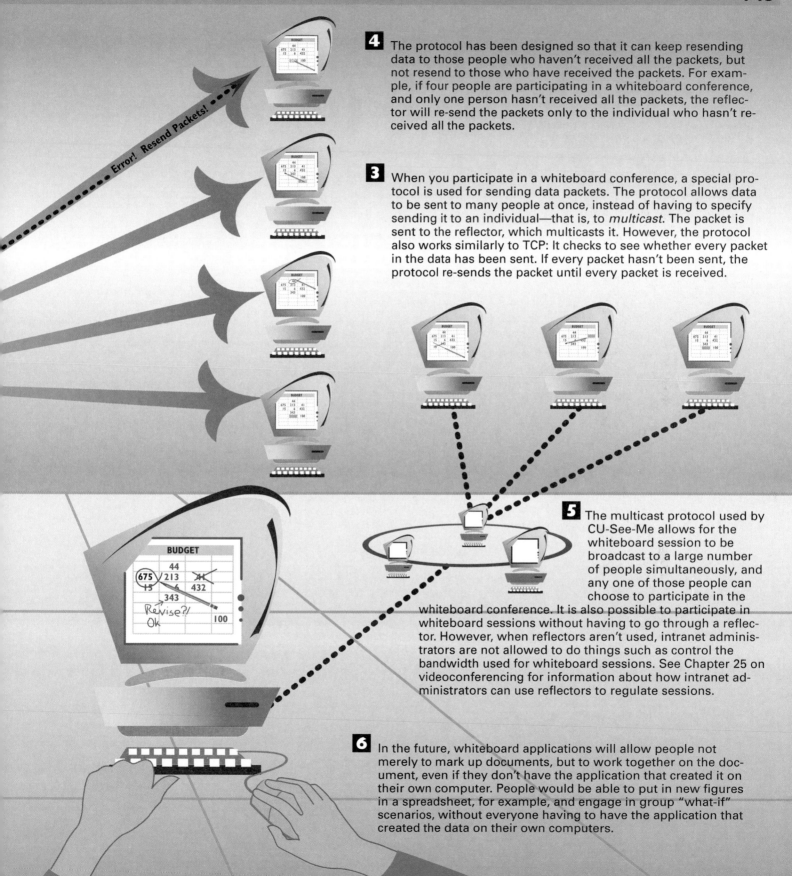

4 The protocol has been designed so that it can keep resending data to those people who haven't received all the packets, but not resend to those who have received the packets. For example, if four people are participating in a whiteboard conference, and only one person hasn't received all the packets, the reflector will re-send the packets only to the individual who hasn't received all the packets.

3 When you participate in a whiteboard conference, a special protocol is used for sending data packets. The protocol allows data to be sent to many people at once, instead of having to specify sending it to an individual—that is, to *multicast*. The packet is sent to the reflector, which multicasts it. However, the protocol also works similarly to TCP: It checks to see whether every packet in the data has been sent. If every packet hasn't been sent, the protocol re-sends the packet until every packet is received.

5 The multicast protocol used by CU-See-Me allows for the whiteboard session to be broadcast to a large number of people simultaneously, and any one of those people can choose to participate in the whiteboard conference. It is also possible to participate in whiteboard sessions without having to go through a reflector. However, when reflectors aren't used, intranet administrators are not allowed to do things such as control the bandwidth used for whiteboard sessions. See Chapter 25 on videoconferencing for information about how intranet administrators can use reflectors to regulate sessions.

6 In the future, whiteboard applications will allow people not merely to mark up documents, but to work together on the document, even if they don't have the application that created it on their own computer. People would be able to put in new figures in a spreadsheet, for example, and engage in group "what-if" scenarios, without everyone having to have the application that created the data on their own computers.

CHAPTER

27

How Document Management Systems Work

WHAT

WHAT do most people in a corporation do most of their working days? Work on documents. Perhaps those documents are budgets in the form of spreadsheets. They might be sales reports. They could be long-range projects. More likely than not, after people have finished working on a document, they send it to someone else, who might make comments on it and send it back, or pass it along to someone else. Paper trails grow.

Complex documents that require several people to work on them, and possibly others to sign off on them, create much larger problems. Think of a company newsletter. Several writers may contribute articles to it. Several editors may work on it. Artists and layout artists work on it, and then it often has to go back to editors to put the finishing touches on it. It may also require that other people *not* involved with its production review it, make comments on it, and send it back for yet another round of revisions, until everyone gives it their final approval.

That process is incredibly time-consuming and fraught with the potential for many errors. There is a way, though, that an intranet can help solve the problem: through the use of document management software. This is intranet-based software that allows groups of people to work on documents together, and that creates a way for work to flow to people, creating an audit trail.

Document management software allows intranet administrators to create systems that track documents through every aspect of their creation. The administrators can set it up so that only one person at a time can check any individual document out of a library—and they can also set it up so that only certain people are allowed to edit or read that document. They can give certain rights to read or work on documents to entire groups, or to single individuals. They can provide a "version history" of every document so that anyone can see who has worked on it, and what changes that person made. And they can give certain people the right to "lock" the document so that no further changes are allowed to be made. Some software even allows for review of older versions of documents to help track these changes.

Many companies are working on intranet-based document management software. This kind of software has been around for some time. The intranet, however, has made this kind of software of greater interest.

Most software works, like much of any intranet, on a client/server model. The documents themselves are managed by special server software. People access the documents and the system often through standard, off-the-shelf browser software such as the Internet Explorer or Netscape Navigator. When they check out documents, they can work on them on their own computer using their own software. But the heart of the system is the server software that allows for the tracking of every document.

How Document Management Systems Work

Document management systems allow people on an intranet to work cooperatively on the same document. There are many different kinds of systems, but the best of them enforce work-flow rules for who can work on a document and when. For example, a document management system would allow people to check documents into and out of libraries to work on; when the documents were checked out no one but the person who checked it out could work on it. The illustration here shows a general view of how a typical system might work.

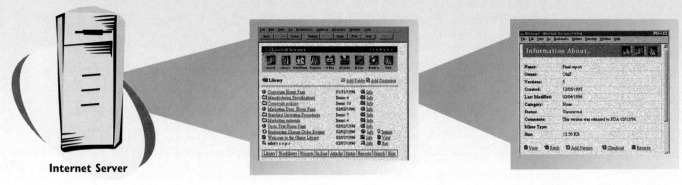

Internet Server

1 The basis of a document management system is a central library of documents, where all the pertinent documents live. From here, people can check out or view any documents they're given the rights to. This document library lives on an intranet server. The entire document management system can be built in HTML format, so that no special client software is needed to run it—normal Web browsers can run it.

2 When someone needs information about a particular document, they can view an HTML page about the document that gives data such as who created the document, how many revisions it has gone through, the last time the document was revised, and the size of the document.

3 Different documents carry different kinds of permission rights. Some documents may allow only certain people to check them out and work on them, but allow everyone to view them. Other documents may let only certain people to view them.

Internet Server

4 When someone checks out a document, other people are locked from using it. This ensures that people can't overwrite each other's work.

5 After the work has been done, the document can be put back into the library. Now someone else can work on the document. The system can also lock the document after a certain point, so that people would be able to view it, but not change it.

6 Document management software is particularly powerful when used in concert with workflow software, or when it has workflow features. Workflow software allows intranet administrators to design a process by which a document moves through various steps until completion. For example, a newsletter may first have to go to a writer, then a designer, then an editor, and then a vice president. Workflow software moves the documents through the steps, creates an audit trail, and makes sure that only people with the proper rights can work on the documents at each step of the way.

P A R T

APPLYING THE INTRANET

INTRANETS enable companies to conduct business better: to keep in better touch with customers, to more effec-

tively sell goods and services, to better integrate all the resources of a corporation, to help employees work better, and to help operate more effectively. In this section of the book we'll look at everything from how intranets can incorporate existing legacy systems to how intranets can be used to deliver corporate information to its employees.

Chapter 28 shows how an intranet can be used to gain access to corporate databases with Web-to-database query tools using the Common Gateway Interface (CGI) and a variety of intermediate software. Intranet users need only type in requests in a Web page, and this technology goes out, searches the database, and sends back the results in HTML format on Web pages. This often makes the databases far more accessible than they were before the advent of intranets.

In Chapter 29, we'll see how intranets can help cut the corporate paper trail and streamline corporate procedures. We'll see how to use an intranet to deliver information to customers without paper, how personnel forms and sales memos have been computerized with an intranet, and many other ways in which intranets can save paper and time. A mobile sales department, in particular, can use the intranet to place sales orders as well as present an up-to-the minute record catalog to music store buyers.

In Chapter 30, we'll look at how legacy systems and data can be incorporated into an intranet. The ways that this can be done are as numerous as the number of companies using intranets. Programs can be written in a variety of languages that use the Common Gateway Interface to access legacy databases. The client/server–based Structured Query Language can be used as well.

Chapter 31 takes a look at the ways in which a intranet can be used to do commerce, both with customers as well as with other businesses. Intranets will increasingly be used for electronic commerce. Companies will post catalogs online, and then people can visit the Web site, browse the catalog, and order goods. In this chapter, we'll look at how the Secure Electronic Transaction protocol (SET) will allow for credit card information to be sent securely over the Internet.

Chapter 32 covers search tools. A well-known problem on the Internet is that it's difficult to find information in the vast sea of data available. The same holds true for intranets. Search tools have been created that go out and essentially create a database of the Web, and then allow people to search through that database and find the information they want. Agents, spiders, or robots traverse the intranet, indexing information that they find. That information is then sent to a server that maintains a database of all the information the agents find. People on the intranet can visit an intranet Web location, and search that database for corporate information. The spiders can also get information from the Web, so that from one site people can search both the intranet and the Internet.

In Chapter 33 we'll look at how people can access their company intranet, no matter where they are. In today's wired world, the separation between the workplace, home, and the road has all but disappeared. People need to be able to get access to corporate information from different locations. We'll see how a new protocol, the Point-to-Point Tunneling Protocol (PPTP), works. This protocol can help companies save a great deal of money, since it allows anyone to dial into a local Internet provider, and from that local call, log into an intranet, even if it's across the country. This saves on long-distance phone bills, and also saves on hardware costs for modems.

In Chapter 34 we'll look at how CyberMusic uses a Web site. Companies need to provide technical support for their products. Providing technical support, especially for companies that sell to a large number of people, can be an expensive proposition. An intranet can help cut those costs. Instead of having to staff many expensive support lines, a company can instead create a public Web site that people can visit that has a great deal of technical support—everything from answers to common problems, to downloadable software to fix problems with hardware, to user-to-user forums where people can exchange answers they've found to common problems.

In Chapter 35, we'll visit again with CyberMusic, this time to solve another nagging problem: how to keep all of its employees updated with the latest company news. Especially in large companies with a number of divisions that are physically separated, disseminating company information is a difficult chore. CyberMusic solved the problem by doing things such as putting up a company newsletter on an intranet Web site, using streaming audio and video technology to deliver the news, using intranet broadcasting to send out news flashes, and other similar techniques.

Finally, Chapter 36 closes out the book, and in it, again we'll be visiting with our mythical CyberMusic record company. This chapter shows how intranets can solve yet another nagging corporate problem: training employees. With technology changing so fast now, training needs to be done for all employees, not just new ones. CyberMusic uses a variety of techniques to do this, including virtual reality, videoconferencing, whiteboard applications, streaming audio, and Web technologies. Like other intranet tools, these all save the company money in the long run, and lead to a better-informed, more effective staff.

CHAPTER
28
Using Web-to-Database Query Tools

THE most important information on an intranet typically is housed in databases. These databases can be on a single site, although typically, they can be found all across an entire intranet.

Most of these databases have been around since long before the Internet became popular, and before any corporate intranets were built. That means that they've been built without TCP/IP in mind, without HTML in mind, and without taking into account any other intranet technologies. Before the intranet was built, they were accessed in a variety of ways, depending on the particular kind of database and access software used.

An intranet can theoretically make it much easier to get at all that corporate data. The use of HTML means that it's relatively easy to build search forms that anyone can use to easily get at data—data that in order to get at, people previously may have been required to know a database programming language.

However, while it's easy to build HTML search forms that let people type in queries, it's not so easy to actually have those queries be sent out to search through a database, and then to have the results be delivered back to whoever did the searching.

That's what Web-to-database query tools are designed to do. They're designed to let anyone, without having to understand database languages, easily get at the vast corporate resources locked up in databases.

Since the databases typically were built before the intranet, some means of getting at them from an intranet, and specifically from the Web, needs to be designed. There are many different ways of accessing corporate databases from an intranet. A popular one is to use the Common Gateway Interface (CGI). CGI enables people on the Web to access resources that aren't directly located on the Web. Through the use of CGI scripts, an intranet programmer can allow someone from the Web to query a database, and have that database send back information that is put into a preformatted HTML page. This makes it easy for anyone, using a standard Web browser such as Netscape Navigator or Internet Explorer, to access corporate databases.

What will undoubtedly prove to be popular is the Structured Query Language (SQL). SQL is a database language that works on a client/server model, as does much of the Web. In the SQL model, the database itself is separate from the software that accesses the data—in other words, the software used to access the database is the client, while the database itself is the server. There can be many different kinds of clients to access the same underlying database. One such client can be a CGI script that takes the input form on the corporate Web, converts its contents into an SQL query, and submits it to the database server. Another client could be a Java applet that allows for the creation of more complex queries and better data display than standard HTML.

How Web-to-Database Query Tools Work

The most important information on most intranets exists on databases that were created long before the Internet became popular, and before intranets were ever created. They use technology built without the TCP/IP protocols or the HTML language in mind. However, there needs to be some way for people on an intranet to access and use that data. A variety of techniques have been developed for doing this that involve allowing people to search the databases from within a Web browser.

1 When someone on an intranet wants to gain access to a corporate database, he or she will typically use a Web browser and visit a particular home page. This home page sits on a Web server that essentially acts as a front end to the database. The database in fact sits on another computer on the intranet, not the Web server.

2 When someone wants to search a database, they use a form built with HTML. After they type in search terms, the search terms are sent using a Common Gateway Interface (CGI) script. CGI is a method that enables databases and other resources to be accessed from the Web. CGI scripts can be written with a number of different tools and programming languages, including UNIX's Perl, or the C programming language.

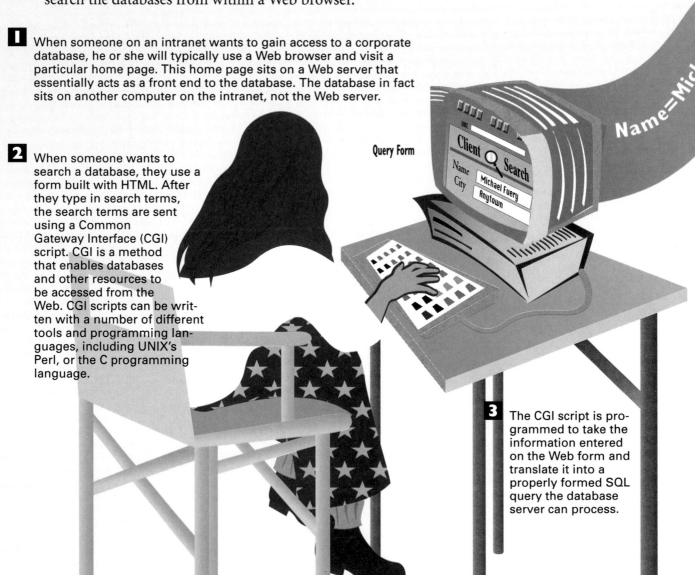

Query Form

3 The CGI script is programmed to take the information entered on the Web form and translate it into a properly formed SQL query the database server can process.

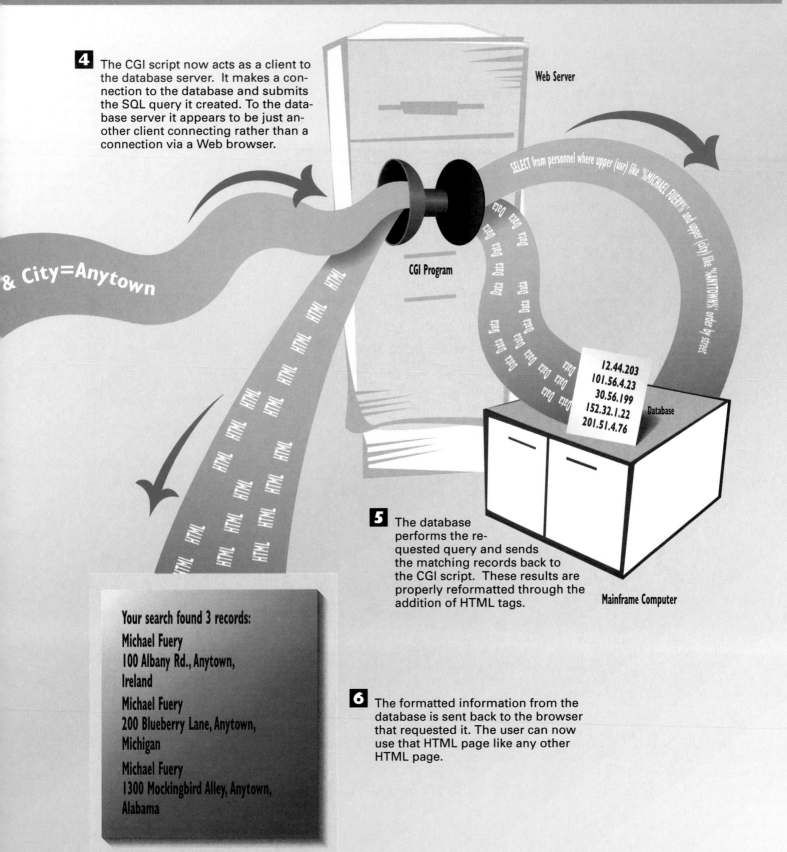

4 The CGI script now acts as a client to the database server. It makes a connection to the database and submits the SQL query it created. To the database server it appears to be just another client connecting rather than a connection via a Web browser.

Web Server

& City=Anytown

CGI Program

SELECT from personnel where upper (usr) like '%MICHAEL FUERY%' and upper (city) like '%ANYTOWN%' order by street

12.44.203
101.56.4.23
30.56.199
152.32.1.22
201.51.4.76

Database

5 The database performs the requested query and sends the matching records back to the CGI script. These results are properly reformatted through the addition of HTML tags.

Mainframe Computer

Your search found 3 records:

Michael Fuery
100 Albany Rd., Anytown,
Ireland

Michael Fuery
200 Blueberry Lane, Anytown,
Michigan

Michael Fuery
1300 Mockingbird Alley, Anytown,
Alabama

6 The formatted information from the database is sent back to the browser that requested it. The user can now use that HTML page like any other HTML page.

CHAPTER
29

How Intranets Can Cut the Corporate Paper Trail

THE typical corporation generates mounds and mounds of paper every day—potentially many tons a year. This is bad for the environment, costly for the corporation, and unnecessarily time-consuming because it requires the company to hire people to maintain and keep track of the paper trail. There are forms that have to be filled out and handled, marketing materials, sales materials and brochures to mail out, sales forms that need to be entered…the list can go on for a long time.

All this paper has many hidden costs—it's not merely the cost of paper that is involved. There are a variety of overhead costs as well. There are sky-high mailing costs. There are often high costs for storing historical material. There is an even more pernicious cost—paperwork causes red tape, and the handling of all that paper slows down how a business can operate and can put it at a competitive disadvantage.

While the "paperless office" has been talked about and pursued for at least a decade, the advent of intranets can finally bring it closer to reality. A combination of communications technologies, Web publishing tools, workgroup applications, and e-mail can cut down on paper costs, help slash mail costs, help eliminate administrative overhead, and allow corporations to react more quickly to business changes and deliver goods and services more quickly to their customers.

The area where paper costs can be cut most—and procedures most streamlined—may be the sales and marketing department. In every aspect of making a sale, from marketing and advertising through making sales calls, to making the sale and then fulfilling the order, paper costs and associated expenses can be cut.

By posting marketing materials on the Web and drawing customers to the site, companies can print fewer expensive marketing materials, such as brochures. Many companies include Business Reply Cards in their marketing materials that people can use to request additional information. Business Reply Cards have many costs associated with them: printing, mailing, and then fulfillment—inputting the person's name into the computer system, then having someone mail out the additional materials. On the Web site, customers can fill out requests for materials. That request is automatically routed to the intranet, where it is sent to the fulfillment department. This cuts down on the printing and mailing costs that Business Reply Cards carry, as well as input costs, since the customer inputs the request, instead of someone employed at the company. A traveling sales staff can input orders on an electronic form on a laptop computer, and then later send that form back to the intranet, again saving on paper and administrative costs.

Internal paper costs can be cut as well. Company newsletters and communications can be posted on an intranet Web server or sent via e-mail. Personnel manuals can be posted as well. Forms for doing things such as requesting time off can be filled out electronically instead of on paper—again, cutting down on paper, overhead, and red tape.

How Intranets Can Cut the Corporate Paper Trail

One of the many benefits of an intranet is that it can cut the amount of paper and paperwork used by corporations, often dramatically. It can streamline corporate procedures and have them done electronically, instead of via paper. And it can also more directly communicate with its customers without having to resort to paper and mailing. Pictured here is an example of how a fictional record company, CyberMusic, uses an intranet to cut paper costs.

CyberMusic employs a sales staff to sell its records to record stores and other outlets, and they carry laptop computers when they travel. Formerly, in order to know the full stock of what records the company carries, they would have to refer to printed material, which easily became outdated. Now, they dial into their company intranet, and access a Web page that contains the up-to-date catalog. When they visit their sales accounts, they can link to the page as well.

Product Availability

Modem Pool

Mobile Sales Force

CyberMusic Order Form

When the mobile sales staff takes an order, they previously had to fill out paper forms, and then send those forms to the data processing department, where the forms would be typed into the sales system. With the advent of the company intranet, the sales staff fills out an electronic sales form while on a sales visit. The form is then sent via electronic mail to the company intranet, where it is routed automatically to the fulfillment and accounting departments. Previously, paper forms had to be routed among all the departments, wasting time and money.

URL

CyberMusic WEB PAGE

Get more Material

Listen to Sound clips

At CyberMusic, a great deal of paper material was generated in sending brochures and related documents directly to customers. CyberMusic has a public Web site, which cuts down on the number of brochures sent out, since people can get information about the company, its records and recording artists directly from the Web. An added bonus is that customers can listen to sound clips as well.

CyberMusic

Please send me more information .... ☐
Free catalog .... ☐
Add me to your e-mail list ☐

CGI

CyberMusic Web Site

CyberMusic used to regularly include extra Business Reply Cards in much of the material it mailed out, so that people could request additional information about the company or its records. Now, people can fill out a form on the company's Web site requesting information, saving on paper and mailing costs. The information is sent via a CGI script to the fulfillment department.

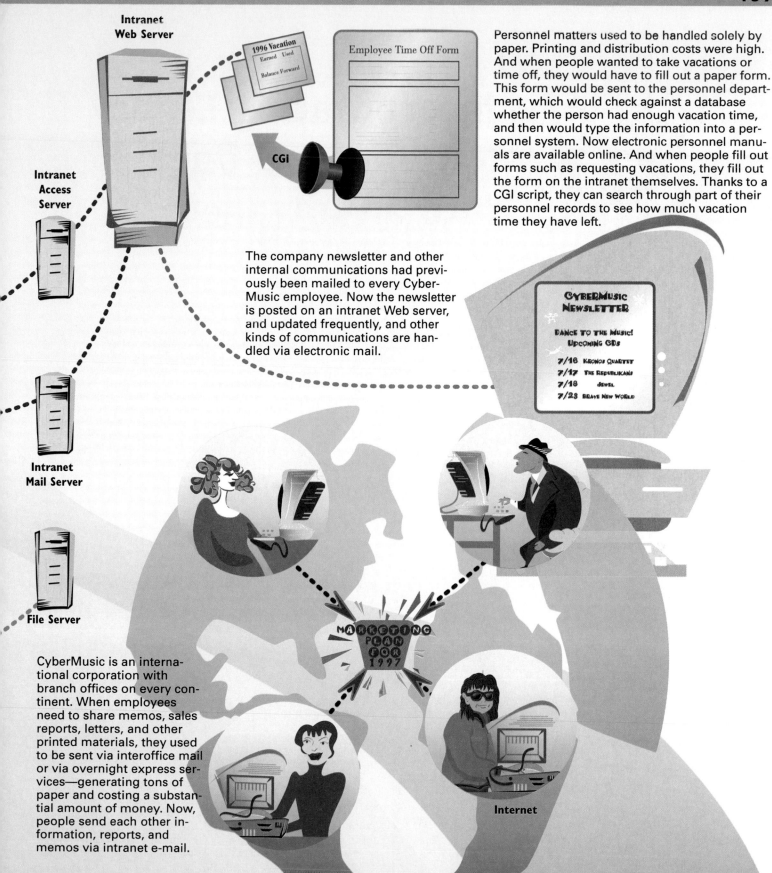

Intranet Web Server

1996 Vacation
Earned Used
Balance Forward

Employee Time Off Form

CGI

Intranet Access Server

Intranet Mail Server

File Server

Personnel matters used to be handled solely by paper. Printing and distribution costs were high. And when people wanted to take vacations or time off, they would have to fill out a paper form. This form would be sent to the personnel department, which would check against a database whether the person had enough vacation time, and then would type the information into a personnel system. Now electronic personnel manuals are available online. And when people fill out forms such as requesting vacations, they fill out the form on the intranet themselves. Thanks to a CGI script, they can search through part of their personnel records to see how much vacation time they have left.

The company newsletter and other internal communications had previously been mailed to every Cyber-Music employee. Now the newsletter is posted on an intranet Web server, and updated frequently, and other kinds of communications are handled via electronic mail.

CYBERMUSIC NEWSLETTER

DANCE TO THE MUSIC!
UPCOMING CDs

7/16 KRONOS QUARTET
7/17 THE REPUBLIKANS
7/18 JEWEL
7/23 BRAVE NEW WORLD

MARKETING PLAN FOR 1997

CyberMusic is an international corporation with branch offices on every continent. When employees need to share memos, sales reports, letters, and other printed materials, they used to be sent via interoffice mail or via overnight express services—generating tons of paper and costing a substantial amount of money. Now, people send each other information, reports, and memos via intranet e-mail.

Internet

CHAPTER

30

Incorporating Legacy Systems and Data into an Intranet

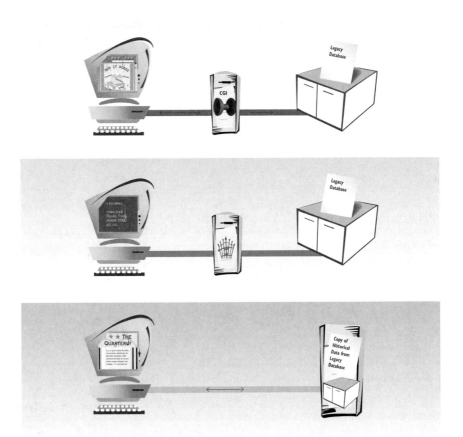

IT'S rare that an intranet has been built entirely from scratch. Intranet designers usually don't have the luxury of creating a logical computing architecture. Instead, they have to take into account existing corporate computing and networking resources. That means attempting to integrate mainframe-based systems, mini-computer-based systems, local area networks, and databases, none of which have been designed with an intranet or TCP/IP in mind. Important corporate information is stored in a variety of databases that are often incompatible—and they have not been integrated into an intranet yet.

That presents a major problem to anyone designing an intranet: how to incorporate all these incompatible systems into their design. As you might imagine, because there are so many different kinds of systems and databases, and because each corporation has designed their intranet differently, there's no single solution—and often, no easy solution, either.

One solution for those who want to give intranet users access to legacy databases is to use the Common Gateway Interface (CGI), a technology that gives access to non-Web-based resources such as databases. CGI scripts—which can be written with a variety of tools, such as the Perl scripting language and the C++ programming language—send the requests to a database, and then return the results in an HTML tagged page.

That solution works, but has drawbacks. One is that the CGI scripts are generally written for a very specific situation—a specific Web page querying a specific database. Often, intranets need greater flexibility, or have a variety of legacy databases that need to be accessed. In that case, several technologies can be used. One that may prove to be very popular is the use of the Structured Query Language (SQL), which is a way of accessing databases. SQL is based on a client/server model. The database acts as a server, and a variety of clients can query the database. With SQL, a database query from the Web goes to intermediate software—and possibly an intermediate server as well—that translates the query into the SQL language. That SQL query is then sent to the database, which returns the data, which is eventually put into HTML format.

Databases aren't the only legacy system that needs to be incorporated into an intranet. Others are local area networks (LANs) or the Systems Network Architecture (SNA), a suite of protocols used to connect IBM mainframe systems. There are a number of ways that an existing LAN can be incorporated into an intranet. The simplest, of course, is to install TCP/IP technology on all the workstations on the LAN, and to install intranet-based servers, routers, and other similar technologies. However, there may be times when the LAN needs to keep its existing technology. In that instance, bridges can be used that will allow data to be passed between the intranet and the LAN. Similarly, a TCP/IP to SNA gateway can be used to connect the mainframe to the intranet.

Incorporating Legacy Data into an Intranet

One of the biggest problems facing many intranet administrators is that they must incorporate systems and databases that were created without TCP/IP in mind—what are called legacy systems. These systems and databases may be mainframe-based, minicomputer-based, or LAN-based. They can be incorporated into an intranet in a variety of ways. Pictured on this page are some of the possibilities.

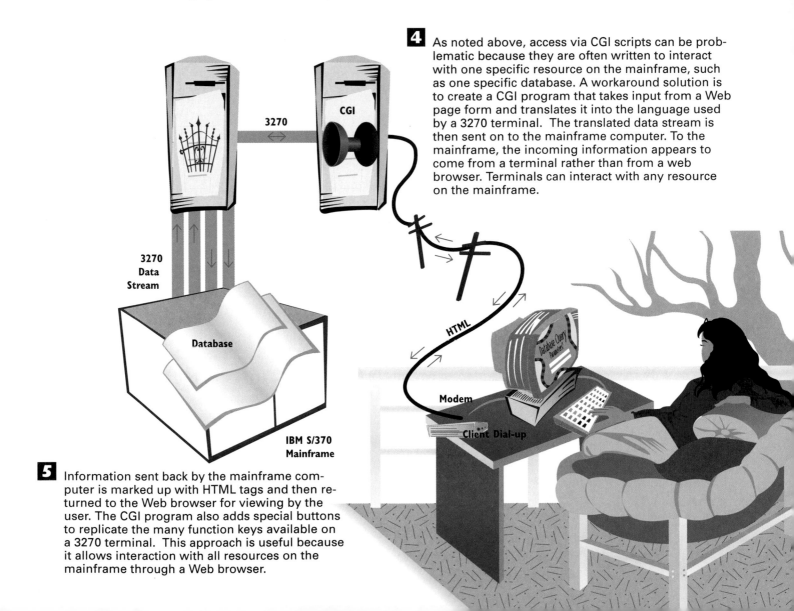

4 As noted above, access via CGI scripts can be problematic because they are often written to interact with one specific resource on the mainframe, such as one specific database. A workaround solution is to create a CGI program that takes input from a Web page form and translates it into the language used by a 3270 terminal. The translated data stream is then sent on to the mainframe computer. To the mainframe, the incoming information appears to come from a terminal rather than from a web browser. Terminals can interact with any resource on the mainframe.

3270

CGI

3270
Data
Stream

Database

HTML

Modem

Client Dial-up

IBM S/370
Mainframe

5 Information sent back by the mainframe computer is marked up with HTML tags and then returned to the Web browser for viewing by the user. The CGI program also adds special buttons to replicate the many function keys available on a 3270 terminal. This approach is useful because it allows interaction with all resources on the mainframe through a Web browser.

1 One of the most common ways of incorporating legacy system data into an intranet is to allow people to search through the legacy database using the Common Gateway Interface (CGI). CGI scripts can be written so that someone can fill out a form on a Web page, and the script translates the information on the form into a format that can be understood by the database. The results of the query are then delivered back to the Web browser after the CGI script has formatted the results with HTML so they are readable by the Web browser.

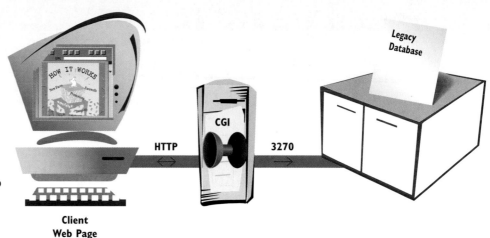

2 One possible way of connecting to a legacy IBM mainframe system is to enable direct access through the use of tn3270 terminal emulation software, which runs on individual desktop machines connected to the company intranet. An SNA gateway sits between the mainframe and the TCP/IP based intranet. The terminal emulation software encapsulates a 3270 data stream in TCP/IP packets. The gateway strips off the TCP and IP headers and wraps the data in the appropriate SNA protocol. To the user, it appears as though they are sitting at a dedicated 3270 terminal.

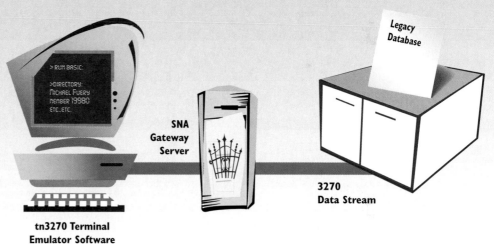

3 Another choice is to retrieve the most popular data from the legacy system and place it in static HTML formatted pages on an intranet Web server. When an individual wants the information, they simply type in the URL for the static page and retrieve it. This solution works fine for information that is static, meaning not frequently updated, such as quarterly financial reports. However, it will not work for information that is frequently updated.

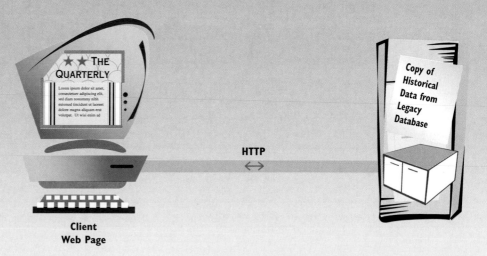

CHAPTER

31

Doing Commerce on an Intranet

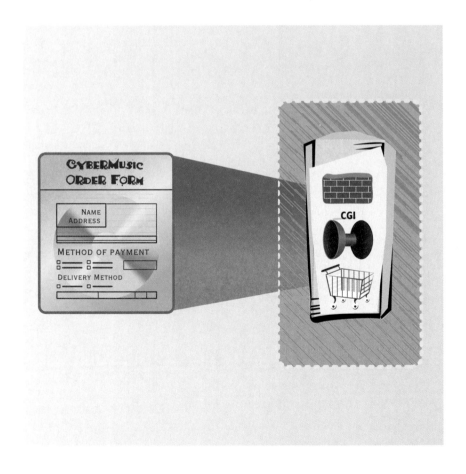

IN much of this book, we've seen how intranets and the Internet can help streamline the ways that companies do business, and change the way that people within a corporation communicate. For many companies, though, the biggest benefit of an intranet can be counted directly on the bottom line—intranets, used in conjunction with the Internet, help the companies do business with their customers. It allows the companies to better market their goods and services, and to take direct orders right online over the intranet. And it also allows the companies to order directly from other businesses as well.

Today, the amount of business done on the Internet and over intranets is relatively small. In the coming years, however, that business is expected to grow to many billions of dollars. The dramatic growth of the Internet has been fueled by business and consumers, and it shows no sign of letting up. The Internet may become one of the primary places that businesses operate—and is expected to be the place where many billions of dollars of goods and services will be bought and sold every year. Because of that, the ability to do commerce is a vital part of any intranet.

Businesses will use intranets as a way to market and sell their products and services. They will accept electronic payment using an intranet as well.

Increasingly, businesses will use the Internet to market and sell their products. Many people will buy things while at home and at their place of business instead of at retail stores—and they will use the Internet to browse through catalogs, and then make purchases online.

There is a major problem that has to be overcome with electronic commerce over the Internet and intranets, however. The nature of the Internet is that it's an unsecured network. As packets travel across it, anyone along the way could conceivably examine those packets. Because of that, there are potential dangers to doing business online—if you pay over the Internet with a credit card, someone could conceivably snoop at it and steal your credit card number and other identifying information. That means that businesses that expect to sell goods and services need some secure way to sell them.

A number of ways of making money payments across the Internet have sprung up to solve the problem. Probably the one that will be most used is the Secure Electronic Transaction protocol (SET)—a set of procedures and protocols designed to make financial transactions on the Internet as safe as possible. SET uses encryption technology to make sure that no one can steal your credit card number; only the sender and the receiver can decipher the numbers. See Chapter 17 for details on how encryption works. Major credit card companies such as VISA, MasterCard, and American Express support SET, as do software companies such as Microsoft and Netscape. With that backing, SET will almost certainly become the standard way for sending secure credit card information over the Internet.

There are other schemes for doing business over the Internet and intranets. In some of them, credit cards aren't used. Instead, people get electronic "tokens" that function as cash. Various terms are being used for this new form of money, partly from vendors offering electronic payment services, including NetCash, CyberCash, .eCash, and emoney. Someone purchases a certain amount of electronic money, and then can use it for online transactions, without having to go through credit card verification for each purchase. There will be other methods of electronic payments online as well.

There are people who believe that the Internet may transform the way that people buy goods and services at least to the same extent, and possibly more, as happened with the advent of mail-order catalogs. Almost any company that sells to the general public will certainly want to use their intranet as a way to help market and sell what they produce.

Doing this requires that a company use its intranet as well as the Internet. In general, the intranet is used as a way to market the goods and services, and the intranet is used as a way to let people actually buy the goods. Today, almost any major company you can name markets via the Internet, while few actually sell anything.

To market what they produce, companies create Web sites on the Internet, outside of the intranet's firewall. What most companies have found is that if all they do is create an advertisement on their Web site, they'll get very little traffic to their site. Few people want to spend their time reading ads online. Because of that, most businesses have found that they need to create compelling content, such as entertainment clips, videos, sounds, and news items. Once they draw people to their site, they can then market their goods and services. Commercial Web sites have also found that word of mouth isn't good enough to draw a crowd to their sites. To ensure that people visit them, they advertise on other Web sites. When someone clicks on an ad, they are immediately sent to the Web site.

While a variety of content such as videos and audio clips may draw people to a site, once people are there, businesses want them to learn about their goods, and ideally to order them. Companies build Web-based online catalogs that promote what is for sale. These catalogs can be as simple as text listings of what's available, or as complex as true multimedia catalogs that include sound and animations. Many companies now have Web sites that include online catalogs, such as L.L. Bean. In addition to catalogs, sites also make available a searchable database of their goods and services, so that people can target what they want to buy, and find information out about it quickly.

Bringing customers to the site and showing them what is available is only the first part of what a company wants to do. More important is to close the sale over the Internet. That's the difficult part, because many people still worry about performing financial transactions over the Internet. However, secure ways of commerce are being developed. At the point where someone actually places the order, they will send information to the intranet. They may not know that they've been transferred, but that's where their data eventually goes. There are a variety of ways to pay online, although the SET standard will undoubtedly become popular.

An intranet comes into play as well after the payment is made and authorized. Since the customer has entered the information about the products being ordered, there's no need for employees to key in an order. The order can be sent over the intranet via electronic mail or via a customized system to the fulfillment department, where the goods are shipped.

Selling directly to consumers is only one way that business can be done with intranets. Many billions of dollars are also spent every year on business-to-business transactions, in which businesses order goods and services from each other. In business-to-business transactions, companies can directly communicate with each other from intranet to intranet, sending data and orders between them over the public Internet. Since much of that data is generally confidential, there needs to be some way of keeping it from prying eyes. The answer is to use Very Secure Private Networks (VSPNs), a technology that allows intranets to use the Internet as if it were a private, secure communications channel. It does this by "tunneling" the private data through the intranet. See Chapter 20 for more information about VSPNs.

For years, a technology called Electronic Data Interchange (EDI) has allowed companies to do direct business with each other electronically. EDI allows businesses to fill out electronic forms and send them to each other, and then have the receiving business act on those forms. EDI is being brought to intranets and the Internet as a way to speed business-to-business transactions.

EDI is not the only way that companies can do business with each other over intranets, however. Intranets can help companies do business with each other in other ways as well. They can post information about what kinds of goods and services they need, and other companies can bid on providing them. They can use it as a way to better communicate with contractors and with businesses they buy goods from. In fact, intranets can help companies do business with each other in so many ways, that there are many people who believe that for many years, the main commercial use of the Internet and intranets will be for business-to-business transactions instead of for transactions between consumers and businesses.

How Financial Transactions Work on an Intranet

Intranets are used not merely to streamline businesses and make them more effective, but as a place to do business as well—to take orders for goods and services and to fill orders for goods and services. In order for this to happen, though, a secure way must be designed for credit card information to be sent over the notoriously unsecured Internet. There are many methods for doing this, but one standard, called the Secure Electronic Transaction protocol (SET), will probably be the primary method used. It has been endorsed by VISA, MasterCard, America Express, Microsoft and Netscape, among other companies. It is a system that will allow people with bank cards to do secure business over intranets. This illustration shows how a transaction using SET might work.

1 Mia visits a Web site that contains an electronic catalog. After browsing through the catalog, she decides that she wants to buy a camcorder. In order to use SET to pay for it, she will have to have a credit card from a participating bank and have been issued a unique "electronic signature" for her computer that will be used to verify that it is she, and not an impostor, that is making the purchase. In SET, everyone involved in the transaction, including the merchant, needs to have electronic signatures identifying them and software that supports the SET protocol. SET also uses public-key encryption technology to encrypt all the information sent among everyone involved in the transaction. See Chapter 17 for details on encryption.

2 Mia fills out an order form detailing what she wants to buy, its price, and any shipping, handling, and taxes. She then selects the method she wants to use to pay. In this case, she decides to pay electronically over the Internet, with her SET bank card. At this point, she doesn't send her precise credit card number, but instead the name of which credit card she wants to use. The information she sends includes her electronic signature, so that the merchant can verify it is really Mia who wants to do the ordering.

3 The merchant receives the order form from Mia. A unique transaction identifier is created by the merchant's software, so that the transaction can be identified and tracked. The merchant's SET software sends back to Mia's computer this identifier along with two "electronic certificates" which are required to complete the transaction for her specific bank card. One certificate identifies the merchant, and the other certificate identifies a specific *payment gateway*—an electronic gateway to the banking system that processes online payments.

4 Mia's software receives the electronic certificates and using them creates Order Information (OI) and Payment Instructions (PI). It encrypts these messages and includes Mia's electronic signature in them. The OI and the PI are sent back to the merchant.

5 The merchant's software decrypts Mia's Order Information and, using the electronic signature that Mia sent, verifies that the order is from her. The merchant sends verification to Mia that the order has been made.

Mia's computer

ORDER FORM

Mia's digital signature

Merchant

Mia's computer

ORDER FORM

363

Merchant

Merchant electronic certificate

Payment gateway electronic signature

Mia's computer

Payment gateway electronic signature

Merchant electronic certificate

ENCRYPTED

363
Unique transaction identifier

Payment instructions

Mia's digital signature

Merchant

Merchant

Unique transaction identifier

DECRYPTED

"V"

Verification

Mia's computer

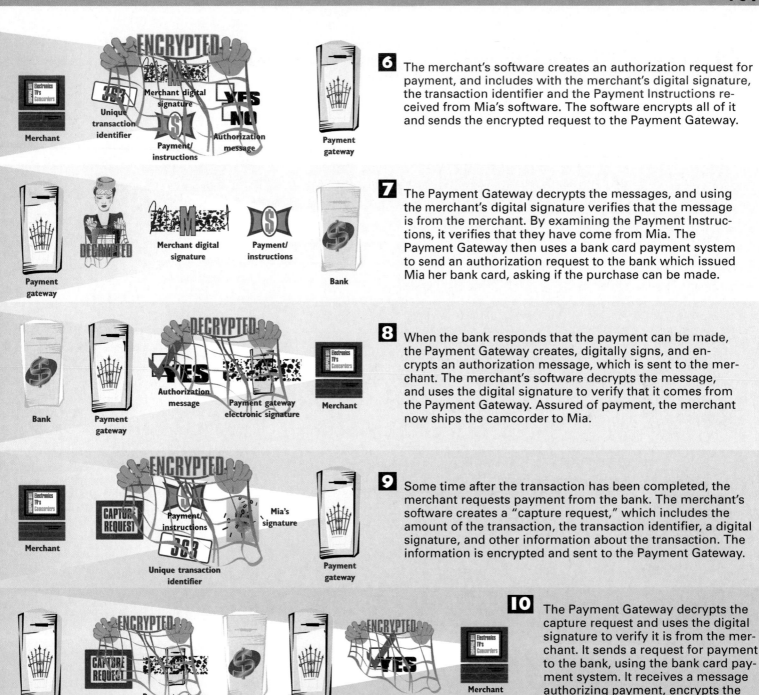

6 The merchant's software creates an authorization request for payment, and includes with the merchant's digital signature, the transaction identifier and the Payment Instructions received from Mia's software. The software encrypts all of it and sends the encrypted request to the Payment Gateway.

7 The Payment Gateway decrypts the messages, and using the merchant's digital signature verifies that the message is from the merchant. By examining the Payment Instructions, it verifies that they have come from Mia. The Payment Gateway then uses a bank card payment system to send an authorization request to the bank which issued Mia her bank card, asking if the purchase can be made.

8 When the bank responds that the payment can be made, the Payment Gateway creates, digitally signs, and encrypts an authorization message, which is sent to the merchant. The merchant's software decrypts the message, and uses the digital signature to verify that it comes from the Payment Gateway. Assured of payment, the merchant now ships the camcorder to Mia.

9 Some time after the transaction has been completed, the merchant requests payment from the bank. The merchant's software creates a "capture request," which includes the amount of the transaction, the transaction identifier, a digital signature, and other information about the transaction. The information is encrypted and sent to the Payment Gateway.

10 The Payment Gateway decrypts the capture request and uses the digital signature to verify it is from the merchant. It sends a request for payment to the bank, using the bank card payment system. It receives a message authorizing payment, encrypts the message, and then sends the authorization to the merchant.

11 The merchant software decrypts the authorization, verifies that it is from the Payment Gateway, and then stores the authorization which will be used to reconcile the payment when it is received as it normally is in credit card transactions from the bank.

Doing Business with Customers Using an Intranet

Intranets may revolutionize the way that businesses sell goods and services. Using an intranet, a company can inexpensively market its goods and services, take orders for them, and then fulfill the order. This illustration shows how a record company called CyberMusic could do business using an intranet.

CyberMusic creates a public Web site on a bastion host in the firewall of the intranet that it uses as a way to draw customers. To get people to visit, it features interviews with musicians, music news, concert calendars, music clips, and contests.

CGI

To further draw people to the site, Cyber-Music advertises its site on the Internet. When anyone clicks on an ad for Cyber-Music, they are immediately sent to the CyberMusic Web site.

Secure Payment System

DELIVERY DEPT.

HANDLE WITH CARE

Fulfillment Department

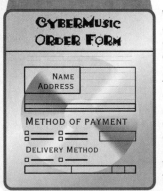

CYBERMUSIC ORDER FORM

NAME
ADDRESS

METHOD OF PAYMENT

DELIVERY METHOD

When the person is done browsing, they go to the electronic checkout counter to pay for the items they've selected. The CGI shopping cart program sends a list of the cart's contents to the checkout counter. The buyer fills out a form that includes information such as their name and address and method of payment. This information is encrypted and sent from the Internet to the intranet through the firewall. The transaction is a secure one because it uses the SET protocol. The orderer, merchant, and credit card company then complete the payment following the illustration on the previous page.

Information about the order is automatically transferred over the intranet to CyberMusic's fulfillment department, which ships out the records ordered.

The site features an electronic catalog that promotes the records that CyberMusic sells. The catalog features music clips so that people can sample records, and has information about the album and its artist. To select an item from the catalog, someone merely needs to click on a link or a button. When this is done, the item is placed in their electronic shopping cart. As they browse through the catalog they can place more items in their electronic shopping cart. A CGI program on the CyberMusic Web site keeps track of the contents of each individual's shopping cart.

Instead of browsing through a catalog, people can do a focused search on the kind of music they're interested in. They can search by type of music, particular artist, date of release and other terms. The search can be done via a variety of database searching techniques, including CGI scripting and SQL technology, both covered in earlier chapters. When they find the album they want to buy, they need to click on a link or a button to drop the item in their electronic shopping cart.

Business-to-Business Transactions Using Intranets

THE MUSIC BOX

Intranets can communicate with one another through the public Internet, instead of by using private leased lines. Leasing private lines can be very expensive, while using the Internet is inexpensive. However, of vital importance when companies do business with one another using intranets is that any transactions be kept private and secure. Virtual Secure Private Networks (VSPNs) allow intranets to communicate with one another over the Internet, while keeping all data secure, by using "tunneling" technology. See Chapter 20 for details on how VSPNs work.

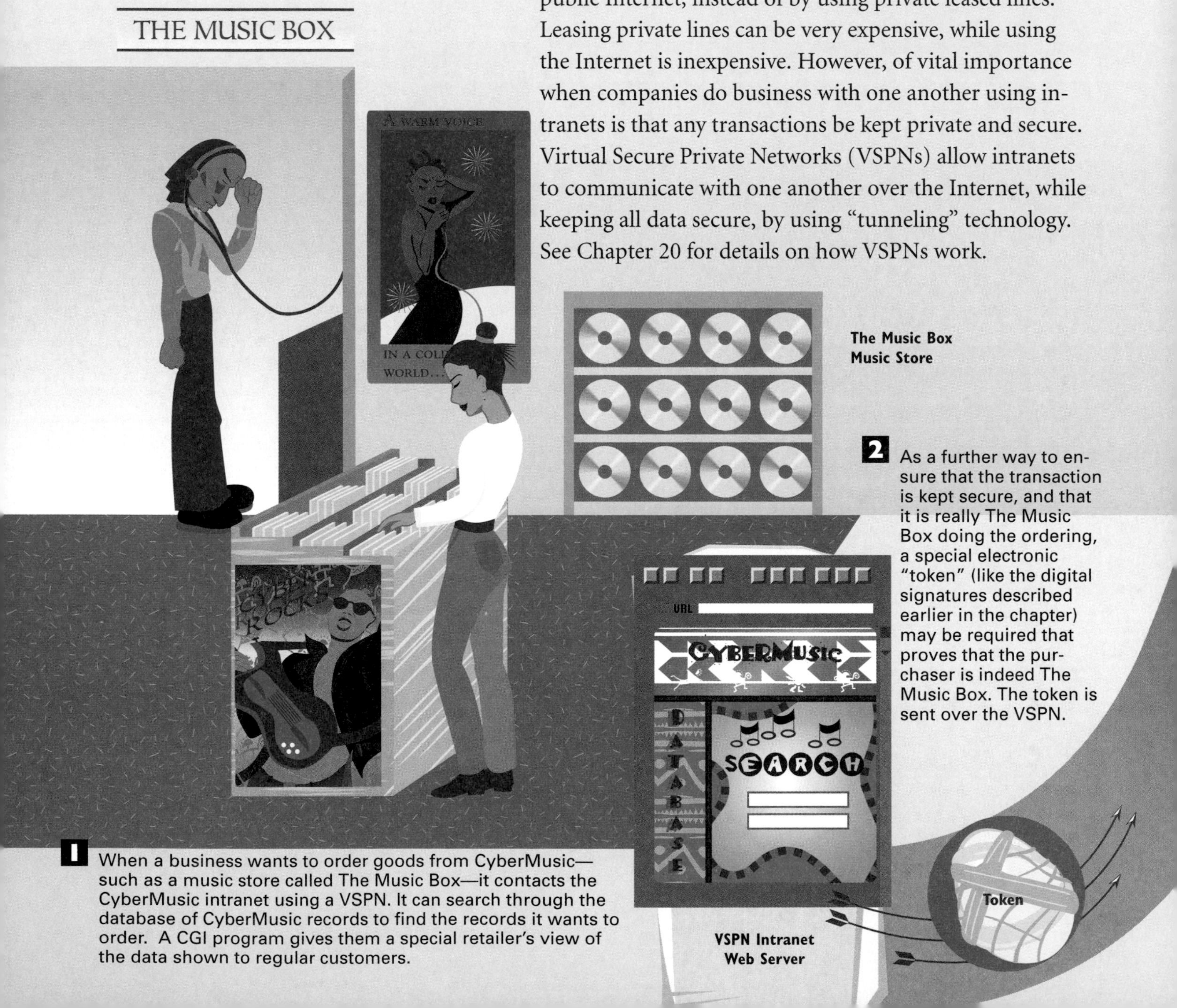

The Music Box
Music Store

2 As a further way to ensure that the transaction is kept secure, and that it is really The Music Box doing the ordering, a special electronic "token" (like the digital signatures described earlier in the chapter) may be required that proves that the purchaser is indeed The Music Box. The token is sent over the VSPN.

Token

VSPN Intranet
Web Server

1 When a business wants to order goods from CyberMusic—such as a music store called The Music Box—it contacts the CyberMusic intranet using a VSPN. It can search through the database of CyberMusic records to find the records it wants to order. A CGI program gives them a special retailer's view of the data shown to regular customers.

3 When The Music Box finds the records it wants to order, it fills out a form. This form may be customized specifically for The Music Box, and will be different from the form used by the general public, and by other companies that do business with CyberMusic.

Token

CyberMusic Order Form

URL

Secure Payment System

Encryption

Authentication

Verification

4 Once it is verified that The Music Box is doing the ordering, the transaction is put through using a secure payment system. There are a variety of secure payment systems that can be used for business-to-business transactions. One is described in "How Financial Transactions Work on an Intranet."

Delivery

CDs

INVOICE

5 Information about the order is automatically transferred over the intranet to CyberMusic's fulfillment department, which ships out the records ordered.

Fulfilment Department

6 CyberMusic can also do business with its suppliers and contractors using an intranet. For example, it can post on its public Internet Web server the fact that it is looking to buy raw, uncut CDs that it will use in the manufacturing process, and have new suppliers submit bids over the Internet. Established suppliers can connect via a VSPN, and submit their bids which are then routed to the appropriate people within the intranet.

CyberMusic Newsletter

ATTENTION!

WE ARE LOOKING FOR UNCUT CDs.

ALL CONTRACTORS WELCOME
SUBMIT BIDS TO:

Intranet

Internet

CHAPTER

32

How Intranet Search Tools and Spiders Work

CORPORATE

CORPORATE intranets can contain an almost unimaginable amount of information. Departments, divisions, and individuals create a wide variety of Web pages, both for internal and external consumption. Human resource information, personnel handbooks, procedures manuals, and newsletters are all posted internally. Databases—both those hosted directly on the intranet and on "legacy" databases on non TCP/IP systems—are available. Add that to all the information that can be gotten via the Internet using the World Wide Web, and you have a serious case of information overload.

There are several ways to help intranet users find the information they need. One way is to create subject directories of intranet data that present a highly structured way to find information. They let you browse through information by categories and subcategories, such as marketing, personnel, sales, research and development, budget, competitors, and so on. In a Web browser, you click on a category, and you are then presented with a series of subcategories, such as East Coast Sales, South Sales, Midwest Sales, and West Sales. Depending on the size of the subject directory, there may be several such layers of subcategories. At some point, when you get to the subcategory you're interested in, you'll be presented with a list of relevant documents. To get those documents, you click on links to them. On the Internet, Yahoo is the most well-known, largest, and most popular subject directory.

Another popular way of finding information—and in the long run for intranets, probably more useful—is to use search engines, also called search tools. Search engines operate differently from subject directories. They are essentially massive databases that index all the information found on the intranet—and can include information found on the Internet as well. Search engines don't present information in a hierarchical fashion. Instead, you search through them as you would a database, by typing in keywords that describe the information you want.

Intranet search engines are usually built out of three components: An *agent*, *spider*, or *crawler* that crawls across the intranet gathering information; a *database*, which contains all the information the spiders gather; and a *search tool*, which people use as an interface to search through the database. The technology is similar to Internet search engines such as Alta Vista.

Intranet search tools differ somewhat from their Internet equivalents. The database of information they search can be built not just by agents and spiders searching Web-based pages. Agents can be written that can go into existing corporate databases, extract data from them, and put them into the database of searchable information. And people on an intranet can fill out forms and submit their information into the database as well. Additionally, since they are built for a specific corporation and its data, the information they gather and the way they are searched can be customized.

How Intranet Search Tools Work

Searching and cataloging tools, sometimes called search engines, can be used to help people find the information they need. Intranet search tools, such as agents, spiders, crawlers, and robots, are used to gather information about the documents available on an intranet. These search tools are programs that search Web pages, extract the hypertext links on those pages, and automatically index the information they find to build a database. Each search engine has its own set of rules guiding how documents are gathered. Some follow every link on every page that they find, and then in turn examine every link on each of those new home pages, and so on. Some ignore links that lead to graphics files, sound files, and animation files; some ignore links to certain resources such as WAIS databases; and some are instructed to look primarily for the most popular home pages.

1 Agents are the "smartest" of the tools. They can do more than just search out records: They can perform transactions on your behalf, eventually such as finding and ordering the lowest-fare airline ticket for your vacation. Right now they can search sites for particular recordings and return a list of five sites, sorted by the lowest price first. Agents can cope with the context of the content. Agents can find and index other kinds of intranet resources, not just Web pages. They can also be programmed to extract records from legacy databases. Whatever information the agents index, they send back to the search engine's database.

Index
Price: $$
Catagory:
Classical

Web Page

Legacy Database of Policy

Administration
Finance
Information Systems
Security

Administration
Finance
Information
Sec...

2 General searchers are commonly known as spiders. Spiders report the content found. They index the information they find and extract summary information. They look at headers and at some of the links and send an index of the information to the search engine's database. There is some overlap between the tools—spiders can be robots, for example.

4 Robots can be programmed to go to various link depths, compile the index, and even test the links. Because of their nature, they can get stuck in loops, and they take considerable Web resources going through the system. There are methods available to prevent robots from searching your site.

Phone Directory
● Index ● By Location
HTML
HTML
HTML

Link 1 ok
Link 2 bad
Link 3 ok

Link
Link
Link
Link
Link

3 Crawlers look at headers and report first layer links only. Crawlers can be spiders.

Web Page

First layer LINKS

HTML
Link
Link
Link
Link

5 Agents extract and index different kinds of information. Some, for example, index every single word in each document, while others index only the most important 100 words in each; some index the size of the document and number of words in it; some index the title, headings and subheadings, and so on. The kind of index built will determine what kind of searching can be done with the search engine, and how the information will be displayed.

6 Agents can also go out to the Internet and find information there to put in the search engine's database. Intranet administrators can decide which sites or kinds of sites the agents should visit and index—for example, competitors to the corporation or news sources. The information is indexed and sent to the search engine's database in the same way as is information found on the intranet.

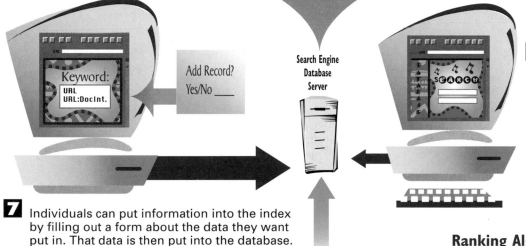

8 When someone wants to find information available on the intranet, they visit a Web page and fill out a form detailing the information they're looking for. Keywords, dates, and other criteria can be used. The criteria in the search form must match the criteria used by the agents for indexing the information they found while crawling the intranet.

7 Individuals can put information into the index by filling out a form about the data they want put in. That data is then put into the database.

Ranking Algorithm

Results

URL: First several sentences
URL: "Title of document"
URL: Tagged HTML results

9 The database is searched, based on the information specified in the fill-out form, and a list of matching documents is prepared by the database. The database then applies a ranking algorithm to determine the order in which the list of documents will be displayed. Ideally, the documents most relevant to a user's query will be placed highest on the list. Different search engines use different ranking algorithms. The database then tags the ranked list of documents with HTML and returns it to the individual requesting it. Different search engines also choose different ways of displaying the ranked list of documents—some just provide URLs; some show the URL as well as the first several sentences of the document; and some show the title of the document as well as the URL.

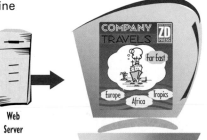

10 When you click on a link to one of the documents you're interested in, that document is retrieved from where it resides. The document itself is not in the database or on the search engine site.

33

How Remote Access Works

THE days of working at an office every day from 9:00 a.m. to 5:00 p.m. and only occasionally working into the night are long gone. Today, people may be telecommuting from home, they may be on the road, and they may work evenings or weekends from their home office. The days of the virtual office are here, and intranets are an important part of making that a reality.

Since intranets hold so much of a corporation's resources, and since so much work these days is collaborative work done via the network, people need access to the intranet in order to do any work. That means they need some remote way of gaining access to the intranet.

Typically, remote access is gained via a modem. The most common method is to dial into a remote access server and its associated modem bank. They dial in using one of the Internet's standard dial-in protocols, either the Point-to-Point Protocol (PPP) or the Serial Line Interface Protocol (SLIP). SLIP is an older protocol and has fast been falling out of favor because the PPP protocol is more robust, especially when it comes to handling errors. Part of the process of dialing in involves identification of the user. Some remote access servers hang up and call the individual back at a pre-determined phone number.

After someone logs into the remote access server, he or she can log into machines on the intranet just like in the office. The intranet's firewall allows packets sent via the remote access server to enter the intranet. Once they've logged in, they have full access to the intranet, although at dial-in speeds instead of at higher speeds available when actually at the office.

Providing dial-in access in this manner is expensive, because corporations have to maintain large banks of modems that can be dialed into, and because they have to pay for the costs of long-distance and 800 telephone numbers.

A solution developed by Microsoft, 3Com, US Robotics, and others is called the Point-to-Point Tunneling Protocol (PPTP). This protocol allows someone to dial into a local Internet Service Provider (ISP), and from there access their intranet. Costs come down significantly, because the call is made to a local phone number instead of a long-distance one, and the banks of modem pools aren't needed.

PPTP also allows for people to use other network protocols, such as IPX or NetBIOS, so they can access parts of the corporate network that aren't TCP/IP-based. And it also allows for secure transmission of data. It does this by encrypting the data being sent, and encapsulating it and the other network protocols inside an IP packet. That IP packet is then sent out over the Internet through a technique called tunneling. On the receiving end, the outer IP envelope is stripped off, and the protocols and data inside the packet used. The person now has full access to the intranet and other corporate network resources, and has done it by making a local phone call.

Providing Remote Access to an Intranet

In today's increasingly mobile world, it's important that people be able to access a corporate intranet from their homes or from the road. This illustration shows how that access can be gained via a new protocol called the Point-to-Point Tunneling Protocol (PPTP).

1 Before the PPTP protocol, when people wanted to gain access to an intranet they usually dialed into a remote access server through its modem bank. After logging into the server, they were then able to get access to the intranet's resources. One drawback of this approach is that it required the corporation to pay for long-distance or 800 telephone access and maintain the modem banks, which can easily cost millions of dollars a year.

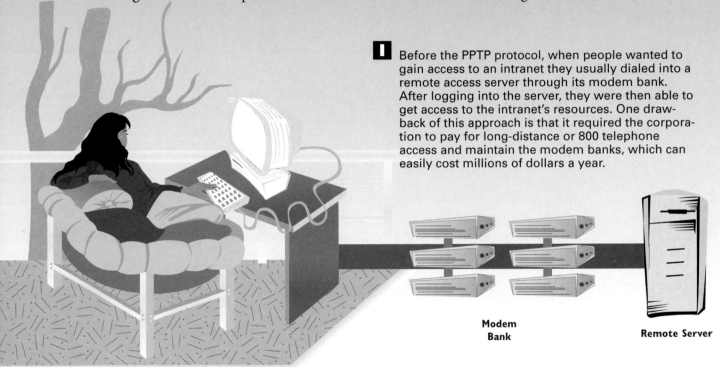

Modem Bank

Remote Server

7 The intranet server strips off the outside envelope. It then decrypts the data inside the envelope. The person can now make full use of the intranet—or other network resources. All packets that pass between the intranet and the user will go through this tunneling technique.

Intranet Remote Server

6 The person trying to get at intranet data will have to log into this server with a user name and password, just as he or she would have to if directly connected to the intranet, as a way to keep out intruders. PPTP uses two protocols for allowing people to log in, the Password Authentication Protocol (PAP) and the Challenge Handshake Authentication Protocol (CHAP). See Chapter 17 for more on how these protocols work.

Authentication
Login Name:
Login Password:

Password Authentication Protocol

Challenge Handshake Authentication Protocol

2 The PPTP protocol allows people to gain access to an intranet by dialing into an Internet Service Provider (ISP) and requesting to be sent to the intranet. The connection to the ISP is made using the normal PPP Internet dial-in protocol. Since ISP calls can be local calls, this cuts down tremendously on telecommunications costs. It also means that the intranet need not have sizable modem pools available to answer every incoming call, another significant cost-savings.

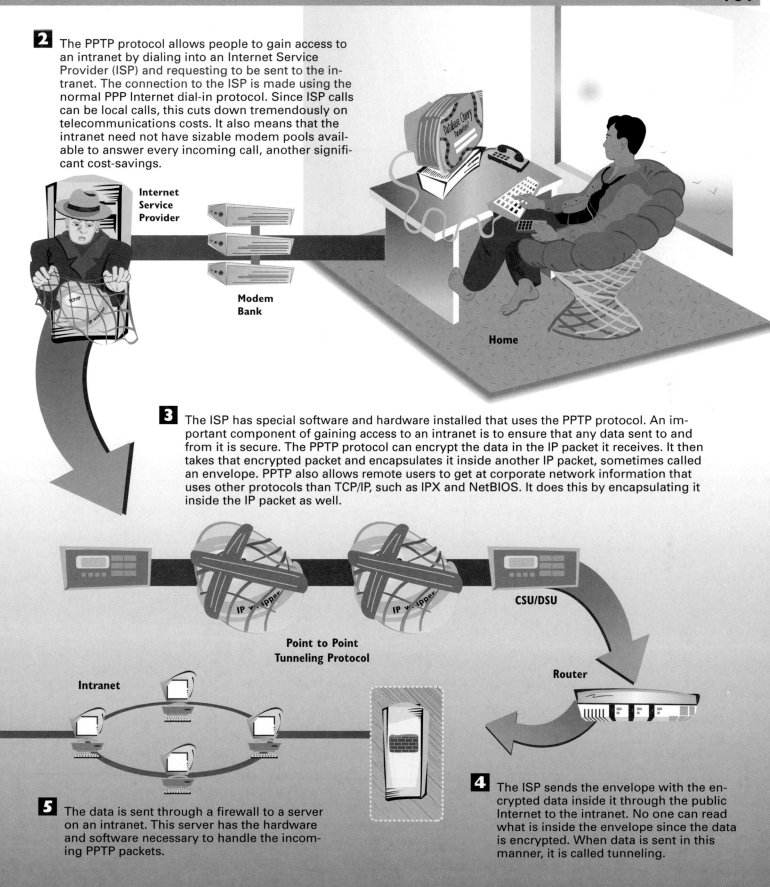

Internet Service Provider

Modem Bank

Home

3 The ISP has special software and hardware installed that uses the PPTP protocol. An important component of gaining access to an intranet is to ensure that any data sent to and from it is secure. The PPTP protocol can encrypt the data in the IP packet it receives. It then takes that encrypted packet and encapsulates it inside another IP packet, sometimes called an envelope. PPTP also allows remote users to get at corporate network information that uses other protocols than TCP/IP, such as IPX and NetBIOS. It does this by encapsulating it inside the IP packet as well.

IP wrapper

IP wrapper

CSU/DSU

Point to Point Tunneling Protocol

Router

Intranet

5 The data is sent through a firewall to a server on an intranet. This server has the hardware and software necessary to handle the incoming PPTP packets.

4 The ISP sends the envelope with the encrypted data inside it through the public Internet to the intranet. No one can read what is inside the envelope since the data is encrypted. When data is sent in this manner, it is called tunneling.

34

How Technical Support Works on an Intranet

ALMOST any company that sells goods and services to consumers—and to a certain extent, that sells to businesses—spends a substantial amount of time, money, and corporate resources providing technical support. It need not be a computer or software company. Even people who buy washing machines or CD players or lamps run into problems with the products and need help.

Providing excellent technical support, especially for companies that need to reach a large number of people, can be an exceedingly expensive proposition. Typically, technical support is provided via the telephone, sometimes using toll-free 800 phone numbers. The cost of hiring and staffing support lines, as well as paying for telecommunications costs, can be staggeringly high.

An intranet can help cut those costs. Instead of having to staff many expensive support lines, a company can instead create a public Web site that people can visit. This Web site can contain an enormous amount of technical support information—everything from answers to common problems, to downloadable software to fix problems with hardware, to links to access user-to-user forums where people can exchange answers they've found to common problems.

In the next illustration, we'll return to our imaginary company, CyberMusic, and see how they use their intranet to help provide technical support to their customers.

When companies provide technical support using Internet and intranet technology, much of what they do is posted outside the corporate firewall, on the Internet. A variety of material can be posted. For example, FAQs (Frequently Asked Questions) can be posted—answers to the most common technical problems. A database of problems and their answers can be searched directly from the Web, using the Common Gateway Interface. Public discussion areas can be set up, where people post their problems, and technical support personnel can answer. And other customers can answer the questions as well. If the product is related to hardware or software, patches to the software can be posted that can be downloaded to solve technical problems. Another bonus in using Web sites to provide technical support is that the company can get people to fill in their names, addresses, and other information—a way of gathering customer names.

While much of what is posted is outside the corporate firewall on the Internet, what goes on inside the firewall on the intranet is still used in a variety of ways to help provide technical support. The databases that are posted on the Internet, for example, are first created on the intranet, and then exported to the Internet. E-mail sent to the technical support department must pass through the corporate firewall from the Internet. And when someone registers to receive technical support, the information from the person is sent in a secure fashion back through the firewall into the Intranet. There, it will be put into a corporate customer database, so that the company can, for example, send out direct mail to all its customers.

Using an Intranet to Provide Technical Support

For companies that sell goods and services to the consumer market, providing technical support can be an expensive, time-consuming chore. Using a combination of a company's intranet and the Internet, technical support costs can be cut dramatically, and better technical support can be delivered. This illustration shows how our imaginary company CyberMusic uses them to provide technical support. CyberMusic manufactures CD players as well as publishes and sells records, so this page shows how they provide technical support for both lines of products.

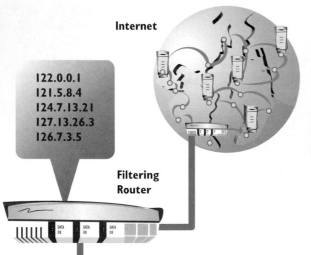

Internet

122.0.0.1
121.5.8.4
124.7.13.21
127.13.26.3
126.7.3.5

Filtering Router

CyberMusic creates a public Web site for technical support that anyone can access over the Internet. They publicize the site in their product literature, in their advertising, and even when people call into their technical support lines, a recorded message suggests that people access the Web site to get immediate technical support. The Web site is located on a bastion host outside the CyberMusic intranet, and is separated from it by a filtering router. The bastion host and the filtering routers are part of the firewall that protects CyberMusic's intranet from the Internet.

Web Server on Bastion Host

CyberMusic has found through the years that only 10 or 12 common problems cause 80 percent of the calls to their technical support phone lines—and these are problems that can be solved quite simply. (For example, a surprising number of people simply forget to plug in the power cord of their CD player.) So CyberMusic posts the problems and answers to them in FAQs on their Web site. This cuts down tremendously on calls to their technical support line.

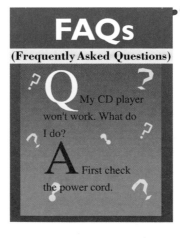

FAQs

(Frequently Asked Questions)

Q My CD player won't work. What do I do?

A First check the power cord.

TECH SUPPORT

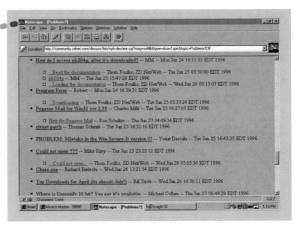

Sometimes the best technical support is provided by people, not FAQs and databases. So CyberMusic has created a number of discussion areas where people can ask questions about their problems, and where CyberMusic technical support professionals can answer the questions. In yet other technical support areas, customers can answer each other's questions. These areas are set up as USENET newsgroups, accessible via browsers such as Netscape Navigator and Microsoft's Explorer.

Not all problems can be solved by reading the FAQs. So CyberMusic uses several other techniques for providing technical support. The company creates a database of common problems and solutions that can be searched via the Web using the Common Gateway Interface. A CGI program takes the user's question, formulates it as a query for the database, submits it, and returns the result of the query in an HTML formatted page.

The company also provides a "mailto" link on the technical support page that when clicked on launches an e-mail program in the customer's browser, with the e-mail address of the technical support staff already filled in. The person can now type in a question, and the e-mail will be sent through the Internet, through the CyberMusic firewall, and then to the technical support department. Once there, a technical support manager uses groupware to route the request to the proper person, and uses the tracking features of groupware to see that the question is answered.

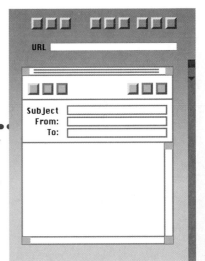

CyberMusic CD's contain more than just musical information on them—they can also be read by a computer and contain interviews and interactive articles about the musicians and other information. CyberMusic has found, however, that some computers have trouble reading the CD's. To solve the problem, they make available special drivers and patches for those computers. The drivers and patches can be downloaded directly from the Web site on the bastion host. This saves CyberMusic a great deal of money in processing, handling, and mailing costs.

CyberMusic, like many companies that sell products to consumers, tries to maintain as comprehensive a list as possible of people who have purchased their products. Most people, however, don't send in reply forms, and so the number of customer names and addresses they have is quite small. CyberMusic uses its Web site to get many more names. One way to get names is to have people type in their name, address, and other information before they can get to a certain area of the Web site—for example, to the discussions or to download patches. Another way is to sponsor contests on the site, such as giving away CD players and records. When a name and address are typed into a Web form, the data is sent through CyberMusic's firewall to its intranet. It's then put in a customer database, where CyberMusic can use it for customer mailings.

CHAPTER 35

Using an Intranet to Disseminate Internal Corporate News

KEEPING everyone in a corporation up to date about the latest news in the corporation is a never-ending, often impossible task. It's particularly difficult in large corporations with many departments and divisions that are geographically separated.

There are many ways that intranets can be used to solve the problem and keep everyone in a corporation informed about corporate news. Corporations can post their company newsletter on intranet Web pages. Because Web pages can be updated so much more quickly than newsletters can be created—and because there is no delivery time involved—the newsletter can be far more up to date than traditional printed newsletters and, with no printing and mailing costs, Web newsletters are less expensive, too.

Intranets can also be used to deliver literally up-to-the minute news flashes. The Java programming language can be used to create news tickers that can flash the breaking news across the top of the newsletter home page. Intranet broadcast technologies can be used that will send out a news flash to everyone connected to the intranet that will run on top of whatever applications they're currently running. And electronic mail can be broadcast to everyone inside a company with important news, such as press releases, or news about quarterly corporate earnings.

An intranet can also deliver more in-depth information in more involving ways. Audio clips and video clips can be delivered via streaming technologies, so that people can listen to interviews with corporate executives, for example, or see news reports about the company.

An intriguing technology for delivering news to intranets is so-called offline news readers. With this technology, corporate news—and news from the outside world—can be delivered to everyone on an intranet.

Offline news readers work on a client/server model. An offline news server carries the latest corporate news. To update the news on the server, someone only needs to fill out an HTML-based form, and that information is put into the proper format for broadcast. Only certain people on the intranet are allowed to update the news on the server.

Since people on an intranet may want to read news about the outside world, not just about the company itself, the offline news server also has on it that kind of news as well. The server gets this news by connecting to another news server on the Internet, which sends it the information.

To read the news, people need an offline news client. The client connects with the server at intervals set by each user, and downloads the news. People can customize their news feeds to get only the kind of news they're interested in. Once the news has been delivered to their local computer, they can use the client software to read the news. They can also click on links in the news stories that will launch a Web browser, and then contact a site that has more information about that particular story.

Disseminating Corporate News and Documents via an Intranet

It's often difficult for people within a corporation to keep abreast of company news. Using a variety of technologies, intranets can broadcast and make available the most up-do-date corporate news. Pictured here is the way that our fictional record company CyberMusic uses their intranet to deliver corporate news and information.

The CyberMusic company newsletter, which is updated weekly, is posted publicly on an intranet Web server. Employees can contact the server at their leisure to read the latest corporate news.

A Java ticker runs across the top of the newsletter page. This ticker is used to display news alerts and the latest news. It is updated every hour of the working day, so that people can read the most up-to-date news about CyberMusic, such as which recording artists have recently been signed, and where CyberMusic records are on the record charts. Every time a person views the newsletter, the most up-to-date news is downloaded for display by the Java ticker.

Mail Server

Electronic mail is used to send everyone on the intranet the same information that is being sent to the outside world. For example, at CyberMusic, every time a press release is issued, that release is also sent via e-mail to everyone in the corporation.

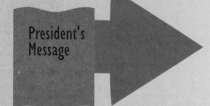

President's Message

News Alert Server

An intranet can be used to deliver instant "alerts" to anyone connected to the intranet. Server broadcasts can be directed to every person connected to the intranet based on their TCP address. These broadcasts are not host specific and appear over whatever application is running. "Offline news readers" can be used as a way to deliver intranet news to everyone at CyberMusic. This software works on a client/server model: The client connects to the server and gets the news. Anyone can then read the latest news while at their own computer. See the next illustration to see how offline news readers work.

CyberMusic Corporate News

New CD Tops Charts

Corporate Discussions

From the Web newsletter, there are links to discussion areas, so that people can discuss the latest happenings at CyberMusic. The discussion areas are used not only to air people's opinions, but also so that anyone in the corporation can publicly post notes about what is happening in their department. These discussion areas take advantage of the Network News Transfer Protocol used by USENET.

Audio Clips

CyberMusic uses streaming audio technology to deliver the news. Streaming audio lets people listen to news reports over the intranet, from their computer. At CyberMusic, this audio news includes clips from the latest records released, and interviews with corporate executives.

Music Videos

CyberMusic also uses streaming video technology, which allows people to see and hear videos across the intranet, while at their computers. Anyone working for CyberMusic can watch any video made by any CyberMusic artist, while seated at their computer, using streaming video technology.

ALERT: RECORDING ARTIST APPEARANCE

You have mail

Using Offline Web Readers to Deliver Corporate Information

One way that intranets can be used to easily and effectively deliver corporate news to people is to use so-called "offline readers"—software that allows people to read news by having it automatically retrieved by their own computer, instead of forcing them to connect to a Web or other intranet server to get the information. Pictured here is a popular offline reader called PointCast. Offline news readers like PointCast can retrieve intranet news as well as news from the Internet.

When an intranet administrator wants to have news delivered to people's desktop computers on the intranet, he or she fills out an HTML-based form that contains all the information to be delivered. The form can include news stories, as well as URLs that people can connect to.

PointCast software on an intranet server converts information in this HTML form into a format that it will use to make the news available.

Administrator

As a security measure, only authorized people have access to filling out the form, or have access to the intranet PointCast server. If someone wants news delivered via PointCast, they will have to contact an individual who has the rights to use the server.

NEWS...NEWS...

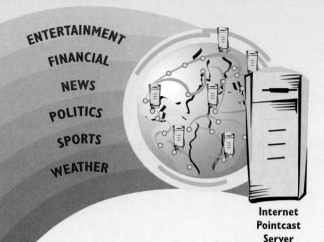

ENTERTAINMENT
FINANCIAL
NEWS
POLITICS
SPORTS
WEATHER

Internet
Pointcast
Server

PointCast can be used to deliver news other than just intranet news, in a variety of topics, including breaking news stories, politics, business, entertainment, sports, financial information, and more. In order to deliver this non-intranet-created news, the intranet PointCast server connects to a server on PointCast's Internet site, and downloads the news. This news now resides on the intranet server, along with intranet news.

In order to get news delivered to them, people on an intranet must have the PointCast client software. People can customize what kind of news they want delivered to them—for example, to get sports but not entertainment, politics but not weather. An intranet administrator can set it up so that everyone will receive intranet news, however.

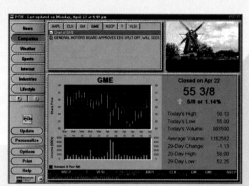

Using the PointCast client, the person can now read the news on his or her own computer. The software can also be set up as a screen saver so that when the computer is idle for a certain amount of time, the news will flash across the person's screen.

At set times determined by each individual, the PointCast client software connects to the intranet PointCast server. The software downloads the news that the person has requested. A person can also manually tell the client software to download the news at any time requested.

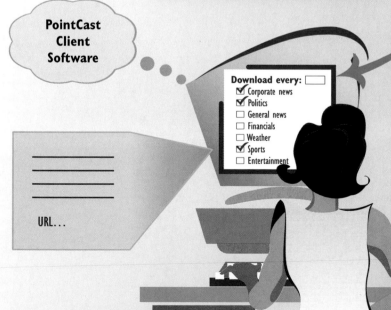

PointCast
Client
Software

Download every: ☐
☑ Corporate news
☑ Politics
☐ General news
☐ Financials
☐ Weather
☑ Sports
☐ Entertainment

URL...

Often, in news and intranet stories, there are URLs to sites that have further information. When that link is clicked upon, an Internet browser is launched, and the specified site is contacted. The person can now read more in-depth news. For example, on an intranet, a brief news story may go out about the company's quarterly earnings. A link to a Web site could be embedded in the story that would have more in-depth financial information, and links to corporate financial database.

CHAPTER

36

Using Multimedia Applications on an Intranet to Train Employees

TRAINING is a large cost in any corporation. Enormous amounts of training need to be done in any company, particularly large ones.

The costs associated with training are not only financial—they are the time devoted to training, and perhaps equally important, the time and money wasted if a company *doesn't* properly train its employees.

Training needs to be done to orient new employees to the corporation itself—things such as teaching about corporate procedures, where to find information, how to fill out forms, rules that managers must follow, and other similar orientation issues.

Another level of training has to do with how to use particular pieces of software at the corporation—for example, how to use the accounting system or a database.

The most complex level of training incorporates not just how to use software or how to follow procedures, but how to actually do business at the company. For example, many companies put new sales employees through a substantial amount of training that encompasses teaching about the industry in which the salesperson is selling, information about the product to be sold, as well as specific sales techniques to be used.

Training is not just for new employees—it needs to be an ongoing process. New products and goods to sell mean people need to be taught about them. New software and business procedures require that people be taught how to use them.

An intranet can help with all these kinds of training. It can cut costs, save time, and ensure that people get better training. On the simplest level, Web pages can be built to train people. The Web can be used as a multimedia training tool by including pictures, video, audio, with the text. It can be interactive as well—people can answer questions, take tests, and try out procedures.

More revolutionary will be intranet-based multimedia applications. Videoconferencing will allow trainers to teach people across the entire intranet. People won't have to be physically in the same room; instead, they can be seated at their PCs. And they'll be able to interact and ask questions using the technology as well.

With whiteboard applications (in which people can see what is on each other's computer screens), a teacher can demonstrate how to use a particular piece of software, and everyone connected can see on their computer screen what the instructor is doing, and can ask questions by doing things such as circling a portion of the screen, and asking questions about it.

Streaming video and audio technologies (which allow people to watch videos or listen to audios without having to wait for them to completely download) can be used for training as well. The ultimate training tool, however, may be virtual reality. A virtual world is built that someone can walk through and interact with in the same way as with the real world. Virtual reality has been used by the airlines and the military, for example, to train pilots.

Using Multimedia Applications to Train Employees

Training employees is a major cost to many corporations. All employees require training on an ongoing basis—training for mundane things such as how to fill out new forms and procedures, to more sophisticated things, such as being given information about new goods and services the company sells. Multimedia on an intranet can be a very effective training tool.

It can be expensive for CyberMusic to fly instructors across the country to teach small classes—many instructors need to be paid, in addition to travel costs. With intranet videoconferencing, however, a single instructor can teach a class live, and people across the intranet and across the country can follow along on their computers via desktop-to-desktop videoconferencing using a videoconferencing program like CU-See-Me. With CU-See-Me, people log into servers called reflectors, and can then participate in a videoconference. They can be seen and be heard by the instructor, and so can ask questions as well. CyberMusic uses videoconferencing to train its sales employees on sales techniques.

Sometimes, particularly with a sales staff, it can be difficult to make sure that everyone can participate in a videoconference at the same time. Additionally, people may at times want refresher courses when a trainer isn't available. To solve the problem, CyberMusic videocasts training videos across the intranet, using streaming video technology. Anyone who wants to watch a training video can click on a link on a Web page to a video clip, and they can watch the training video at their own leisure. The video clip is played from a streaming video server.

For in-depth training on how to use a particular piece of software, CyberMusic uses whiteboard applications. Whiteboard applications allow many people to view what is on each other's computer screens. An instructor can teach, step-by-step, how to use a piece of software, and everyone connected to the whiteboard can see what he is doing on their own computer screen. The instructor can also mark up the screen, and everyone connected can see what he is marking up. CyberMusic uses whiteboard applications for training its accounting department how to use a new accounting system. CU-See-Me reflectors allow for whiteboard applications.

Audio technology can be used for training as well—in particular one called RealAudio. People can click on a link on a Web page, and when they do so, they will hear an audio clip. The clip can also display HTML Web pages as it plays the audio clip. In the case of CyberMusic, RealAudio is used to teach its employees what records are in their catalog. People can click on music clips from all their recording artists, and as they listen, can view Web pages with pictures and information about the artists. The audio clips are played from a RealAudio server.

Virtual Reality has long been used in training applications—notably by airlines and the military in training pilots. In virtual reality, virtual worlds are built that people can walk through and interact with. At CyberMusic, virtual reality is used to teach recording engineers how to handle a recording session. A world has been built in which engineers have to not only handle the technical aspects of how to use the recording hardware, but even have to contend with rock artists gone awry, intent on destroying the recording session.

INDEX